The stamp on the front of the binding and the emblem on the title page is taken from a wineglass of the 1780's.

A dog of the breed called "Keeshond" was the symbol of the Patriot party in the Netherlands. Their rivals, followers of the Prince of Orange, carried an Orange tree in their shield.

That tree should not be confused with another tree so prominent in the arsenal of late eighteenth century emblems, the tree of Liberty, which, according to Thomas Jefferson "must be refreshed from time to time with the blood of patriots and tyrants."

The Orange tree did not need any fertilizer, according to the Dutch Patriots. On the contrary, a little leg-lifting by the Patriot dog was needed to reduce that tree to its proper size.

On the dust jacket, citizens "of reflection" are cheering the Patriot leader Henrik Danielszoon Hooft in front of the Town Hall of Amsterdam, while Ceylonese bearers are passing with Jacob Haafner in a palanquin.

Pieter Ondaatje and Henrik Hooft are high in the skies overshadowing their descendants Christopher Ondaatje and the author.

This book was published in the Netherlands in 1994 by "De Prom" in Baarn under the title "De burgher en de burgemeester."

The American edition was made possible by grants from:
the Jaffé-Pierson Stichting in Amsterdam,
the K.F.Hein Stichting in Utrecht,
the Elise Mathilde Fonds in Utrecht,
the John Adams Instituut in Amsterdam,
Stork N.V. in Naarden.

The author is very grateful to Richard J. Wolfe of Newton, Mass., who has helped to produce this American edition by generously making available his time, his long experience in publishing and his knowledge of history.

Hendrik Hooft

PATRIOT AND PATRICIAN

To Holland and Ceylon in the steps of
Henrik Hooft and Pieter Ondaatje,
champions of Dutch Democracy.

SCIENCE HISTORY PUBLICATIONS/USA
1999

First English edition.

Published in the United States of America
by Science History Publications/USA
a division of
Watson Publishing International
P.O. Box 493, Canton, MA 02021-0493

© 1999 Hendrik Hooft

A major portion of this book, excluding the chapter "Tea for Mrs. Washington," and new material on John Adams and John Quincy Adams, was published by de Prom in the Netherlands in 1994 under the title *De burgher en de burgemeester*.

Hooft, H. G. A., 1939–
   [Burgher en de burgemeester. English]
   Patriot and patrician / Hendrik Hooft. — 1st English ed.
     p. cm.
   Includes bibliographical references.
   ISBN 0-88135-261-6
   1. Netherlands—History—1714–1795. 2. Netherlands—History—Batavian Republic, 1795–1808. 3. United States—Politics and government—1789–1797. 4. United States—History—Revolution, 1775–1783—Influence. 5. Netherlands—Relations—United States. 6. Washington, George, 1732–1799—Influence. 7. United States—Relations—Netherlands. 8. Political culture—Netherlands—History—18th century. 9. Democracy—Netherlands—History—18th century. I. Title.
DJ208.H6613   1999
949.2′04—dc21   98-46828
                                                                                                                     CIP

All rights reserved. No part of this book may be reproduced in any form by any electronic or mechanical means (including photocopying, recording, or information storage and retrieval) without permission in writing from the publisher.

Set in Plantin by Wellington Graphics.
Printed and bound in the United States of America.

Contents

Foreword
6

I
Under the Breadfruit Tree
9

II
In the Backwaters of Utrecht
19

III
On the Shrimp Market
25

IV
A Different Kettle of Fish
37

V
Dutch Dessert
45

VI
The Winds of Change
53

VII
A Forgotten Citizen
73

VIII
Jewels in His Head
87

IX
The Cautious Coup
107

X
The Pear is Ripe
119

XI
Tea for Mrs. Washington
137

XII
The Pear Drops
149

XIII
Exits and Entrances
163

XIV
Hope and Disappointment
183

XV
The Losing Horse
191

XVI
Shadows and Clearance
201

XVII
Missing Links
221

Regrets Only
239

Bibliography
240

Provenance of the illustrations
247

Index of personal names
249

Foreword

It was about ten years ago that I met Christopher Ondaatje for the first time. He was sponsoring a fundraising effort for a Toronto chamber orchestra of which I was a board member.
On a winter evening he received a number of potential benefactors in his Pagurian gallery amidst scenes of bearskin-wrapped explorers, frozen on canvas in dogsledges in the icy silence of the snowclad forests, and of red Indians, sticking pink salmon in pristine streams, rozy in the setting summer sun.
Meanwhile the beneficiaries of the event sat playing Viennese waltzes.

I was aware that the Ondaatjes were Ceylonese " burghers," descendants of the Dutch who had occupied the island between 1650 and 1796.
I asked Christopher how he was related to Pieter Quint Ondaatje, a famous eighteenth century Dutch political figure who had come from Ceylon.
Christopher seemed pleased that I knew about his family.
We met again and continued to talk about Pieter Ondaatje in Holland and the Dutch in Ceylon. My interest in this Ondaatje was more than general. He had been the champion of a democratic movement of which one of my own ancestors had been the figurehead and rallying force.

Pieter Ondaatje had written a short autobiography which was published well over a century ago, together with a sketch of his life and times, by a Mrs. Davies, an English scholar of Dutch history.
Although this ancestor of mine, Henrik Danielszoon Hooft, had been the most popular Dutch statesman of the 1780's and is mentioned in every study of that period of Dutch history no one so far has written his biography. Fuller research has been impeded by the disappearance of Hooft's papers. Only recently some of his letters turned up in the State Archives in the Hague amongst the papers of a family related to him by marriage.

After our musical introduction Christopher and I continued to meet regularly. The present took over from the past. Foreign exchange markets were in a turmoil, the postwar economic boom was drawing to an end. We were discussing new chances for finance.
Christopher divested himself in time of all his active investments, went abroad, travelled and wrote books.

FOREWORD

We continued to see each other. Our conversations returned to travel and history.

Christopher wrote a book about his return to Ceylon and the places which he had visited as a young boy together with his father, a journey which culminated in a reconciliation with his past. Then he made his come-back to Bay Street.

Shortly thereafter we went to Sri Lanka together. We looked at the Dutch past, present Ondaatjes and investment possibilities for the future.

On our way we visited Holland, walked in the traces of our ancestors and looked for ties between Pieter Ondaatje and Henrik Hooft.

Our journey and further discoveries in books and archives, in churches, inns and country houses revealed a whole network of ties.

The lives of most of the historical figures of the late eighteenth century in the Netherlands came together like threads spun by the spinster-sister of the Fates, or by the giant spiders of Ceylon.

The Fates of history wove the warp and the spiders of Ceylon the woof on which I have knotted a texture of intertwining destinies, a carpet covering distance and time.

> Socrates: I myself, Phaidros, like to disentangle things
> and knot them together again.
>
> from Plato's *Phaidros*

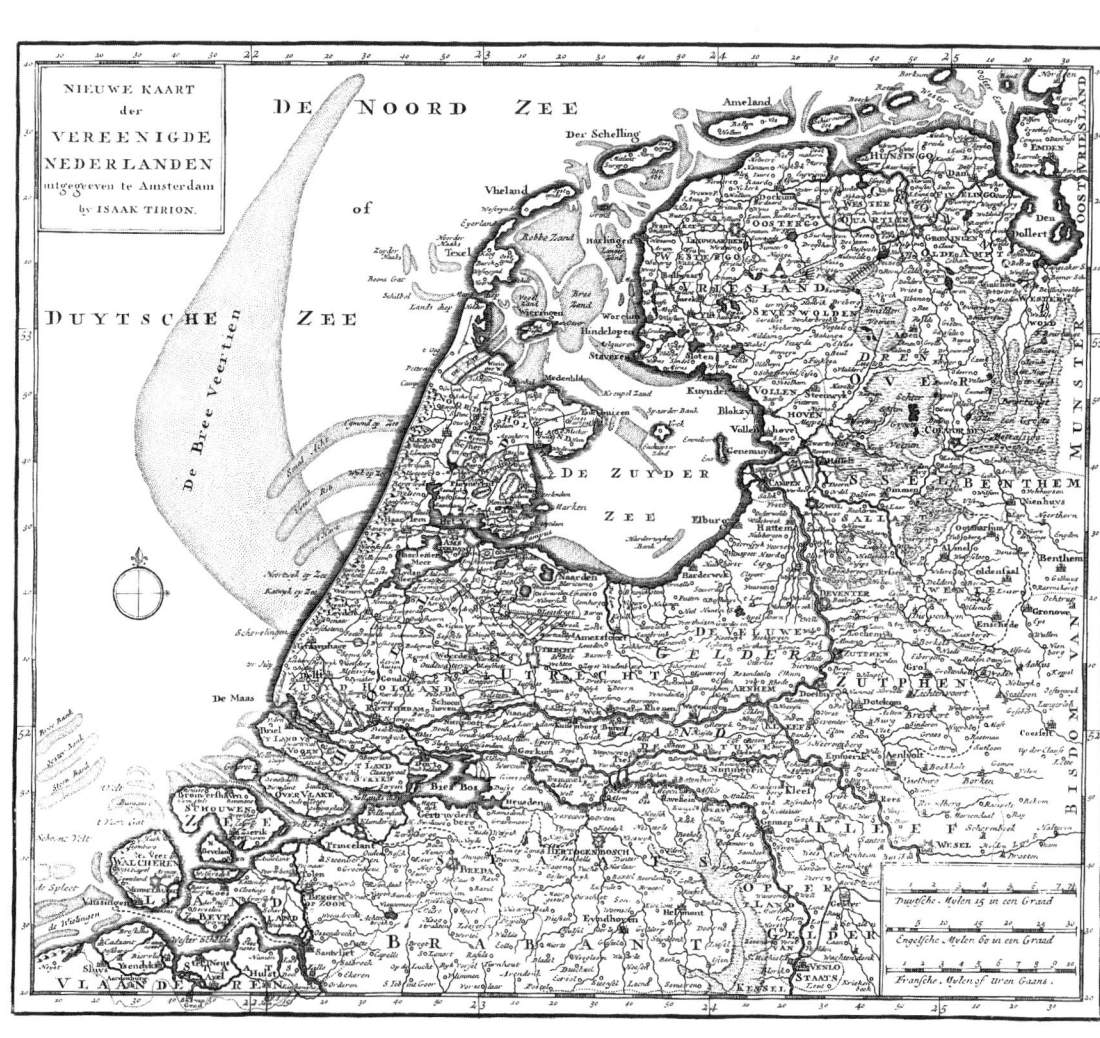

CHAPTER I

Under the Breadfruit Tree

Christopher Ondaatje under the Breadfruit tree looks, lost in thought, over the Bay of Galle.

"I can almost see the ship now" Christopher Ondaatje says. We are looking out over the bay of Galle on the tip of Ceylon's South-West coast. "Pieter Quint must have felt like me. I left Ceylon when I was 14, and I did not return until I was 57. Pieter Quint was the same age when he left but he never came back." In the wide bay there is not a ship to be seen.

On the 16th of November 1773 an East Indiaman was sailing out. A boy stood at the bulwarks on portside. His name was Pieter Ondaatje. His cousin Simon de Melho stood next to him.
They watched the dark grey walls of the town grow smaller and smaller. At the mouth of the bay the ship heeled to the force of the North-East monsoon. Galle

CHAPTER I

blended into the blue-green coastline and the blue-grey mountains until even the red-white-blue flag flying on the Utrecht bastion and the fluted white and blue gable of the Dutch Reformed Church could no longer be distinguished.
Only last Sunday they had been in that Church listening to the sermon of the Reverend Petrus de Silva, Pieter Ondaatje's uncle by marriage.
The two boys had stayed with their aunt at the rectory in Galle. She must have been quite pleased with her two nephews, who had done so well at the Dutch School in Colombo that they had been selected for further education in the Dutch Republic. If they continued to do well, they would become Reverends like their fathers and her own husband and then they would come back and rise to the pinnacle of society in Dutch Ceylon and rub shoulders with the top merchants and administrators of the VOC, the Verenigde Oostindische Compagnie – the Dutch East India Company.

Galle lies on a peninsula, well defended by the sea, the bay and its ancient walls.

View of Galle.
by J. W. HEYDT, 1744.

Adam's Peak seen from a ship in the roads of Galle.
by H. B. HOPPENSTOCK, c. 1816.

Christopher and I are standing on the ramparts of Fort Akersloot rising from the waters of the deserted bay. The fort had been the residence of the Dutch Commander; a one-storeyed building with thick, ochre walls and a high, red-tiled roof. The house is set back from the parapet to leave room for a small garden. An enormous breadfruit tree stretches its branches over the garden, the roof and the shoals at the foot of the ramparts. Christopher gazes pensively over the bay, leaning on a weathered Dutch cannon while his sister Gillian wanders through the high rooms behind us.
She lived here when her husband was on duty in these waters as head of the pilot department. He had told us about the breadfruit tree, the first on the island, over 200 years old.
"Nobody on Sri Lanka has to die of hunger. You just climb a jack tree or a coconut palm or a breadfruit tree and you have enough for a meal."
Overshadowed by 200 years of branches and leaves we have our minds fixed on Pieter Ondaatje sailing away, seeing the island slowly sink beyond the horizon; Galle first with the palmgroves along the coast, then the hills and the blue mountains and finally the next day Adam's Peak.
Why was it Pieter Ondaatje never came back to Ceylon? Did he not become a minister as the VOC had intended?

CHAPTER I

The Lords Seventeen, the mighty Board of the Company, needed Dutch-trained clergymen to edify and teach the local population. Gain was the aim of the Lords XVII, but the One Lord above all was entitled to His share, and an ample supply of literate and God-fearing locals was good for business.

The VOC had established a Dutch Seminary in Colombo where the fear of God was instilled together with a respect for learning. Bright local boys connected with the Dutch were given a chance to study all the subjects they would be taught at school in the Netherlands and, if they showed particular promise, they were sent to the Republic to study theology and become clergymen.

Pieter's own father and his uncle de Melho had been students at the Dutch Seminary and eventually both became headmaster; two brothers of his father had studied there as well.

The Ondaatjes were a bright family, and respectable too, although they were not of Dutch descent. They had come from South India, notwithstanding their Dutch sounding name. And although the surnames of their relatives de Melho and de Silva sounded Portuguese, their ancestors too had come from South India, as so many of the Ceylonese.

They had inter-married with the European settlers and become Christians; they had even given clergymen to the Dutch Reformed Church. Pieter Ondaatje's father, the Reverend Willem Juriaan Ondaatje, while studying in the Dutch Republic, had married a girl from Amsterdam. Pieter was half Dutch.

And Christopher Ondaatje, my companion on the walls of Galle? What does he have of a Dutchman? His mother was a Gratiaen, a family already prominent in Ceylon in the eighteenth century, originally from the Flemish city of Brugges in the Southern Netherlands, now Belgium. His grandmother's name was Jonklaas, very Dutch as well. But Christopher does not speak Dutch. Not even the Dutch families in Sri Lanka speak Dutch anymore. Dutch had already been forgotten in the nineteenth century when the English established themselves. In the 150 years that the Dutch held the coasts of Ceylon, they had never imposed their language; in fact, they themselves had been speaking Portuguese with their servants, the local people, the King and often even in their own families.

The Portuguese had been there before them, and Portuguese had become the lingua-franca; it was easier on the throat than the guttural Dutch.

It was in Portuguese that the King of Ceylon concluded the first contacts between the Dutch and the Ceylonese, a Portuguese ultimatum at that: "Que bebem vinho, noa he bon. Deos fes justicia. Se quisieres pas, pas; Se quires guerra, guerra" – He who drinks wine is no good. God will do justice. If you look for peace, peace. If you want war, war.

He who drank wine and was no good, was Sebald de Weert, vice-admiral of a Dutch fleet visiting Ceylon in 1603, the second Dutch expedition to come to Ceylon.

A year earlier, a Dutch fleet had appeared on the East coast under the command of Admiral Joris van Spilbergen. He had been sent with three ships, named the *Sheep,* the *Lamb,* and the *Ram,* to investigate rumors that there were "great and profitable opportunities for trade in Ceylon, its stones are rubies and sapphires, cinnamon scenting its forests, and the most common plants furnish precious perfumes; elephants run there in herds . . . while brilliant peacocks and the bird of Paradise occupy the place of our rooks and swallows."
Dutch trading expeditions had already explored the Indies further east and clashed with the Portuguese established there. Now Ceylon had drawn the attention of the Dutch merchant adventurers.

The Portuguese had been colonizing Ceylon for over 100 years. The Ceylonese under their local Kings had been fighting the Portuguese and each other. Eventually one local chieftain had succeeded in establishing absolute supremacy

The first contact between the Ceylonese and the Dutch. The Emperor Vimala Dharma Suriya and Admiral Joris van Spilbergen hand in hand, 1602.
from HISTORIAEL JOURNAEL, 2ND EDITION, 1605.

over the Ceylonese and called himself "the great and mighty Emperor of Ceylon, Vimala Dharma Suriya."

The Portuguese held the coasts, the Emperor the interior. The Emperor knew that the Dutch and the Portuguese were enemies and rivals. Believing in the universal maxim "my enemy's enemy is my friend," he welcomed Admiral van Spilbergen and his flock of Sheep, Lamb and Ram as friends and allies against the Portuguese, those ravenous wolves in human shape.

The Emperor decided to court the Dutch. Spilbergen was invited to the capital Kandy, a formidable journey of some weeks, up mountains and over passes and narrow ridges, deliberately left inaccessible. Imperial elephants and palanquins – beds carried by bearers – were provided to Spilbergen who was received by the Queen and the royal children in their private chambers. The Emperor even started to learn Dutch: "Kandy is nu Holland" – "Kandy is now Holland," he decreed. Gifts were exchanged, some business was done and a treaty drafted of mutual support against the Portuguese. So far, so good. The Dutch were going to help the Emperor, and the Queen thought Spilbergen was a perfect gentleman.

A second fleet with less pastoral names appeared that same year. The vice-admiral, Sebald de Weert, went up to Kandy as well, but this time we do not hear of any idyllic encounters with the Emperor and his family. De Weert must have been a tough man. The strenuous ascent to Kandy had only whetted his appetite. He proceeded to climb Adam's Peak and visited the famous place of pilgrimage for all religions on the island, the first European known to have done so. While the vice-admiral was taking the measurements of the footstep on the top, which Buddhists claim as Buddha's footprint and Muslims as Adam's, the Emperor kept in touch with his arch-enemies, the Portuguese. He thought he had better keep a foot in both camps.

The next year de Weert appeared again off the east coast of Ceylon. The Emperor was now positively plotting with the Portuguese and wanted to give them a proof of his steel. A conference was arranged on shore with some of the Dutch.

After having drunk his Imperial Majesty's health somewhat liberally, de Weert heard Vimala Dharma Suriya say in plain Sinhala: "Bandapan me balla" – "bind this dog." When de Weert drew his weapon he was killed and so were his companions, whereafter the Emperor sent his laconic message to the Dutch fleet, reverting to Portuguese: "If you look for peace, peace, if you want war, war." A realistic linguist. It might after all not be worth his while to learn Dutch.

One year later. No longer hand in hand but hand-to-hand: Vice-admiral Sebald de Weert and his men murdered, 1603.
from DE BRY, 1607.

Fences, however, were mended, and the Dutch did all the serious fighting for the Ceylonese against the Portuguese.
The Emperor's successor, Raja Sinha II, continued to use the Dutch to throw out the Portuguese.
Finally in 1656 the last Portuguese stronghold, Colombo, fell after a siege in which the defenders fought like lions.

The Portuguese aim had been to convert the Ceylonese to Christianity and colonize the entire island including the highland center. The Dutch were only interested in a few fortified strongholds on their shipping route to the East Indies. Their main interest otherwise was the cinnamon trade. A treaty with Raja Sinha II gave them the desired strongpoints and exclusive trading rights in local products in exchange for military help to the Ceylonese. Raja Sinha used to call them "his Hollanders," and his Hollanders humored the Emperor's pathological self-esteem by pretending they were only guarding, not occupying, His Imperial Majesty's forts, and administering the areas where they held sway on H.I.M.'s behalf, not governing them in their own right.

As long as the Dutch could make profits they were prepared to send envoys who prostrated themselves before the Emperor and brought him fresh supplies for his private zoo. They had come for trade and trade needs peace and good neighborly relations. Provided the Emperor kept his side of the bargain the Dutch were prepared to leave him alone in his capital in the mountains of the interior.

Often when talking to our Ceylonese friends I was surprised at their nostalgia for the Dutch. The stiff British would never think of kneeling before the Ceylonese Emperor. On the contrary, the first thing they did after they took over from the Dutch was to invade the Ceylonese capital and deport the whole Imperial Family. The days of the Dutch seemed idyllic in comparison. Would our Ceylonese friends admire the Dutch as unreservedly if they had still been there in 1948 instead of giving up power in 1796?

Christopher, too, is convinced that the Dutch were better rulers than the English. "They did not impose their class system on this society. And they were the first to educate boys born in their colonies, and even sent them to the Netherlands to complete their studies at Dutch Universities."

But why did Pieter Ondaatje not become a clergyman like his father and return to follow a respectable career on the island where he was born? Indeed, did he ever study Theology in Holland?
He went to the Latin and Greek School in Amsterdam for four years and entered University where he studied Theology, all appropriate steps for becoming a Protestant Minister. But his restless mind seems not to have been satisfied with Theology alone. He followed courses in the faculties of Philosophy, Medicine and Law as well, and took two doctoral degrees: the first in Philosophy at the University of Utrecht with a thesis on perception, mind, matter, memory, the laws of gravity and Keppler's laws, and the second in Law at the University of Leiden.
He was in his eighth year at University when he graduated with a doctoral degree in Law. But he had used his time for many other pursuits besides his academic studies.
His two theses, written in Latin, were published. He had to defend them orally, in Latin, during the solemn ceremonies which used to grace doctoral graduations at Dutch Universities.
Soon he would use his oratorical gifts for less academic pursuits and speak simple Dutch.

It so happened that in the period of 1782 to 1787, when Pieter was studying to become a Doctor and "Meester" (abbreviated 'Mr.' in Dutch), political earthquakes shook the solid Dutch and led to civil war, foreign invasion and mass emigration.
Only during their War of Independence, the so-called Eighty Years War [1568–1648] had the Dutch experienced such upheavals, but then the nation had been united. Now province stood against province, town against town, one member of a town council against another, family against family.
Now the old quip of "the Seven United, d i s u n i t e d Netherlands" achieved a dreadful real meaning.
Pieter found himself in a hornets' nest. However, it set his spirit on edge; he used his words to gad, his pen to sting and became a famous figure for every schoolboy who has learnt his lessons of Dutch history.

> Eight years did I myself apply and studied more and more.
> Medicine, Law, Philosophy even, alas, Theology.
> And still I wonder why, despite a doctoral degree
> I am no wiser than before.
>
> freely translated from Goethe's *Faust*

P.P.J. Quint Ondaatje, A.L.M., Ph.D. et J.U.D.

CHAPTER II

In the Backwaters of Utrecht

In Amsterdam, Pieter Ondaatje lived with his maternal grandparents. His grandfather Pieter Quint came from a large family. Their father had become a citizen of Amsterdam in the beginning of the century. Most Quints were artisans, milliners, glovemakers, coffin-makers. Pieter's receptive mind and impressionable character might have lacked inspiration in the modest circle of his grandparents, but this was amply made up for by the stimulus which he received from the Latin and Greek school and from Amsterdam itself.
The city was cosmopolitan and vibrating, intersected by waterways and canals, and surrounded by water and water meadows. From every point of view ships or masts could be seen. The smells of brackish water, fish and tar reminded Pieter of the waterfront of Colombo. Amsterdam was at that time the second largest commercial center of the world, only recently overtaken by London. Its streets overflowed with seamen and bargemen, merchants and tradesmen, with moneymen and middlemen, visitors and foreigners, with low life and high life. When Pieter went to Utrecht – only thirty miles inland from Amsterdam – to start his studies, he came to a different world.

Utrecht with some 30,000 inhabitants was a small city compared to Amsterdam with a population of 200,000. Utrecht still found room within its Medieval fortified walls. The town was dominated by the Dom Tower, the highest churchtower in the Netherlands.
It had retained a certain ecclesiastical solemnity from the past when the town and the province, also called Utrecht, had been the territory of a prince-bishop, the first and foremost bishop of the Netherlands, whose seat was founded in the seventh century. But in the early 1500's, the prince-bishop had been forced to give up his wordly powers; and bishops vanished altogether when Utrecht joined the Reformation.

Life in the town of Utrecht was brightened by the students of the old university and graced by many patrician and noble families with estates in the province of Utrecht and elegant houses in town along the two main canals or grachten, the Oude Gracht and the Nieuwe Gracht. Utrecht was very old and very elegant. The Medieval church properties had been secularised and acquired by those patricians and nobles who lived in the elegant houses on the Oude and Nieuwe Gracht. These prebends provided ample incomes to their wordly holders for

CHAPTER II

The Town Hall and the Dom Tower in Utrecht.
by JAN DE BEYER, 1746.

whom the collection of rent was not a very time-consuming business. There was much disposable income and free time in the elegant quarters of Utrecht. Its inhabitants lived an undisturbed and quiet life.
And the students, that other group of outstanding inhabitants of Utrecht? For them, too, life was not over-difficult nor were their studies over-exacting.
Utrecht did not have much industry and trade. The rest of the population depended for their living on rentiers and students. The University employed only a dozen of professors and hardly any staff or administration.

The city had not grown in size since the Middle Ages.
Cattle grazed along the city walls. Large pleasure gardens stretched behind the better houses in town. On the street-side, along both sides of the moat-like deep canals overshadowed by trees, these houses presented a line of uninterrupted facades with large windows and imposing front doors behind flights of stone steps.
Century-old lindens and beech trees grew in the gardens; the city walls were planted with avenues of elms. From a distance the city looked like a forest, with church-towers rising above the treetops, the tallest, the Dom Tower, visible for miles around.

Trekschuiten, passenger-barges drawn by horses along streams and canals, connected the city of Utrecht with the heart of the Dutch Republic: the large province of Holland and the cities of Amsterdam, Haarlem, Leiden, Delft, Dordrecht and Rotterdam. The trekschuit was a comfortable, cheap, and sociable way of travelling.

From the roof cabin of the trekschuit the passengers could enjoy the beautiful views along the river Vecht between Utrecht and the castle of Muiden near Amsterdam. The river was lined with mansions surrounded by parks of broderies and parterres, full of topiary and lined with high trimmed hedges.

Each country place vied with its neighbors in the luxury of the house and the splendor of its symmetries; pools like mirrors, fountains and waterworks, marble nymphs and fauns in niches in the darkgreen walls of clipped yew, entry-gates crowned with gilded scroll-work and intricate wrought-iron railings along the river.

The borders of the Vecht were covered with a double line of water gardens and water palaces, all facing the grey and slow river, covered most of the time by a grey and low sky. Each garden-palace on a few acres only, a small-scale reproduction of the favorite designs of the Sun King of Versailles; more than one hundred of them on both sides of the river.

The Triumphant river Vecht.
from DE ZEGELPRALENDE VECHT, 1719.

CHAPTER II

The "trekschuit", a convivial means of transport, picking up passengers at the "pleasure" house of Suypestein [Boozeston].
by CORNELIS TROOST.

The city of Utrecht displayed its origin as the seat of the Medieval Bishop by the large number of churches and former monasteries hidden between the houses, gardens and canals, or rising from the cobblestone pavements of irregularly shaped squares. At full and half hours bells chimed, the Dom Tower taking the lead with a psalm or one of the hymns sung on Sundays in the austere whitewashed brick churches of the Reformed Religion.
At dusk the vigil was rung from the Buurkerk, and the wooden gateways of the four city gates were closed. Until 10 o'clock, pedestrians could still go in and out by giving a tip to the watchman, who would open a small door in the huge gateways, but at the sound of the "knaves" bell from the Dom Tower the entire city was locked up until dawn next day. The nightwatch started their hourly rounds while the members of the town militia were on duty in the guardroom of the Town Hall in case of burglary or fire. Needless to say that burglary rarely occurred; the patricians could sleep undisturbed and in safety. Even all beerhouses and public places had to close at the sound of the "knaves" bell at 10.

Nobody would have believed that great changes were soon to be brought about by this same town militia, this rather somnolent epitome of law and order, after it had been stirred from its Medieval slumber and taken inspiration from the example of the American revolutionaries.
Small, old-fashioned Utrecht, a backwater of the Dutch Republic, would establish representative democracy before the rest of the Netherlands, and more amazingly, before the French, the most revolutionary reformers in the whole of Europe.
The bridge between the New World in Boston and Philadelphia and the new order in France would be the city of Utrecht.
It would turn out to be a drawbridge in true Dutch fashion, no sooner let down than drawn up again by the bridge-keepers of the old order.

None of the reformers of Utrecht became more prominent than Pieter Ondaatje. He would be cut off on the wrong side, be banned from the Dutch Republic and live in exile in France to witness the terror and killing which he and his companions had avoided when they had their year of glory.
But those who build bridges receive their honors when people start to cross over.

> "Place one foot of a compass in the middle of Holland
> and extend the other leg 50 miles and strike a circle,
> and you would include more learning and more
> information, and more riches than any other spot on
> the globe of the same extent."
>
> Benjamin Waterhouse, an American medical student
> at Leiden University around 1780.

CHAPTER II

Henrik Danielszoon Hooft [1716–1794].
SILVER PORTRAIT BY HENDRIK ROODENBERG.

CHAPTER III

On The Shrimp Market

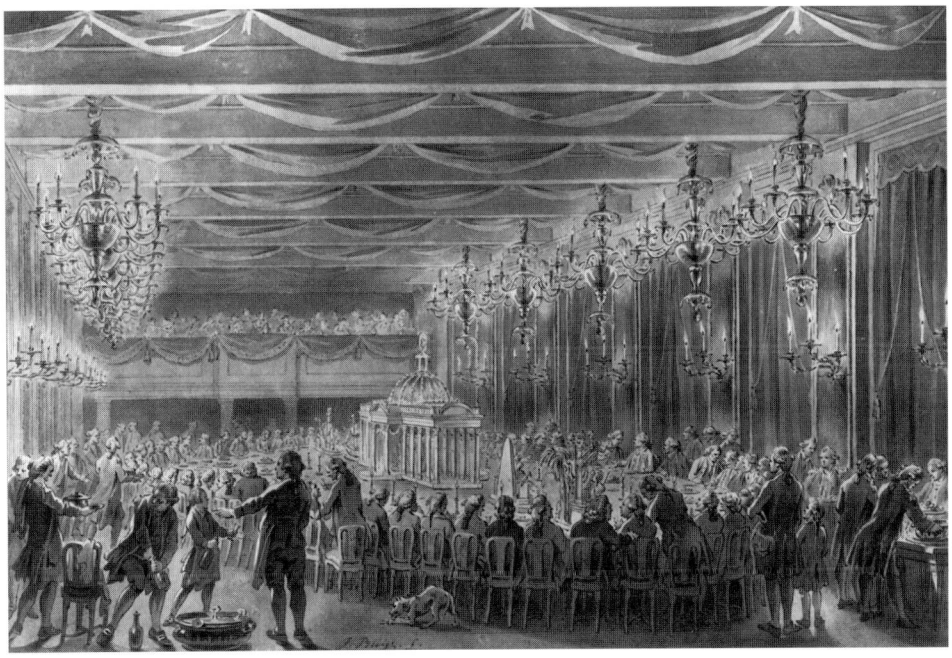

The Shrimp Doelen and the Temple of Freedom.
by JACOBUS BUYS, 1786.

On the 26th of April 1783 some seventy worthy gentlemen gathered together for a solemn, almost ritual, banquet in one of the old halls of Amsterdam. Since the Middle Ages the crossbowmen of the town militia had met in the Crossbow Doelen (Handboog Doelen) alongside the shrimp market on the Singel canal, one of the original moats defending the Medieval city walls. In the Golden Age, that is the seventeenth century in which the Dutch Provinces had become fabulously wealthy, the city of Amsterdam had tripled in size and had spilt over into three concentric rings of canals with flanking houses, on all sides of its old round city core: on all sides, save to the North where lay "het IJ," Amsterdam's harbor. The fleets, heavy with gold and silver from the America's, silk and spices from the Tropics, and wood and grain from the Baltics, anchored in het IJ and – visible from many parts of Amsterdam – reminded citizens and visitors that

CHAPTER III

Amsterdam and the rest of the Republic depended for luxuries and peace on ships and cargoes.

These seventy gentlemen gathering at the venerable venue known as the Shrimp Doelen were very aware of the importance of ships and cargoes; many of them were merchants and shipping magnates themselves.

At the head of the table sat one of Amsterdam's burgomasters, Henrik Hooft Danielszoon,* at that time sixty-seven years old, a gaunt man with small eyes, a nose like a parrot's beak and an old-fashioned periwig.

On his right sat Joan Derk van der Capellen tot den Pol and on his left John Adams, the official representative of the United States of America.

The Hooft family had been merchants since the Middle Ages. They came from one of the small shipbuilding and fishing towns North of Amsterdam in a part of the Province of Holland called West-Frisia. Holland, the largest province of the Seven United Netherlands, had been made habitable by its people with their own hands. These age-long efforts had reinforced the natural sturdiness and self reliance of the Hollanders and West-Frisians. Their tightly knit families who had inherited the reins of local power from their ancestors, together with the family's ships and property, bent for no one in their marshy and watery element.

The first Hooft who entered the stage of anecdotes perished at sea in his late seventies with one of his sons. As he had seven more, the Hooft name survives to this day.

Old Willem Janszoon Hooft must have been a successful captain and shipowner, as he managed to give to five of his sons a ship each. Once, in the early 1500's, the old captain and his five sons were sailing through the Danish Sound in a single procession, one ship after the other. They were on their way to the Baltic Sea with a cargo of dried fish, salt and cheese which they would exchange for timber and hides from Russia, and grain from East Prussia. The Danish King, one of the many named Christian, happened to be nearby as toll was collected. "What is your name?" the Danes asked father Hooft and the other five skippers. When they got the same answer "Hooft from Amsterdam" six times, the King was informed. He invited this enterprising firm of Hooft & Sons to his castle and gave all of them free passage for life.

Some half century later, when the Dutch were fighting their War of Independence, a grandson of the old captain, Cornelis Pieterszoon Hooft, together with a small group of like-minded Protestants, took over the government of Amsterdam from the Catholic and pro-Spanish faction which had ruled the city

---

* In Amsterdam it had been customary since the Middle Ages to add to one's name the Christian name of one's father with the suffix "zoon" (son) even if the family had a proper family name. This patronym was sometimes put behind the Christian name, sometimes after the family name.

before. This Hooft became burgomaster in 1588, was reelected many times, and died in 1626.

During his life the city of Amsterdam grew at a phenomenal pace, both in size and importance. For those who nowadays visit Amsterdam, that cosy mixture of middle class virtues and excessive freedom, it is difficult to imagine that the city in the seventeenth and eighteenth centuries was a splendid, virtually independent city-state, the Venice of the North.

Amsterdam contributed more to the Province of Holland than all the other cities together. Thanks to Amsterdam, Holland in its turn could make the other Dutch provinces follow and act as one nation as long as all remained aware that the welfare of that nation depended on trade, the fleet and open seas.

Cornelis Pieterszoon Hooft [1547–1626].
Father of Pieter Corneliszoon Hooft, the famous Dutch poet, historian and dramatist.

CHAPTER III

The seven provinces which formed the United Netherlands had less than two million people. The Dutch had realized that they were too few to build up armies for an aggressive policy of power.

They could defend themselves by ships and by inundating large tracts of land. God had made the world, the Dutch had made Holland and Zeeland, and could also unmake it into an archipelago of habitations surrounded by water whenever they were threatened by invasion. During the War of Independence, more Spaniards had been drowned than shot. The French in 1672, and again in 1793, found these waterworks impassable.

The Republic lived like a fish in water; water was a matter of life and death. To survive in this precarious way the Dutch needed ingenuity, both in mastery of their environment and in international statecraft. The Republic strove to make a living from sea and land, and to stay in the middle of the great opposing European powers. Neutrality was the only way by which the Dutch could hope to remain middle men. A neutrality secured by armed ships. Money was necessary for this policy, money which could be made from cargoes carried in ships and escorted by navies, provided and guided by Amsterdam. Its families ran the city as a virtual state in the state, as fathers , masters and merchants.

There was nothing new in families running entire cities. This had happened in all towns in the Netherlands since the earliest times; the power of these often interrelated families was restricted by age-old liberties, or privileges, given to corporate bodies composed of other citizens, such as town militias and guilds of tradesmen and artisans.

The nobility, which played such a large part in other European countries, had lost most of its political influence in the Netherlands after the War of Independence. Only in the so-called "land" provinces of Gelderland, Overijssel and Utrecht did the nobility still play a dominating role. Large estates locked their noble owners into local office. If a father or elder brother happened to run the family estate, a young nobleman usually joined the armed forces or the diplomatic service and lost his local influence.

The land provinces were economically unimportant. To the monies levied by the seven provinces for those activities which they had decided should be communal – in fact, only the army and navy and foreign affairs - the province of Holland contributed around sixty percent, Friesland eleven percent, Zeeland nine percent and the other four provinces around five percent each. Amsterdam alone paid around fifty percent of Holland's contribution.

The sea province of Holland was dominated by cities. Eighteen towns had a seat in the provincial government, called the States of Holland and West-Frisia. In those days the inhabitants of a province were not politically active as individual voters but were represented by corporate bodies or Orders, town people by the Order of the Cities, and nobles and farmers by the Order of the Nobility. A citizen in his city was represented by the "Vroedschap" – Council – consisting of "Vroede Vaderen," "wise fathers." In most cities of the Republic, Council was composed without any influence of the citizens which it was supposed to represent.

A Municipal Council usually consisted of thirty to fourty councillors from whom were appointed each year a small number of burgomasters. Council appointed aldermen, "schepenen," who acted as judges.

In the States of the province of Holland, the Order of the Cities had eighteen votes, the Nobility only one. Decisions were taken by a majority of these nineteen votes.

Although Amsterdam had only one vote out of nineteen in the States of Holland, it usually succeeded in making Holland do what it wanted by wielding carrot and stick.

This intertwining of commerce and politics, the many local centers of power and wealth and the lack of a central administration drew a great number of able citizens into the government of their cities and provinces. Contrary to other important European countries of that period, there was in the Netherlands not one social pyramid but fifty or sixty; at least 500 families shared power and influence.

In the Middle Ages each province of the Netherlands had been ruled by its own indigenous family of sovereign Counts or Dukes. Through marriage and inheritance, various provinces had come under the same sovereign and in the 1400's most provinces were ruled by the House of Burgundy, a cadet branch of the Royal House of France. At one time even the prince-bishop of Utrecht was a bastard son of the Duke of Burgundy. Eventually, all provinces, seventeen in total, were united under the heir of the Burgundian Empire, Charles V, King of Spain and Emperor of the Holy Roman Empire.

Whenever the Burgundians needed money they called together the estates: the clergy, the nobles and the cities of their Netherlands hereditary territories. These estates, meeting as the "States General" would decide on the request for money, usually consenting in exchange for certain privileges or liberties, such as non-interference in the appointment of city councillors, or no billeting of troops without the consent of the affected. The King-Emperor, Charles V, and his son Philip II, King of Spain, continued to convoke the States General. After the start of the Dutch rebellion the States General met on their own initiative and acted as the link between the rebellious provinces.

They had, however, no other role than being a forum for the delegates of the various provinces. In later days the States General were sometimes compared to a conference of ambassadors. These delegates were not entitled to vote without a specific mandate of their province and were definitely not allowed to interfere with provincial and municipal privileges and independencies.

In 1579, during the early phase of the War of Independence, the seven Northern Provinces which became the Dutch Republic drew up a solemn treaty among themselves, the Union of Utrecht, which confirmed provincial independence and granted only limited powers to the States General.

CHAPTER III

Count William of Nassau, Prince of Orange [1533–1584].
from P.C. HOOFT'S DUTCH HISTORIES, edition 1703.

The Dutch Republic had been born out of an armed rebellion, which was tolerated, supported, and later led by a German nobleman with vast possessions in the Netherlands, William Count of Nassau, who was also Prince of the tiny principality of Orange in the South of France.
The Prince of Orange spent his private fortune on raising a regular army for the rebels, and to Europe's amazement he and his brothers managed to rally seven of the seventeen internally divided Dutch provinces to a common cause and expel the Spaniards from the Northern Netherlands. Because he was diplomatic and could hide his thoughts, his enemies called him sly which led by a mistranslation to his famous nickname of William the Silent. In fact, he was affable and forthcoming.

The cause which united a population, still only partly Protestant, was freedom of religion and freedom from centralized and arbitrary taxation. Both freedoms formed a Dutchman's most holy tenet: to enjoy his conscience and his purse in liberty.

While the struggle with Spain was continuing under the two sons of Prince William of Orange, Prince Maurits and Prince Frederik Hendrik, its nature changed from a war of liberation to a campaign of consolidation of territorial gains and of prize taking of ships, cargoes, forts and colonies.
Particularly profitable were privateering expeditions against Spanish South America, rich in silver, and the Portuguese East Indies, the Portuguese regretting forever the union of their Crown with Spain.

Prince William of Orange was born a Lutheran, brought up as a Catholic and practiced a French version of Calvinism. He was deeply religious and extraordinarily tolerant, but could not enshrine guarantees for an equal treatment of all religions before his death. The Calvinist Dutch Reformed Church became the official State Church to which all who wanted public office had to adhere. But other churches were tolerated and respect for religious dissent became ingrained in Dutch society and in the national character.

The rebellion had been defended on the grounds that the Sovereign, King Philip of Spain, had violated the rights and privileges which had been granted by his ancestors in the Middle Ages to the various cities, corporate bodies and provinces of the Netherlands. The King's men had persecuted heretics – non-Catholics – and sentenced them to death in special courts, and the Dutch were taxed without the consent of their Estates.
The States General in 1581 formally forswore their allegiance to the Sovereign. "A prince of the realm, appointed by God, is chief over his subjects to preserve and guard them from all injustice, ill-treatment and coercion, like a shepherd his sheep. The subjects have not been created by God for the pleasure of the prince, to submit to him in everything he may command whether it be godly or ungodly, right or wrong, and to serve him as slaves."
If he does not treat his subjects like children or sheep entrusted to his care, he cannot be considered a Prince, but a "Tyrant" and may be deposed.
Having forsworn their Sovereign, the various Provinces themselves ended up with the sovereignty, so to speak, by default.
Full sovereignty includes the right to enact laws, to tax, to administer justice, to declare war and peace, to negotiate treaties. But the Provincial States had to share areas such as justice, taxation and lawgiving with cities proud and jealous of their age-old liberties. A second restriction on full provincial sovereignty lay in the Union of Utrecht; in that treaty the provinces had solemnly sworn to use their common mouthpiece, the States General, for foreign affairs and war and peace.

CHAPTER III

Two principles lay at the creation of the new Republic:
One, provincial supremacy, gave the Dutch Republic its archaic, individualistic character: a commonwealth of sovereign provinces with a common institution in The Hague, the States General with limited powers.
The other principle was embodied in the words which the States General had used to forswear allegiance to the Sovereign who had become a tyrant. It acknowledged the right of subjects to depose their rulers.
It would give citizens a good argument against any higher power, be it burgomaster, town council or Provincial States, if those citizens thought that the authority had broken the conditions under which it had been given the right to rule. Subjects do not have to accept everything their rulers decree and rulers have to act as "shepherds" of the sheep entrusted to their care.
The echo of those words would come to disturb the peace of the periwig rulers of the cosy Dutch towns and provinces two hundred years later.

Prince William fell in 1584 at the hand of a murderer openly incited by the King of Spain.

The assassination of the Prince of Orange, 1584.
from P. C. HOOFT's Dutch Histories.

Days before his death, the States of Holland had been discussing whether to offer him the sovereignty of their province. Cornelis Pieterszoon Hooft had delivered a speech in the Council meeting of Amsterdam against such a move. He cited many Biblical examples of monarchs who had devoured their sheep. And besides, he added, we have now managed some years quite well without a Sovereign, so why should we change? If, however, the matter would come to a final vote in the Council of Amsterdam, Hooft insisted that the town militia should first be consulted. Council resolved accordingly. This was the last time that bodies representing the common citizen would be reckoned with. Soon the States of Holland decreed that town councils should no longer consult their militias, although the States had no right to interfere in such a municipal matter.

The next one to appeal to the old tradition to consult the town militia in city matters is . . . Pieter Ondaatje, in Utrecht, two centuries later.

The Netherlands remained a republic, faute de mieux.
But the House of Orange was still around.
What place was there for a princely family in a republican confederation?

In the old Burgundian days, and under Emperor Charles V and his son, King Philip of Spain, the Sovereign would appoint to each province separately a Stadhouder which means literally "someone who holds a position on behalf of someone else," a lieutenant.
Prince William of Orange had been Stadhouder of Holland, Zeeland and Utrecht before the outbreak of the rebellion. He had resigned from all his royal commissions and had joined the rebels. The States of Holland, Zeeland, and Utrecht had appointed him as Stadhouder again, although the King whom he was to represent had been deposed.
When the provinces became used to the idea of being their own Sovereigns, they did not abolish the post of Stadhouder but continued to appoint one themselves. The young son of William the Silent, Prince Maurits, was appointed Stadhouder in all provinces, except Friesland and Groningen, where his cousin was elected Stadhouder.
Theoretically a Stadhouder had now become the executive of the province which had appointed him, its first servant. He was made responsible for the maintenance of the Dutch Reformed Religion and for the administration of justice.
But most important in a nation which would still be at war for nearly sixty years after the death of William of Orange, the Stadhouder had also been made the commander in chief of the army and the navy, raised by the States General; a commander with far reaching authority, but always under the ultimate control of the Lords High Mightinesses, as the States General came to be called.

CHAPTER III

This would inevitably lead to trouble because the supreme command became in fact, if not in law, hereditary to the House of Orange-Nassau. People started to consider the supreme commander as a sort of monarch, which galled all upholders of the true republican constitution, among whom the patrician families of the towns of Holland were the staunchest and those of Amsterdam the richest and most powerful. In peacetime the adage "who pays the piper calls the tune" usually decided the outcome of the struggle for supremacy, but in wartime weapons could be stronger than the republican constitution and the strings of the purse combined.

In the seventeenth century, the Dutch Republic was engaged in war a great deal: war with Spain until 1648, two naval wars with England, and an invasion by France in 1672, followed by an occupation of part of the Republic for nearly two years. Thereafter war with France until 1713.

During the two hundred years of the Dutch Republic's existence, one can observe a see-saw between Holland led by Amsterdam on the one side and the Princes of Orange on the other. Now Amsterdam and Holland are up and the Prince is down, now the Prince is on top and the patricians are off balance.

Sometimes the Princes of Orange were not only down but out. Between 1650 and 1672, there was no Stadhouder in most provinces.

Then, in 1672, when the French invaded the Republic, a young Prince William was hastily appointed as Stadhouder: William III, the last direct descendant in the male line of William the Silent. Eventually he would become King of England, too. He was said to rule the Kingdom of England like a puppet of Parliament and the Republic of the Netherlands like a King.

After his death in 1702, no Stadhouder was appointed in most provinces until 1747. Then, a second French invasion paved the way for Stadhouder William IV and his son William V, both unimpressive scions of a side-branch of the House of Orange.

Prince Maurits, the son of William the Silent, was considered to be a military genius. He had become involved in religious and political factions in the early days of the Republic and had come out with greater power than before. In Amsterdam he had appeared at the head of troops to depose some councillors and burgomasters who displeased the party which Maurits backed and to replace them by others. This was a blatant infraction of the Union of Utrecht and of the rights and privileges of the city. The only person who dared to stand up to Prince Maurits and delivered a long speech in which spades were called by their name, was old Burgomaster Cornelis Pieterszoon Hooft, by then seventy-two years of age. The Prince sat quietly through the speech. The old burgomaster had been a personal friend of his father, William the Silent, who had often stayed in Hooft's house in Amsterdam. When Hooft had finished, Prince Maurits replied somewhat familiarly:

"Good father, it has to be thus for the time being. The needs of the time and of the country require it."

Hooft, during his long life at the helm of Amsterdam, had shown on earlier occasions that he dared to speak his mind and that his ethics were high, exceptionally high for the age of greed and naked display of power in which he lived.
He had fearlessly denounced colleagues who had enriched themselves by real estate transactions based on inside knowledge. He had all his life maintained that government should be in the hands of a few only, the wealthiest and most experienced members of society, but he expected those to serve the interest of the citizens first and never use their positions for personal gain. He called this his aristocratic system of republicanism.
He had warned time and again against the danger that this aristocratic republican system would degenerate into a self-serving oligarchy. He beseeched the "Regents," as the ruling class now started to be called, to remember that they were being watched closely.
"The Regents can be deemed to stand on a stage from which their actions are observed and judged by the great and the small, and we should not believe that all the wisdom of the community is to be found in the chambers of government only. In this city alone there are so many wise and good men of judgement outside this Council, who are watching things closely."
Therefore, Hooft added, should we Regents avoid "any suspicion that we are pursuing private profit to the detriment of the common good."

"All the world is a stage " was not borrowed by Hooft from Shakespeare.

Joan Derk van der Capellen tot den Pol [1741–1784].
by L. J. CATHELIN after J.A. KALDENBACH.

CHAPTER IV

A Different Kettle of Fish

The banquet on the 26th of April of 1783 in the Shrimp Doelen in Amsterdam reminds us of the stage. The gallery was filled with musicians and a choir presented "Odes to the Fatherland," composed by a certain Pieter Vreede, a cloth manufacturer who thus musically made his first entry on the stage of Dutch national history. We will meet him fifteen years later in the role of co-head of government in a tragedy in which Pieter Ondaatje would be a stagehand. The banquet had nothing tragical.

Next to Burgomaster Hooft sat a man on whom the eyes were directed of all who professed reforms: Joan Derk van der Capellen.
He came from an old family of one of the land provinces and had inherited the fine castle of Appeltern and ownership and seigneurial rights over the landed estates of Alforst, Boeleham, Hagen and de Pol, of which he was "de Heer," the Seigneur or manorial Lord. He was adressed as Baron van der Capellen tot den Pol.
The democratic citizens were proud that even in the Order of Nobility people could be found who saw the need for reform of the system. The reformists had come to be known as "Patriots." Many called themselves by that name, merely to show their dislike of the old order, embodied in the Stadhouder and his Orangemen. Amsterdam was Patriot because it was proud, liked to be independent and disliked a Prince of Orange. Other Patriots were democratic by conviction. The rank and file were self-employed tradesmen and free thinking intellectuals of the broad middle classes. They wanted a say in the way their cities were run. The mob was fickle, could easily be persuaded one way or the other, and would in the land provinces follow their Lords and masters in being Orangemen. Most of the "Dominees," the Dutch Reformed ministers, resented the Regents as the wordly powers placed over them, and therefore tended to glorify the God-ordained House of Orange, however weak its temporary representative might be.

This banquet was very much a Patriot affair.

On the other side of Burgomaster Hooft sat a patriot of a different nation: John Adams, the official representative of the Congress of the United States of America.

CHAPTER IV

John Adams, envoy of the North American States [1735–1826].
by R. VINKELES.

His presence in this Patriot gathering showed how big a role the events in the former British North American colonies were playing in the growing unrest in the Netherlands.
In the wake of the American rebellion, a war had broken out between England and France. The Dutch Sea Provinces, Amsterdam at the head, saw new markets for their shipping and provided the American colonies discreetly with guns and powder. The English were the big competitors at sea and in the Indies. Besides, the American struggle resembled the War of Independence which the Dutch had had to fight themselves two hundred years earlier.
No true Dutchman could hear the news from the new world without sympathizing with the rebels.
At least two manor farms in Holland had been called "America," and one had been decorated with American prints and a bust of George Washington. A Dutch busy-body had written an "American Bible", prescribing to his fellow rebels

overseas how to set up a republican government, and dedicated it to John Adams, that expert on republican constitutions. Taciturn George Washington was revered by Dutch Americophiles as their own William the Silent born again.

In 1780 the Republic had been dragged into war with England. It had been waged entirely at sea, but the Dutch navy was not prepared. Prince William IV, and Prince William V had blocked a naval reinforcement program which Amsterdam and Holland had been advocating since the 1750's.
The Orange faction wanted a strong landarmy which would give the Stadhouder more power, or at least a heavy stick behind his back. Amsterdam had not forgotten that Prince Maurits had appeared at the head of an army to depose the town council; that Prince William III, after the retreat of the Sun King, had occupied with the army under his command the three land provinces as if they were enemy territory and had rammed down their throats a new regulation of government, the infamous "Regerings Reglement," which gave him as much power in those three provinces as any petty potentate in a tiny German principality.

The two forces in the eighteenth century Republic, the Regents and the Stadhouder, were so delicately balanced that everything was blocked if the two could not compromise and agree.

The Regents in the four provinces which were not dominated by the Stadhouder through a Regerings Reglement, were accustomed to compromise. They were from merchant stock although by now leisure and pleasure were more in vogue than hard work and risk taking. As investors and international bankers they remained realists who knew by experience what course would be most profitable. They were not motivated by dynastic ties with European royal families or by the prestige that drives those who live in the world of armies and courts.

William V was three years old when his father died. That prince, William IV, had been brought up at the very provincial, very parsimonious mini-court of the Frisian Stadhouders in Leeuwarden. He was a hunchback and had a flippant, careless character. The branch of the Father of the Fatherland had died out with William III, the King-Stadhouder, married, but without children, to Mary Stuart, whose sister Anne ascended the British throne. Between 1702 and 1747, four of the seven Provincial States of the Dutch Republic had preferred not to appoint a Stadhouder at all. This changed when the French threatened to invade the Republic in the War of the Austrian Succession, one of those gentlemanlike affairs where the English commander at the start of the battle of Fontenoy had ridden up to the French lines and, doffing his three-cornered hat, shouted:
"Messieurs des gardes françaises, tirez les premiers."
The French commander replied, "Messieurs, nous tirons jamais les premiers, tirez vous-mêmes."

CHAPTER IV

Civilities must eventually have led to some compromise because the battle was fought and won by one side or the other.

When the French armies approached the territory of the Dutch Republic in 1747, no such reciprocal civility was shown. Even if the French would have invited the Dutch to shoot first, the Dutch would not have answered in such high spirits. Their usual response was more down to earth; they would inundate large parts of Holland. But the farmers were not prepared this time, as they had been in 1672, to flood their fields and farms. The Regents of the four provinces who had been ruling without a Stadhouder had not made themselves sufficiently popular in that near-half century to expect any sacrifices from the population. On the contrary, the mob in the cities rose up in revolt and clamored for a Prince of Orange, energetically encouraged by the agents of the House of Orange who resorted to the time-honored incentives of genever – Dutch gin – and stuivers – 5 cent pieces. Such was the predicament of the patrician Regents in the town councils whose overriding concern was public order, that Prince William IV was called from his rural court in Friesland and offered Stadhouderian dignities in all the provinces of the Republic, hereditary at that, in the male and female line.

In the cities the mob slunk back to their hovels. No more gin and stuivers for some time.

No Stadhouder had ever been so secure of his position and succession. Yet William IV was not the man to consolidate his gains. Henpecked by his prim and sharp-tongued Hannoverian wife, a daughter of King George II of England, he frittered away the esteem he had enjoyed from the people who had looked upon this Stadhouder-in-waiting from the mythological House of Orange as a saviour from all evils: from the French, the oppressing Regents, taxes, high cost of living, cattle pest, inundations, adulterated genever.

William IV died unmourned, except officially, in 1751.

His son never knew his father. The English Princess, his mother, died when the boy-Prince was 11 years old. He was educated by a guardian, Duke Frederic of Brunswick, popularly known as the Fat Duke, who was far from popular. A debt-ridden bachelor, intriguing, bad tempered, he brought up the boy in awe of himself and suspicious of everybody else, the gentlemen of Amsterdam most of all.

William, who was small, popeyed, and fat, was fobbed off with military trivia and taught to think of himself as a soldier. But his real interest lay in the law. He had the mind of a law clerk, at home in all the intricacies of the Dutch constitution, its many privileges, precedents, treaties and traditions. It enabled him to become a real stickler for his rights and privileges.

The Duke encouraged him to do simple chancery work. William loved to correct drafts, change a word here and there, find a better expression. In later days his private secretaries would be driven to exasperation by the delays he caused by his petty-mindedness, coupled with erratic work habits and no system or order in his correspondence. Important communications went unanswered because they got lost in some coat pocket, to be found months later, if at all. Unread

Prince William V [1748–1806].
by J. F. A. TISCHBEIN, 1789.

letters piled up and were stuffed in closets which had to be shut by shoulder-force.

The Prince himself could not be pushed about. He was intelligent, though not broad-minded. He quickly sensed people's hidden motives, spoke English, French and German fluently, had a self-deprecating wit, but lacked dignity and did not inspire confidence. He was no leader by nature and had been spoiled by his mentor. Still a boy he had been married to the niece of King Frederic the Great of Prussia. That cynical monarch had a high regard for his niece but a low regard for her husband.

Princess Wilhelmine did not have an easy life. She had been brought up to follow, but was a leader by nature. With great tact she managed to cultivate the small stock of dignity left to her husband and played the second fiddle.

In William V's time, the President of the Order of Nobility of Utrecht was Gijsbert Jan van Hardenbroek. He kept a diary in which he recorded political and Court gossip. All his entries are verbatim reports with no comments; we are overhearing private conversations. Those with the Stadhouder reveal more of the character of William V than any psychological study could do. The picture which emerges is scattered over thousands of pages. The reader has to put the fragments together.

One day van Hardenbroek visits William V who confesses to him:
> I wish I were dead, that my father had never become Stadhouder. To abandon everything now would be churlish, otherwise I would say goodbye to their Lords High Mightinesses and would quit being Stadhouder. I feel I am not capable for this job. I wish I were dead. I cannot and I will not last for another year in this way. I work as hard as I can, even to the point of damaging my health and still I cannot satisfy people; that grieves me, that hurts me, and truly I am too weak. Even so I believe that people think that I am good, which is true, but I feel that I have not sufficient capabilities to be in charge of so many affairs. My head turns round and I know hardly what to do and what not. Let the people choose the Pensionary of Holland and the Burgomaster of Amsterdam in my stead. Those two are anyhow in charge of everything.

No "talk of graves, of worms, and epitaphs" but stammerings of self-pity to which the dignified van Hardenbroek replies with a kinder version of the Bishop of Carlisle's answer to Richard II: "My lord, wise men ne'er sit and wail their woes."

Prince William's education had made him insecure. He clung to his rights and privileges as his only anchor and often said he preferred to be chased away rather than to give in one inch. He would have been a good figurehead ruler in some sleepy principality. Unfortunately he was the Stadhouder of all the provinces of the Dutch Republic, the times were not particularly quiet and his powers were such that he could block every activity. There was a general feeling that industry and trade were stagnating and now the nation was at war with England, with the Stadhouder's first cousin, the equally insecure and stubborn King George III.

The war with the American colonies had opened the gates of political discontent in England, too. The standard complaints of the Age of Reason were boisterously voiced: Parliament was unrepresentative and corrupt, the Crown had too much power.
King George III by conscientious application and painful experience grew gradually capable of sensible determination and realistic compromise and made the way free for an effective government under the twenty-four year old William Pitt, the Younger. Pitt's father, William the Elder, had presided over King George II's government and as a prefiguration of Winston Churchill had ensured that England won the Seven Years' War. Pitt the Elder had started his political life as a Whig "patriot boy." The term patriot did not gain as much political currency

in England as it did later in the American colonies and in the Dutch Republic. Pitt the Elder became popular as "the Great Commoner" and claimed that he spoke with "the voice of England." When no longer in government, he became a champion of liberty and of conciliation with the Americans.

When Pitt the Younger became the leader of the government, he had seventeen years ahead of him to steer his King and his country through the shoals of domestic reform and the cliffs of Continental wars. American independence settled, John Adams, one of the guests of honor at the Shrimp Doelen dinner, had been promoted from Envoy to the Dutch Republic to Minister at the Court of St. James. When King George III received him, he said, "Sir, I was the last man in my Kingdom to consent to your independence and shall be the last to do anything to infringe it." The King was a good loser. His cousin, Prince William V, had less common sense. He did not know how to win and did not know how to lose.

In the Republic the system had come to a stalemate. The Regents of Holland were blocked in any breakthrough they might attempt, be it in repairing the fleet, giving new life to trade and industry or reforming the system; the Stadhouder used his power to work against these Regents, but did not take the initiative for necessary reforms.

For two years, 1781 and 1782, the English had blocked the seas. The annual supply of goods from the colonies was held up, commerce and industry in the Dutch Republic lay supine. The Dutch fleet was no match for the British. The Regents and Amsterdam who had insisted on strengthening the fleet were proven right. The stalemate had led to defeat.

The Dutch were watching how the American people had broken a stalemate and how they were establishing a free society based on the People and on Reason. If William had spent his time studying *"Common Sense"* by Thomas Paine, and *"The Declaration of Independence"* inspired by Thomas Jefferson, instead of the constitution of his own United Republic, now called that Gothic Ruin, he might have seen where his chances lay.

The reasoning part of the nation, as the nobleman van Hardenbroek observed, wanted change. If William had sided with these reasoning and reasonable citizens, the broad base of the Dutch Patriots, he would have stayed on top with dignity and grace.

> "We hold these truths to be self-evident, that all men are created equal, that they are endowed, by their Creator, with certain unalienable rights, that among these are life, liberty, and the pursuit of happiness. That to secure these rights, governments are instituted among men, deriving their just powers from the consent of the governed, that whenever any form of government becomes destructive of these ends, it is the right of the people to alter or to abolish it. . . ."
>
> from the Declaration of Independence of the
> United States of America, 1776

The honor of the Dutch Maiden in jeopardy.
by C. VAN CUYLENBURGH

CHAPTER V

Dutch Dessert

The seventy gentlemen gathered at the dinner in the Shrimp Doelen in Amsterdam have by now finished four courses and many bottles of wine. As an entremets Pieter Vreede had recited a patriotic poem which he had composed himself and the choir had sung a fresh cantata. While the plates were being changed a group of men appeared carrying pieces of mirror-glass and what looked like stage props.
Under the direction of a head-confectioner and a master-pastrycook the bits of shiny glass were laid out on the table in scrolled patterns, like the broderies of a formal garden. On top of these mirrors the men quickly put together some buildings of gilded pastry and adorned them with figurines of pastel-tinted sugarwork. The warm light of the chandeliers, caught in these fragmented mirrors, sprinkled glowing sparkles on the compositions which rose before the spectators.
At one end of the table emerged a temple of Freedom, some five feet high, with seven Corinthian pillars, representing the seven provinces of the United Netherlands.
The golden Sun of Liberty shone at the top. Naked toddlers of icing surrounded an altar inside the temple and were picking up freedom charters which lay around discarded. Some of them held gilded coats of arms of Baron van der Capellen tot den Pol and Henrik Hooft Danielszoon.
At the entrance of the temple a less sweet scene provided some drama heavy with allegorical meaning:
A harnessed Gothic Knight, an Orange banner broken in his hand, was on the point of ravishing the Dutch Maiden, who remained serenely in her seat while a hero in Roman attire was attacking the knight.
Everyone recognised in this hero one of those brave Batavians, valiant ancestors of the Dutch. The Batavian was carrying a shield with the words: the Omnipotence of the People.
No one had any doubt who that thwarted knight, forced to impotence, was supposed to represent.
The second table piece, conjured out of the pastry cook's hat, made a less tasteful impression. A haggard looking old man with a long beard and a gown stood on top of a funeral tomb. It was not difficult to guess who he was: Johan van Oldenbarnevelt, after William the Silent the most important statesman the Netherlands had known.

He had kept the Provinces united after the murder of the Father of the Fatherland and had educated and coached his young son, Prince Maurits, for his role as commander of the army of the States General. While Maurits consolidated the territorial victories, van Oldenbarnevelt, the Advocate of Holland as he was styled, acted like a prime minister and dominated Dutch and even European politics in the first decades of the seventeenth century.
Master and pupil fell out with each other. Maurits allied himself with the political and religious opponents of the Advocate and lent his support to a judicial murder.
The great statesman was publicly beheaded in his seventy-first year. On his walk to the scaffold, he had supported himself with a walking stick which became a symbol for his tragic fate and is still preserved and immortalized in a contemporary poem which Dutch schoolboys used to learn by heart.

To make sure that all the banqueters would get the point, the gowned old man of coated sugar was leaning on a candy stick.

For the party assembled here and for their like-minded predecessors, Johan van Oldenbarnevelt had long been the upholder of the privileges for which the War of Independence had been fought and the defender of the constitution which gave ultimate power to the States of the provinces. He had insisted that the States General stay in command of their commander in chief. For the Patriot party, van Oldenbarnevelt was the victim of the tyrannical House of Orange, and a martyr of Freedom.

The sea, that quintessential element of the Dutch, was symbolized by a column as high as the Temple of Freedom. A banner with the words "Mare Liberum" reminded the observers more of the past than of present facts. Three sea wars had forced the British to respect the Dutch fleet and Admirals such as de Ruyter and Tromp. Now the Dutch did not dare to venture outside their harbours. Reality was reflected on the table: a leopard, symbol of stealthy and prying Albion, was seen threatening Justice on top of the column. The confectioners however had sugared the pill. The leopard was attacked by the Dutch Lion, the French Cock and a Snake. Had not a warship of the United States recently flown a flag with an emblematical snake and the words "Do not tread on me." To us, a snake does not seem quite the appropriate national emblem.
We do not know whether it struck a chord of national pride with the third guest of honor, John Adams, the resident minister of the United States of America. He was certainly flattered – if not amused – by the fourth table group which was placed right in front of him. The American Maiden, rather emancipated with the cudgel of Hercules and in the skin of a lion, was holding down with one hand the crowned figure of Tyranny, stretching out her other hand over the Altar of Independence to the Dutch Maiden. In our own time the Dutch Maid[en] is known as a trademark for a detergent; two hundred years ago, she stood for Freedom. In her left hand she held, not a broom, but a lance topped with the Hat of Liberty, the symbol of freedom since Roman days, and with her other hand kept at bay two rather unattractive ladies: Ambition and Flattery who were trying to prevent her shaking hands with her American colleague. A palmtree of spun sugar decorated with the flags of the United States and the Republic, overshadowed this show of goodwill.

It was thanks to the efforts of each of the three guests of honor that hands could be clasped so sweetly in front of the banqueters.
A year earlier the province of Holland had finally twisted the arm of the other provinces and coerced the States General into recognizing the new Republic of the United States of America. Holland had been driven by Amsterdam and Amsterdam by a group of forward-looking Regents and merchants and by all who called themselves Patriots. The driving force in the Town Hall had been Henrik Hooft, the principal Burgomaster on and off since the early '80s.

Hooft and Joan Derk van der Capellen had been friends for a long time. They addressed each other in their letters as "dear cousin." When Joan Derk had suffered the humiliating experience of being kicked out of the Order of the Nobility of the States of his province because of being too independent-minded and too outspoken, Hooft had written him a letter of consolation and comfort: "Please don't be dejected. A jewel cannot shine before it has been polished. Only thereafter can one appreciate its worth. The time will come that you will be called one of the most valuable treasures produced by our Fatherland."

A few months before the banquet, Baron van der Capellen tot den Pol had been reinstated in the Order of Nobility, his honor vindicated before the whole world. Now Burgomaster Hooft proposed a toast on van der Capellen's rehabilitation. Father Hooft's glass was filled with rainwater. "All his life he only drank rainwater and beer," writes a biographer. Beer was not quite appropriate for banquets.
A medal in gold, specially struck for the occasion, was presented to Joan Derk. All other guests received a silver copy.
Two hundred years later a large national exhibition, bookshelves full of publications about van der Capellen and a statue, although not in his own country but in the gardens of the Villa Borghese in Rome, prove how right his friend Hooft had been.

John Adams, on Hooft's other side, had his own reasons to look up to the Dutch baron.
Joan Derk had been the first Dutchman to take up the cause of the American Revolution. Already in 1775 he wrote "We are a people who also have been called rebels and have fought themselves free."
When John Adams arrived in the Dutch Republic in 1780, he had no instructions from Congress and no official letters of introduction. He knew no one in Amsterdam where he settled with his two young sons. One of them, John Quincy Adams, entered Leiden University at fourteen years of age to study law. He had to interrupt his studies within a year to accompany the American envoy to Russia as secretary and French translator. John junior followed in the footsteps of his father and became resident minister of the United States in the Netherlands in 1794. In later life, when he was elected as the sixth President of the United States, to the delight of his by then eighty-nine year old father, he still spoke Dutch.
Father John started to learn the language, but when he became America's second President after George Washington, in 1796, he had forgotten most of it. When John Adams arrived in Amsterdam, his prospects were not so high. The Stadhouder refused to see him and obstructed all overtures from the rebellious colonies of his first cousin.
Although the Republic made a show of neutrality, the English realized that the Dutch were sympathizing with the Americans. When a draft was discovered for a commercial treaty between Amsterdam and the new United States, England declared war on the Dutch Republic.

A street demonstration in Rotterdam in 1782. A Dutch mob follows the American flag.
by DIRK LANGENDIJK.

Although the treaty had been conditional upon peace between the British and the Americans it provided the "praetextum belli" which the British had been looking for. On Christmas Eve of the year of our Lord 1780 they fell upon the Dutch commercial fleet and empire. The one and only battle fought in this war, at the Doggersbank in the North Sea, remained undecided. Both sides claimed victory. The mob in Dutch cities was elated. English flags were trampled underfoot, Dutch and French flags, and the thirteen stripes of the American Confederation, were carried around in triumph.

For the Americans, it did not really matter who could claim victory in the Battle of Doggersbank. The English fleet had been tied up and damaged sufficiently to prevent it from relieving Cornwallis at Yorktown. In this way, Dutch arms and lives contributed to the victorious conclusion of the American War of Independence.

John Adams had arrived in August of 1780 and had written a letter to Burgomaster Hooft who was known for his pro-American feelings. He was warmly received by Hooft in his house on the Herengracht. Joan Derk happened to be staying there as well. The gruff and difficult American who needed money, the highly strung country nobleman who needed sympathy, and the avuncular patrician who needed company, got on well together.

CHAPTER V

Hooft and van der Capellen helped John Adams to raise money for the Continental Congress.

Amsterdam was still the most important capital market of the world. The Americans had already in the earlier years of their struggle for independence tried to tap the deep pockets of the Dutch. Johan Derk was one of the first to put his, modest, money where his pro-American mouth was, a mouth which had since 1778 proclaimed the idea that the Americans should raise loans in Amsterdam. He had written letters to Jonathan Trumbull, Governor of Connecticut, and William Livingston, Governor of New Jersey. The issue of Dutch loans had been discussed in Congress. A list of potential Dutch investors had circulated there; this list was headed by Henrik Hooft's daughter in her own right, for she was the sole owner of her maternal grandfather's banking house. She figured for a total of 40,000 guilders (the equivalent of US $2–3 million now). Her father was second on that list with 10,000 guilders.

During the Anglo-Dutch war, started by the English under the pretext that Amsterdam had been too hot on dealing with the United States, some American states did try to place loans in Amsterdam, but they were rather coldly received. For the wealthy Dutch, it was one thing to open their hearts to their American fellow patriots, but to open their purses was quite a different matter. Those, however, who like father and daughter Hooft eventually subscribed for the first bonds of the United States of America earned a high rate of interest and were repaid in full and on time. Dutch bankers and bondholders became more and more important for the Americans. Already in 1788, of the $10 million foreign debt, more than half was held by the Dutch.

Van der Capellen in the meantime not only helped to raise money but also organized popular petitions. All over the Netherlands thousands of people signed, demanding that the States General in the Hague should formally acknowledge American sovereignty.

John Adams himself did not remain passive. In his "Memorial" to the States General which supported his application for recognition of the United States, he reminded their Lords High Mightinesses of their own heroic past:

"The origins of the two Republics are so much alike that the history of the one seems but a transcript of the other, so that every Dutchman instructed in the subject must pronounce the American revolution just and necessary or pass censure upon the greatest actions of his immortal ancestors; an action which has been approved and applauded by mankind and justified by the decisions of heaven. . . ."

In April of 1782, the Lords High Mightinesses acknowledged American independence. John Adams could finally come out of the woods; the Stadhouder received him as first plenipotentiary minister of the United States of America at his palace near the Hague, called "Huis ten Bosch," House in the Woods.

The Dutch Republic was the second nation in the world to recognize the United States, after France.

Joan Derk wrote to the Court in Versailles that this diplomatic move, so important for the United States at that moment, had only succeeded thanks to the influence and activities of Burgomaster Henrik Hooft. Hooft had also, a few months earlier, turned around the Council of Amsterdam. The big city had been sitting on the fence and without her support the States General could not move. When Hooft announced Amsterdam's decision to John Adams, "he, Adams, had been so moved and affected that the tears had burst from his eyes."
A popular petition was an old and respected way for citizens to approach their Councils or States with particular wishes of a domestic nature. Van der Capellen had used it as a weapon for broader political aims. His initiative would open floodgates of ink in the next few years.

A short while before an anonymous pamphlet had appeared which shook the nation.
"*Aan het volk van Nederland,*" "To the People of the Netherlands." Most provincial governments banned possession and distribution of this "seditious libel." It adressed the readers as citizens of one single nation, in itself a new sound in a republic of sovereign states and autonomous cities.
The pamphlet called the citizens to arms, literally, as it advocated the formation of bodies of citizen-militias; these should be independent from the town councils which controlled the old "schutterijen," town watches.
Since Rembrandt's Nightwatch, these town militias had become more picturesque and less effective. They were now the playground of the Regents, famous for their banquets. The change of time becomes apparent when we look at the large group-portraits commissioned from the most fashionable painters of the day. Until 1650 the paintings show martial and sober figures, the sons and grandsons of the heroes of the War of Independence: Huydecopers, Hoofts, Hasselaers, Bickers, de Graeffs.
A hundred years later their sons and grandsons appear to have doubled in weight, the dignified costumes of the Golden Age have been exchanged for elegant velvets and lace, short clipped hair disappears under curly powdered periwigs, beards and mustaches no longer adorn the flabby babyfaces.

The pamphlet preached a return to independent militias made up of able, arm-bearing citizens who will choose their own officers. Look what the citizen-militias of the Americans achieved in their struggle for freedom.
John Adams was one of its surreptitious readers. He translated the pamphlet for the Congress, together with the placards condemning its distribution and possession, and wrote to its President: "Who and what caused such a sense of self esteem? The American Revolution!"
The most revolutionary part of the pamphlet was an indictment of Prince William V. He was blamed for all the disasters which had recently befallen the Dutch Republic. It contained a veiled incitement to take away the powers from such an incapable Stadhouder. Less revolutionary was the call for Citizen Committees, freely elected by the able citizens (males between twenty and sixty,

CHAPTER V

of some means) to assist and advise city councillors and to supervise the city's government.
No call for direct democracy, not even for representative democracy.
No summons to a drastic change of the old constitution.
All hope is vested in a return to the Golden Age when Regents were the shepherds of their flock; but a flock capable of defending itself and able to make itself heard.
Would old Cornelis Pieterszoon Hooft have agreed? Did Henrik Danielszoon Hooft agree? Did he know that the writer of that anonymous pamphlet, which was found one night in all major Dutch towns some one and a half years ago, was sitting next to him?
For almost a century the identity of the author of the most famous political broadsheet ever published in the Netherlands was clouded in mystery.
One person had a suspicion. William V, the target of its most incendiary part. He had asked one of his courtiers: could that impossible baron by any chance be the author?
Prince William carried the pamphlet around in his pocket and joked that he was now liable to banishment by the judicial authorities of which he was himself the formal head.
Gijsbert Jan van Hardenbroek, the Dutch Saint-Simon, relates that when "that baron" died suddenly, one and a half years after the banquet, Prince William became silent as the news was given to him and got drunk that evening.

The evening of the banquet, however, nobody drank too much although glasses were raised for many toasts: to the age-old freedoms and privileges of the provinces of the Dutch Republic, to the treaty of friendship and trade with the United States concluded recently, and last but not least, to the Sovereignty of the People. John Adams could be satisfied.

> "Arm youselves, elect those who must command you . . .
> and in all things proceed like the people of America, with
> modesty and composure.."

From *"Aan het Volk van Nederland"* by Joan Derk van der Capellen tot den Pol.

> "I dare not say in what a multitude of ways he has
> served us. Posterity will, perhaps, know them all."

John Adams, writing about Joan Derk van der Capellen.

CHAPTER VI

The Winds of Change

The bold, short and uncompromising indictment of William V and the plan of action published in van der Capellen's "Aan het volk van Nederland" appealed to the bold, young and enthusiastic. This was different from the drivel ladled out in party broadsheets for and against the Prince and the system.
Two friends at the University of Utrecht made it the subject for discussions in the literary circle they had founded: Jacobus Bellamy and Pieter Ondaatje.

Pieter was now in his fourth year at University. He had been following lectures in many subjects, even in medicine to which he might have felt attracted for some atavistic reason. Had not his great-great grandfather been a doctor? As physician of the King of Tanjore in South India, he had been so famous that the first Dutch Governor of Ceylon had invited him over to Colombo.

Jacobus Bellamy [1756–1794].

CHAPTER VI

But Pieter concentrates on mathematics and science and is preparing for his graduation in the autumn of 1782. He is keen on new thoughts and new feelings. Change is in the air when the breeze is from the South; new thoughts blow in from east and west and feeling flows from hearts straight into poetry, music and tears.

His friend Bellamy has a great following among the young. Girls swoon over his love poems. Young men try to imitate them.
Together the friends publish a poetical and philosophical magazine. If the fruit of their pens becomes too personal or too political, they write under pseudonyms which are known to everybody. Bellamy signs "Zeelandus" and Ondaatje writes "Adolus the Observer."

Change is in the air and never more so than for Pieter Ondaatje in the year 1783.
A remarkable year on many accounts.
In France the first journey by air is made. A manned hot-air balloon takes off from the square in front of the Royal Palace at Versailles and makes a safe landing nine minutes later.
Manned? Well, the travellers are: a cock – the national symbol – and, less typically French, a meek lamb and a tame duck.
In the same year Pilatre de Rozier and the Marquis d' Arlandes follow the animals' example.

Pieter Ondaatje, "Indo-Ceylonensis" as his thesis lists him, becomes a burger, a citizen of Utrecht. He swears the oath, pays the fee and receives his citizens-certificate. He now fully qualifies for all the rights of a true citizen of Utrecht. Passive rights for the most part; the citizen has lost his most important right, namely to vote for those that are to govern the city.
City Council has become an oligarchy and councillors are appointed by the Stadhouder.

Threatened by the French invasion in 1672, poor Utrecht, together with two other land provinces, was abandoned by Holland and Zeeland, which withdrew behind their inundated border zones and turned themselves into islands.
The French occupied the land provinces but got bogged down and retreated. Conduct of the war had been entrusted to William III, the stand-by Stadhouder, now installed by necessity.
Upon liberation the land provinces were treated like occupied foreign territory and a regulation was imposed which gave the new Stadhouder virtually absolute power, the Regerings Reglement of 1674. It had been abolished in 1702 upon William III's death but reimposed in 1747 when, under the threat of a new French invasion, William IV had become Stadhouder.

In the city of Utrecht every October each councillor was "loose," meaning that the Stadhouder could reappoint him or let him go, as he pleased. Yearly, therefore, gentlemen were seen grovelling at audiences in the Hague to recommend themselves for election or reelection.

Each year the Stadhouder appointed two burgomasters and seven aldermen from a proposal by Council containing two names for each post .

It had become the tradition to write to the Stadhouder in advance to request whether the two candidates which were to be proposed by Council would please His Highness. The Prince would then graciously respond to Council that one or both candidates pleased him or that one or both displeased him, in which case Council had to propose new names. Council, after having assured itself of the Stadhouder's pleasure, then submitted a formal proposal of two candidates and the Stadhouder chose and appointed one.

Never had the King of Spain been invested with so much power in his Dutch provinces.

No wonder that the same gentlemen from Utrecht who had to go on pilgrimage to the Hague to beg for reappointment hated the Stadhouder and themselves for having to comply with such an obsequious system.

Even more galling for the Regents than the yearly reminder of their subservient position was the daily reality of a person who since the year 1747, when the Regerings Reglement had been reimposed, had acted as the man on the spot for the Stadhouder: Willem Nicolaas Pesters, the Lieutenant-Stadhouder, more widely known as the ex-colonel.

He had become the most hated person in the whole province, he and his brother, with whom he worked hand in glove.

The ex-colonel was by now a man of sixty-six years old, tall and slim, with sharp features and a restless and intriguing nature. Although he wielded more power than anyone except the Stadhouder himself, he had never held any formal office. He lived the life of a country squire for most of the year on his estate of Wulperhorst near Zeist. In winter he resided in his house "Onder de Linden" on the Nieuwe Gracht in Utrecht.

He was rumored – by whom nobody knew – to have served gallantly in the army of the Emperor in the War of the Austrian Succession; in fact the Emperor had enobled him as Baron of the Holy Roman Empire. But in the same way as he shunned office in Utrecht, he avoided using his title and preferred to be called the ex-colonel. The people called him "Lanky Klaas."

His younger brother, Jan Pesters, was as laid-back and lazy as the ex-colonel was active and meddlesome. He lived on an adjacent estate with the languid name of "Cattenbroek" – Cats Pants –, in a comfortable country house built by their grandfather who had been Prince William III's confidant and secretary. Utrecht had to swallow Prince William's Regerings Reglement together with the Pesters family.

CHAPTER VI

Willem Nicolaas Pesters [1717–1794].
by J. VAN SELM after J. FOURNIER, 1752.

They would remain in Utrecht throughout the upheavals of the late eighteenth and early nineteenth century, stay rich and become respectable, now freely using their title of nobility and adding the French sounding "de" in front of the family name. Some of them inherited the energetic characteristics of Lanky Klaas, and my great-grandfather, the great-grandson of Jan Pesters, preferred fermenting beer over fomenting trouble and founded the Amstel Brewery.

The ex-colonel had developed a system of ruling the rulers. In the wake of the Stadhouder's come-back in 1748, he had divided the city Council into two groups of twelve members each, a young group and a group of elderly worthies, and played one off against the other. He was so much on top of things that he was compared to a coachdriver of two twelve-in-hands.

He chose one particular Regent, Arnout Loten, to become his postillion. Loten was rewarded with the post of burgomaster, which he fulfilled on and off for many years.
The ex-colonel had an equal influence over the first order of the States of Utrecht, the so-called "Elected."

The States were composed of three orders.
The "Elected" held the place of the First Estate of old, representing the clergy. The eight gentlemen who sat as the Elected drew the income of the old ecclesiastical properties. The Stadhouder appointed them for three years.
The second order of the provincial States was the Nobility.
The third order was made up of the five cities of the Province, dominated by the City of Utrecht.
Decisions in meetings of the Provincial States were taken by majority vote, each order casting one vote. The Stadhouder controlled the Cities and the Elected. The order of the Nobility was regulated by old rules which even the Stadhouder could not bend. Although he was its formal president and appointed its members, a nobleman once appointed sat for life, which guaranteed some independence.
In the middle of the assembly hall of the States of Utrecht stood an elaborate chair, reserved for the Stadhouder. In the town hall of the city of Utrecht, there was a similar chair, raised on a low dais between the seats of the first and the second burgomaster. The Stadhouder had never sat there but it reminded the councillors at each meeting that the Stadhouder was watching them.
Although Nicolaas Pesters preferred to hide behind the power of the empty chair, his brother had a seat in the Order of the Elected, as did his own son and the father-in-law of brother Jan. The son of his brother was a member of the Council of the City of Utrecht. Other family members, too, were strategically placed in influential and profitable positions of government.

Had he left it at that, nobody would have openly objected. After all, every oligarchy works that way. But such was the over-bearing nature of the ex-colonel that he did not stop at advancing his family and relatives. He had to put even his servants and retainers into every small post which was for the giving in the city and the province. For years the humble jobs of skippers of the provincial trekschuit, letter carriers, city porters, gate watchers, had been given to favorites of the ex-colonel. When foreign servants, Germans and other non-Utrecht creatures, were appointed in the place of citizens, protests reached the Town Hall. City Council decided to lend an ear and put an end to this most blatant form of Pesterian favoritism. The first sheep of popular protest had been allowed to pass. Soon many would follow.

In early 1783 a petition signed by 600 men was presented to the City councillors. It requested Council to put new life into the rusty town militia.

A well known lawyer, Adrianus Hoevenaar, was the driving force behind this petition. Hoevenaar had a daughter Christina, married to the sharpest journalist of the whole Republic, Johan Christiaan Hespe. The couple lived in Amsterdam where he published a fiercely democratic newspaper, called *"de Politieke Kruier,"* – the Political Wheelbarrowman. Dung to throw at the Stadhouder was provided to the reader by the wheelbarrow.

Since the outbreak of the disastrous war with the English, the struggle against the Stadhouder had been kept up by the pen. The pen will soon bring people to their feet, the people, not the mob, moved by a feather pen, not by stuivers and genever, although no Dutchman can be moved without at least a drop of Dutch Courage.

Council graciously grants the petition and the town militia resumes its old duties with new energy, new uniforms and new weapons. All male citizens between eighteen and sixty years of age are obliged to serve, except professors, clergymen and students, who can ask to be exempted. Students, however, enthusiastically enlist, amongst them Pieter Ondaatje who is made an ensign in one of the companies called "the Black Boys." It has nothing to do with his dark complexion. The company was already named "the Black Boys" in the sixteenth century and happened to be the one serving the quarter of town where Ondaatje lived in lodgings, which he shared with his great friend, the poet Jacobus Bellamy.

The city fathers don't foresee any problems. Each of the eight companies is commanded by a member of Council; the commander in chief is the second burgomaster.

At the same time a totally new development is set on foot.

A second petition is submitted to Council asking permission to form a society for voluntary military training, open to all male citizens including members of the town militia. One of the self-appointed officers is one P.P.J. Ondaatje.

If Council had studied Joan Derk van der Capellen's pamphlet as attentively as William V had done, it would have been apprehensive. Council, however, is well disposed. Who knows, these active citizens might play Council's hand against the Stadhouder's iron fist. One of the few who sees the writing on the wall is the ex-colonel, but his two teams are out of hand.

The new society assumes the high sounding name of "Pro Patria et Libertate." Ondaatje's friends fill the rank and file: Adriaan de Nijs, born as he in the East; and a student of independent means, who never writes any exams and who answers to the name of Friederich Boguslav von Liebeherr, of German-Polish extraction, born in Makassar in the Dutch East Indies.

This colorful group dresses up in colorful uniforms.

They are not the only ones.

Everywhere else in the Republic, Freecorps are being formed after the American example recommended in such convincing terms by the famous pamphlet.

Illustration of the accoutrements of the armed Militia and Freecorps of the Netherlands, 1787.

In the summer, parades and demonstrations of military prowess are given outside the City walls of Utrecht. A special guest of honor attends: Baron van der Capellen tot den Pol, with wife and only daughter.
Pieter Ondaatje is presented to the great man. He joins his fellow officers for a lunch, hosted by the Patriot sympathiser and Councillor Paulus d' Yvoy. Joan Derk is not well; a year later, he is dead.
 But Pieter Ondaatje has met the father of Dutch democracy in person. He will continue van der Capellen's work.
Bellamy describes the ceremonies at the parade to his sweetheart in glowing terms. "Tears were in my eyes."

CHAPTER VI

After a summer of marching and exercising with sabres and muskets, that other weapon was taken up again, the pen. The Freecorps submitted a petition to Council.

This time it did not contain a request for banners or new sashes. The Freecorps demanded that Council would no longer ask the Stadhouder in advance whether he agreed with the two candidates which Council wanted to propose for burgomaster and alderman.

Council immediately agreed to the demand and sent a deputation to the Stadhouder to give him notice of Council's decision. From now on, Council would simply submit a proposal with two names. This was the opening shot at the hated Regerings Reglement of 1674.

William was taken aback but agreed that the practice was not contained in so many words in the Reglement.

Council saw the first glimmer of freedom; the first hope of a slackening of the leash. What they ultimately wanted was: appointment for life for every councillor from a binding proposal of two candidates. If they could obtain appointment for life, they did not mind having to submit a proposal of two names to the Stadhouder as long as their proposal would be binding and the Stadhouder would be obliged to appoint one of the two proposed.

This was already the practice in many cities of Holland.

There, Regents were appointed for life and had concluded cozy agreements amongst themselves. During the eighteenth century, these so-called Contracts of Correspondence had become real time-tables for advancement. A father who was part of this network could tell the mother of a patrician baby in the cradle in what year the boy would be a member of the Treasury, when he would appear on the binding proposal as City councillor and when he would be proposed as alderman or burgomaster. If the baby avoided getting into trouble he could be sure of his career, "as sure as, wanting to know what time of the day it was, he would look up to the clock of the Dom Tower," said one Patriot critic in Utrecht. The small victory of Utrecht's Council did not yet open the door for such untrammeled oligarchy. It had not changed the situation that each October every councillor could be discontinued by the Stadhouder.

The small victory had been won not on Council's own initiative but by a petition of the Freecorps. Would these Freecorpsmen now go back to playing at being soldiers?

In October of 1783 the Stadhouder reappointed all sitting Council members for another year.

However, there were two vacancies. Until now it had been tradition to ask the Stadhouder whom he would like to see proposed for a vacancy during the year in the same way as for the annual renewal of Council.

The Freecorps presented a second petition in which it maintained that the Regerings Reglement did not mention ad-interim vacancies and that such posts were therefore at the free disposition of Council.

Council realised that this was more potent medicine than the first dose administered to the Stadhouder, and delegated the matter to a commission of councillors, in the meantime communicating the petition to the Prince.

The Stadhouder wrote to Council insisting upon full compliance with the Regerings Reglement. He would fill any vacancies in the usual manner.

Early in 1784, Council made a truly bold move. It decided henceforth to fill vacancies themselves without any outside interference. Within twenty-four hours, a new councillor was appointed for one of the vacancies.

The first shot had hit the target: the Stadhouder and the Reglement. Prince William shot back; he fired off a letter to the Provincial States of Utrecht, relying on his control of that body. The States, however, realized that their powers did not give them the right to interfere in internal municipal matters.

The States decided to invite the governments of the five voting cities to find out directly from their citizens the causes of their complaints. The tide started to flow away from the Stadhouder.

Spring of 1784 saw frenetic activity in Utrecht. Council had given the citizens five weeks to deliver their written complaints and suggestions for improvement. An anonymous pamphlet appeared with a masterful indictment of the Reglement of 1674 exposing how it had been imposed against the laws and with brute force. The pamphlet was ascribed to Ondaatje's pen.

CHAPTER VI

Ondaatje was very visible in a campaign organized by the members of the Freecorps. Not only did they voice their complaints, they drafted a totally new provincial constitution, complete to the last issue and paragraph, covering both the organization of the Provincial States and the workings of the City of Utrecht. Law student Ondaatje's hand can be detected in this work. It is unlikely that he was the only brain behind the new draft.

The draft aimed at a fundamental redress of the iniquities of the Reglement of 1674 and at a return to the more democratic ways of government hallowed by the past. As there had been many ways in the past, most of them obscured by the mist of time, an appeal to history could cover any system desired. The draft for a reformed city constitution was in fact an amalgamation of old and new ideas.

The first change, revolutionary – or reactionary if you prefer to invoke the past – was that the Stadhouder no longer had any role in the appointment of councillors.

Ondaatje and his draftsmen had devised a complicated system of appointment and controls, leaving most of the existing order intact. In those days every would-be reformer tried to avoid the accusation of advocating for direct democracy.

It provided for primary elections, by indirect vote. All male citizens of independent means choose a body of representatives, a Citizens Committee as recommended in van der Capellen's pamphlet, dubbed as "Ondaatje's Meentemannen" when the draft became public.

"Meentemannen" – "common men" – had existed for a short time in the Middle Ages in Utrecht.

Each time a vacancy in the City Council had to be filled, these Meentemannen had to draw up a list of qualified candidates. Through a process of cascading ballots the list of candidates would be narrowed down to two, one of which the sitting City Council had to choose. A councillor would sit for life. To avoid the danger that a Council appointed for life would become a cozy oligarchy – or "aristocracy" as people said in those days – the Meentemannen would also exercise a vaguely defined control over Council.

These were not exactly ultra-democratic novelties , opening the gates to mob rule, the bogeyman of the Regents. Ondaatje himself wrote a year later that "unrestricted democracy is abhorred by every reasonable human being as ending up in anarchy." The son of Reverend Ondaatje had even allowed for the sensibilities of a society still very much under the influence of the Dutch Reformed Church.

One of the qualifications for those wanting to excercise public office, apart of course from possessing independent means, was membership of the Dutch Reformed Church. In Utrecht, where one third of the population was Catholic – and Patriot – a Catholic might become a Meenteman, but did not qualify for city father.

Although reformers were talking about the "Sovereignty of the People" and the "Majesty of the People," the concept that political rights belonged to self-perpetuating representative bodies and not to individual citizens was still so strong in Europe that no one suggested taking the next logical step and granting to the People directly the right to vote its representatives in and out of power. Traces of election of representatives were preserved in the House of Commons of the British Parliament, and were present in the mind of everyone with a classical education; but it fell to the rebels against the British Parliament on the other side of the Atlantic to take that next logical step.

Eleven other proposals were submitted, one inspired by the "aristocratic" councillors. They, too, proposed appointment for life but wanted sitting councillors themselves to draw up a list of two candidates for each vacancy. They did not mind that the Stadhouder would make the final election, because with a binding proposal by Council and appointment for life, Utrecht would revert smoothly to an unfettered, self-appointing oligarchy.
Utrecht and the other cities sent all proposals to the States who within three months published a draft for a revised regulation.
The old Reglement of 1674 was called "shameful" and "abominable." Furthermore, it had been reimposed upon the province "by violence." Thus spoke the States of Utrecht. The empty seat had lost its threat.

The States' draft for a new regulation proposed that the Stadhouder would appoint city councillors for life from a binding proposal by the sitting Council – exactly as the majority of the Regents in Utrecht would like – but with the proviso that the citizens should have "some participation in order to avoid cabals and similar disorder." How much participation and in what way was left up to the cities to work out with their citizens in their own municipal bosoms. This went a long way in the direction of the democratic Patriots. The Prince was furious when the matter was discussed with van Hardenbroek. William wanted to cling to the Reglement even "if in Utrecht no stone would be left unturned."

Another stalemate loomed on the horizon: the States wanted to change the Regerings Reglement, the Stadhouder did not.
People in those years believed in the contract theory of government. The rulers ruled by explicit or tacit agreement of their subjects. What to do if one contract party wanted to change the terms, or worse, invoked the invalidity of the agreement, and the other party did not want to renegotiate?
Frederic the Great had all his cannon embossed with the letters : "URR," ultima ratio regum. The cannon was the final argument of Kings. But in the Dutch Republic this kind of argument was not acceptable and, besides, the Stadhouder did not have sufficient cannon and the Freecorps were rapidly adding some of these final arguments to their arsenal. William V was not of the same caliber as Frederic the Great, who had often shown that before he played that last trump he had other cards up his sleeve.

CHAPTER VI

Back view of the Town Hall of Utrecht.
The righthand building harbored the "Stadskelder" inn.
J. VAN LIEFLAND, 1857.

Prince William was not a fighter, neither was he a poker player; he was stubborn, despondent, listened to the wrong people and talked too much, did nothing when he could have used a favorable opportunity and, when he should have kept quiet, wrote a letter. So he wrote a letter to the States protesting against their draft for a new Reglement. The States merely confirmed receipt.

However, the States had admitted, cautiously, that "some influence" should be allowed to the citizens. Here lay a chance. The Utrecht Freecorps grabbed it and mobilized the citizens to widen the chink opened by the States. They deposited a list of twenty-four names, all Freecorpsmen, at an inn called the "Stadskelder," right behind the Town Hall.

They announced in the newspapers that during a fortnight all "citizens and residents," without further qualifications or restrictions, were invited to sign in support of the Freecorps' draft of a new Provincial Regulation. A notary public would be present and citizens would be asked also to sign a proxy authorizing the twenty-four Freecorpsmen to represent them in the matter.

After fourteen days, the Freecorps reported to City Council that 1,215 citizens had signed up and that the twenty-four had been duly "constituted" to deal with the issue. One of them was Pieter Ondaatje.

In the past, groups claiming to represent the people had often enough approached the authorities with specific wishes. In this case a group, the Freecorps, had methodically made sure that some of them were delegated formally by specific citizens for the purpose of establishing new rules of government, rules which had been published in advance and had been approved by 1,215 voters. These 1,215 citizens and residents represented about twenty-five percent of all males in Utrecht of twenty-two years and over.

The concept that the most fundamental layer of sovereignty consists of the people, taken together as a body politic, was not new. Ideas that the people could delegate the power to rule over them, and also could revoke such delegation had been alive in classical antiquity and were resurrected again in the Middle Ages and during the period of the Reformation in Europe. Philosophers and statesmen had abstracted such thoughts into theories of pacts and contracts on which all civil societies were supposed to be based. Jean Jacques Rousseau had popularized these theories in his *"Du Contrat Social"* of 1762. He had called the most fundamental of such contracts, the one whereby individuals agree that they will henceforth form a people or a nation, a "convention."

American politicians had gone one step further. They had felt that the ground rules of government, in other words the constitution, had to be established by a specific, purely constitutional activity. For that purpose, the people would elect delegates who would sit together in a convention, solely for the purpose of drafting a constitution. Having done their work, they would submit the constitution to the people and disband. Existing institutions, claiming to represent the people, such as Councils, Estates or Parliaments, were not the proper bodies to establish, or drastically change, the constitutions of which they were but the children.

The Americans had not borrowed such ideas from Rousseau.

Already, some 150 years earlier, on the soil of Massachusetts, the Pilgrim Fathers had sown ideas which did not derive from any state of Nature or from Greek and Roman Antiquity, but from the Bible with its message of a Covenant, and of rights and duties belonging to the people. These ideas had taken root and were producing a new variety of fruit between 1776 and 1780. Simple farmers had declared: "the law to bind all, must be assented to by all."

CHAPTER VI

In 1779, elections were called for a special convention. All adult males of the State of Massachusetts were allowed to vote. The sole purpose of this convention was to draw up a new constitution for the Commonwealth, as the state was still called by its colonial name.

A previous draft formulated by the sitting Legislature and submitted to the electorate had been voted down.

One of the delegates to the constitutional convention was John Adams. He was asked to draft a new constitution. Adams had read Rousseau. His library harbored four copies of *Du Contrat Social*. But I doubt whether his practical, legal mind had much time for the imprecise brain products of that son of a Swiss watchmaker.

The preamble of John Adams' draft sounded more like the Mayflower Compact brought up to date by a few of the more fashionable terms from the Social Contract. It referred to "a voluntary association of individuals" as the base of a body politic, and "a social compact by which the whole people covenants with each citizen, and each citizen with the whole people, that all shall be governed by certain laws for the common good." Puritan Massachusetts, where according to a later poet "the egg of democracy was laid," provided the constitutional convention of 1779 with enough homegrown material to make a purely local egg dish, in which the Pilgrim Fathers, Locke and Rousseau and other ingredients from John Adams' store of constitutional knowledge were scrambled together. For the highlight of the preamble, Adams had suggested: "We, therefore, the delegates of the people of Massachusetts, . . . agree upon . . . the following Constitution. . . ."

Significantly, the convention added to the words "agree upon", the highly charged words "and ordain and establish."

Adams' draft, including the addition of these portentious words, was adopted by a referendum in which all male adults again had the vote. It has lasted with some further amendments until today. And the formula, "We the people ordain and establish," was seven years later adopted for the constitution of the United States of America.

I believe that what happened in Utrecht in 1785 can be compared to the steps taken to establish the new constitution of Massachusetts. The difference was that in Massachusetts the government was encouraging proper procedures and in Utrecht it was not. In Massachusetts, things could be done in an orderly and timely fashion, with publicly supported elections and referenda. In Utrecht, the Freecorps had to improvise. It hit upon the expedient of powers of attorney attested by notarial deeds, so familiar to the property-owning and mercantile Dutch. The Freecorps had assumed the role of a constitutional convention, and had drafted new provincial and municipal regulations, in other words a new constitution for the Province. They had solicited popular support and had received, in the convivial surroundings of a Dutch inn, 1,215 votes to ratify their draft and to confirm their position as delegates. The formal procedures in Massachusetts and the improvised happenings in Utrecht led to the same result:

a new constitution, drafted by a "convention" and supported by the people, came into effect. The authorities accepted the voice of the people in the one case freely, and in the other case under pressure.
Did Ondaatje and his Freecorps take a leaf out of the Massachusetts book? I do not believe so.
Although the constitution of Massachusetts had been translated and published in a Dutch newspaper, in French, in 1780, the contents of Ondaatje's draft were totally different from John Adams' new democratic concept which provided for direct elections of both the executive and the legislative bodies by a wide franchise. Utrecht's draft contained only a feeble effort to shake off the suffocating burden of the Dutch past, the Glorious Golden Age. It looked back even further to Utrecht's Middle Ages with its "Meentemannen" who were to conduct ballots for the appointment of councillors and were to act in some way as supervisors. The simple step of giving the people the right to vote their councillors in and out of power was apparently still too revolutionary.
Ondaatje and the Freecorps had been more daring in the manner in which they had put their draft constitution on the table and had legitimized their own position as delegates of the people. They had made the best of the controversial situation in which they had to operate.
Ondaatje and his men had sensed that whenever a constitution has to be established, or drastically altered, the people have to get involved directly in some formal and extraordinary manner. They had sensed that the people are the constituent power, as we would call it now, and that this constituent power should be exercised in a solemn, even ritual, way.
In Utrecht they did not imitate the Americans, but they were on the same track. Some whiff of these new ideas and practices must have reached Utrecht from across the Atlantic. No wonder. After all, ideas of change were in the air.

During the next five months both sides, the twenty-four and City Council, were engaged in dogged skirmishes waged in petitions, replies, deadlines, delaying tactics and reminders, supported by petitions from the town militia containing such veiled threats as: "we do not carry arms for nothing."
It had taken the Provincial States only three months to grab the bull by the horns and publish the draft for a reformed regulation; City Council had been beating about the bush for five months and had not come forward with a draft for the chapters dealing with city matters.

March of 1785 approached. Everyone expected a showdown. The last deadline set by the twenty-four and the deputies from the militia was March 7.
Just before that final date a sudden storm broke from an unexpected quarter.

On March 3, City Council decided by sixteen votes against thirteen to appoint a Mr. Jonathan Sichterman to a vacant position as councillor. Council was using its newly conquered freedom to fill ad-interim vacancies without the Stadhouder. Sichterman was known for his conservative views and had signed a petition against Ondaatje's draft.

The twenty-four, along with the sixteen deputies from the eight companies, had already requested Council before Sichterman's appointment not to elect anyone who had publicly declared himself against their wishes. They had specifically singled out Mr. Jonathan Sichterman as not acceptable to "the People."

The next evening, the "Stadskelder" was full of people. The twenty-four were in a meeting in one room, the sixteen in another.

Genever, beer and tobacco added to the excitement. The majority of the twenty-four and of the sixteen representatives of the militia voted to demand Council to revoke Sichterman's appointment.

The next afternoon the two committees met again in the inn for the sober job of drafting a petition. It was already Saturday, and Monday Sichterman would be sworn in.

Before dinner time many pipes had been smoked, many i's dotted and many t's crossed. They were all home by six o'clock, except for a small group which walked to the burgomaster's house. They asked respectfully whether a deputation might be admitted in a full meeting of Council before the swearing-in ceremony, planned for Monday. The burgomaster, to the amazement of posterity, agreed to call an extraordinary Council meeting for the next day, a Sunday. Utrecht was a small city, and all Regents lived within walking distance from each other. It was early March; no one had moved to his summer house yet and nobody had anything else to do on Sundays but to go to Church in the morning and wait until it was Monday.

Council, on Sunday, agreed to receive the deputation the next day at 9 in the morning.

The two committees met again that Sunday afternoon in the Stadskelder, which was doing good business thanks to Mr. Sichterman. Ondaatje had worked hard and now proposed a draft for a speech. It was accepted and he was asked to lead the deputation next morning and to deliver the address.

Monday, 7th March 1785, at 9 sharp in the morning, the deputation of six was ushered into the Green Chamber; six extra chairs had been arranged in a row. The gentlemen bowed to each other and exchanged civilities.

When everybody was seated, Ondaatje was asked to deliver the address of the deputies, authorized by 1,215 citizens and eight companies of the town militia.

Nobody in Council raised objections. Nobody remarked that the proxies of these 1,215 limited the proxy holders to negotiate and draw up a new regulation of government for the city and did not cover other items such as a veto over the appointment of new councillors before the new regulation had taken effect. The wise city fathers, many of whom had studied law, just sat and listened. They were overawed by Ondaatje's speech.

Did it dawn upon these Regents that their only weapon was an impressive wig and that the base of their authority was age-long deference of the people, who only now were beginning to ask questions and to wonder why they should keep quiet? Who would uphold the Regents' authority if the town militia itself, together with the Freecorpsmen, would turn against them?

Council postponed a decision until the 11th of March. Prince William V was following developments closely from his residence in the Hague. Now, he remarked sarcastically, this very same Council which made use of the voice of the people to attack his due rights and privileges, was "like the Sultan of Turkey: under the thumb of the Janissaries," the palace guard who made and broke the Sultans in the years of decline of that empire.

On March 11, the innkeeper of the Stadskelder is busy at an early hour. This time a large number of people has been mobilized. Something more exciting is going to take place than a new series of meetings.

Council meets at 9 am. After long deliberations, the majority decides to postpone the swearing-in of Mr. Jonathan Sichterman until Council has adopted a new municipal regulation. It seemed a reasonable compromise, but Ondaatje had already convinced the twenty-four plus the sixteen to reject it. Council politely invites a deputation to the Green Chamber to inform them of their decision. Ondaatje and his five reappear, are again offered chairs, and listen. They ask leave to consult their backers. In the Stadskelder, Ondaatje pleads for the hard line. No compromises. After heated arguments, the twenty-four and the sixteen agree with Ondaatje.

Older and wiser Hoevenaar is so appalled by this intransigence that he resigns on the spot as deputy.

In the meantime the councillors have gone home. Ondaatje's friend von Liebeherr goes in search of the burgomaster and leaves a note at the burgomaster's door asking for a new meeting of Council to receive a deputation. "If this is refused, we will not be responsible for the consequences." At 6:30 in the evening, the councillors meet for the second time that day. People by now have closed their shops and are coming home from work. What is happening at the Town Hall? Let us go and see. Some know what is going on: "Council is trying to humiliate our deputies." "We will show them who we are." One of the ushers comes to fetch Ondaatje and his colleagues in the Stadskelder. "Let us slip in through the back door," he suggests, "there are too many people in front." But Ondaatje replies as a Roman Tribune of the People: "We will go in through the Royal entrance." The people standing packed together around the old Town Hall let them through.

The speech which Ondaatje now delivered was short and almost peremptory. Here is the voice of the people: "Sichterman is unacceptable. We insist, let us hope for the last time, on a final answer which has to be given now. Otherwise do not blame us for the baleful consequences."

After these few and carefully chosen words, the deputation was led to an adjacent room where Ondaatje took the secretary of Council aside and told him that the hour of truth had come. Would the voice of the people be listened to

CHAPTER VI

and would their reasonable demands be accepted? If not, then this matter would become the talk of the town and the province; yes, of the whole Republic. He added confidentially that the citizens were restless and had forced the twenty-four to remain in meeting all day. The people insisted on a definite answer. All entrances to the Town Hall were occupied by the people who – although unarmed – would not allow any councillor to leave before Mr. Sichterman's appointment had either been revoked or definitely confirmed. If Council decided to confirm Mr.Sichterman, the deputation and the twenty-four would not consider themselves responsible for the regrettable consequences. In that case they requested Council to announce their decision directly to the people, and not through the twenty-four as these would no longer want to be mediators. And then Pieter Ondaatje spoke the famous words: "The People declare that their eyes have been opened. They will fight for their rights not as '48 men, but as '85 men.'"

In 1748, the people had relied on the Stadhouder to restore the liberties which they deemed trampled underfoot by the Regents. Now they were wise enough to demand and – if necessary – to seize their rights themselves.

Ondaatje knew that the secretary would report each and every word to the councillors inside. Had he said all this to their faces, he would have committed a grave breach of protocol which required politeness and deference from an eighteenth century citizen addressing his lawful government.

And indeed everything Ondaatje had said to the secretary privately was reported to Council and can still be read in the minutes of that meeting.

When Ondaatje and his five colleagues were called in again, they hear that Council has resolved to renounce the election of Mr. Jonathan Sichterman and that a new day would be set for filling the vacant post.

In the extract of the resolution, which was given to the deputation, no mention was made of Council's motives, but the full minutes of the meeting stated that the decision was taken "in order to prevent dreadful consequences and mishaps which are to be feared." From the minutes, it appears that the vote was unanimous. Afterwards nineteen councillors claimed that they had voted out of fear, and had therefore been coerced by force.

After communicating the eagerly expected decision to the deputation, the burgomaster added: "Gentlemen, you see the condescendence of Council to the good citizens of Utrecht. We expect that you will now explain this to the people and admonish them to go home peacefully and quietly." Ondaatje, obligingly, replied: "Noble and worthy Gentlemen. This proof of magnanimity strikes us, this generous behaviour of Council, added to the firm conduct of Utrecht's citizens, will be an eternal monument for this and future generations. We recommend the good citizens to the protection of your Noble Worships."

Was he sarcastic? What protection were their Worships capable of offering?

Ondaatje complied with the burgomaster's request. Standing at the top of the stairs of the Town Hall, he addressed the crowd. A general hurrah greeted the news of the decision, but Ondaatje imposed silence and said:

I have to tell you something more. You can see from this the magnanimity of your Council. This line of action taken by Council joined to the determination of our citizens will be an eternal monument for this and future generations. Go home quietly and peacefully, tell this to your wives and children and impress on your grandchildren how harmony between such honest Regents and the citizens can accomplish everything.

The newspapers, which reported the happenings in detail and all the speeches verbatim, concluded that the people uttered a loud long cry of joy which could be heard for miles around in the quiet night-air of the city.
As in the grand finale of a Mozart opera, everyone leaves the scene cheerfully. Only the singing is missing, but Dutchmen do not sing together, except in Church.
The worthy gentlemen return to their houses undisturbed by anyone, but most of them are much perturbed.
This is not a Mozart opera, it does not turn out to be the joyous finale: the Regent's bowing to the Peoples' will.
Even before the councillors adjourned, two of them had handed in their resignation. Seventeen more followed suit three days later.
Adrianus Hoevenaar, who had already resigned as one of the twenty-four when Ondaatje had convinced the others to take a hard line, published a personal declaration in various newspapers, distancing himself from Ondaatje's addresses to Council and from "such strong and pressing measures."

One of the councillors who resigned was Paul d' Yvoy who had so far been one of the backers of the democratic movement and had in fact voted with the minority against the appointment of Sichterman. He had been the host of the dinner for Joan Derk van der Capellen on that summer day when the Freecorps had shown what it was worth and Pieter Ondaatje and his fellow officers had graced his table with their presence.
His thundering resignation speech was widely reported in the Dutch newspapers: "The sovereign of the city has been insulted by a misled part of our good citizens who deprived the councillors of their right of free access and exit and free deliberation; who occupied the Council Hall and all entrances, and carried arms, some of them swords and some others muskets."
He refers to "a disgraceful insurrection" and to "insults by the conceited Pieter Philippus Jurriaan Ondaatje."
"There we sat, on the seats of honor, but treated like schoolboys. We had to agree with the demand of the twenty-four and sixteen if we did not want to see the crowd force its way into the Council Hall."
We know that no one was armed or harmed. But the Regents who were brought up in fear of mob terror were easily intimidated. They knew how to bend when the wind blew from the Stadhouder or Klaas Pesters. But now the wind came from a different quarter and Ondaatje had blown them off their feet.

CHAPTER VII

A Forgotten Citizen

Christopher and I are standing in front of a modest house in the Lange Nieuwstraat in Utrecht. A simple old-fashioned Dutch front, two storys and an attic. To the right and left and on the other side of the street are rows of old houses, all different and yet similar.
The house which interests us is marked number 18.
We ring the doorbell. Nobody answers.
It is a winter morning. A short distance away looms the Dom Tower in all its Gothic brick solidity and sandstone grace, sharp and clear against the deep blue winter sky. On the facade of the house between the windows on the first floor we notice an unobtrusive stone slab, some dates and a name: "Jacobus Bellamy."
"They forgot to mention Ondaatje," I say to Christopher. "We have to put that right," he replies.
Nothing seems much changed since Pieter Ondaatje went in and out of that door, except the traffic, at this hour of the day mainly bicycles.

In the summer of 1783, Bellamy moved in with Pieter Ondaatje and took the room with the two sash windows at which we are peering. One window is slightly ajar.
Are we allowed a glimpse into the past?
On the same floor at the back Ondaatje had a room, the room with the "closet bed."
Their landlord was a grocer, Hendrik van Renswoude, who ran a modest shop on the ground floor. When you opened the door, a little bell gave a jingling sound. Bellamy's letters to his beloved in Zeeland give an idyllic picture of their student life in lodgings.
"I am sitting in front of the window. The maid is coming up with our dinner. Ondaatje plays the flute and sends you his compliments."
Against this backdrop of the solid and secure life of small town Dutch burgers, a cloak and dagger show went on." My head fumes from all the turbulence in our room. I am fed up with the constant clamor of these political friends. In the other room there is such a noise that you cannot hear or see a thing. Officers from Leiden and the Hague, burgomasters from Wijk bij Duurstede etc, etc."
Thus wrote Jacobus Bellamy in the fall of 1783.
The resurrection of the town militia, the birth of the Freecorps "Pro Patria et Libertate," the popular petition movement, every happening in those heady days was discussed or conceived in those small rooms on the Lange Nieuwstraat 18. And on the plaque commemorating this house, the nerve center of the revolution in Utrecht, only the poet is mentioned, the man of action left out.

CHAPTER VII

On our walk through old Utrecht, Christopher is full of plans. "We have to do something about a statue for Ondaatje," he says. We walk along the Oude Gracht and stand on the wide bridge, more like a small square in front of the Town Hall. The Medieval cluster of buildings where the Council and burgomasters met in the eighteenth century was demolished in the early 1800s. But the dignified building which replaced the Town Hall does not seem out of tone. The location is unchanged. Here Ondaatje went in "the Royal Entrance," here he stood at a later occasion amongst the crowd and was seen by a passer-by who wrote "he was directing the mob with a little stick," like the conductor of an orchestra.

No sign is left of the Stadskelder, the inn where the addresses were rehearsed which made Pieter Ondaatje's name famous throughout the Republic.

We eat bread and cheese and drink milk in a place overlooking the site where that den of smoke, beer and genever once stood.

We stand under the Dom Tower, and look at the buildings of the University of Utrecht; a nineteenth century statue of the brother of Prince William the Silent gives the square a pompous air. He was the ancestor of that branch of the House of Orange-Nassau which produced the hapless William V. It reminds Christopher of the statue he wishes for Pieter Ondaatje.

Now I want him to look eye to eye with William V. We have already been running in the family for too long, Ondaatje and Hooft.

Off we go to the museum of Utrecht in one of the old convents of the city, in search of the Stadhouder's chair. That chair which stood empty at every meeting of the States of the province and kept every Regent attending in awe.

I had corresponded with the Museum in an effort to get a photograph. We chase down an official who remembers that the chair has been in storage for some time. I explain that I would like to take a picture of my friend and the chair.

The name of Ondaatje opens every door in the historical museum of Utrecht. Even the doors of a gloomy warehouse in a derelict area outside the city, heavily protected by electronic devices which Christopher and I immediately manage to set off. The chief of the storage department is so proud of heading this historical expedition that he remains cheerful while he allays the alarm which we have raised. Big caves without daylight with furniture stacked four rows high. The chief brings us straight to the chair as if he shows it to visitors every day. We pull it out, a dull looking thing. An orange flag happens to lie close by. We use it as a backdrop. The chief apologetically informs us that he has instructions not to allow anybody to sit in the chair. Our sense of history is keen enough not to think of committing such sacrilege. I take some pictures of Christopher standing next to the chair and ask him to look at it with a disapproving air.

Do I notice someone else standing behind the chair looking disapprovingly at us?

A FORGOTTEN CITIZEN

In twilight, we walk along the Nieuwe Gracht. The old trees, now bare, are dripping with cold fog. Water is forming on the ice of the frozen canal, one story below the bridges. The most elegant houses are near the ramparts of the city walls which are planted with trees, called Onder de Linden – under the lime trees. No one is walking there except Christopher and me. All sounds are muffled by the fog. Do I feel the ex-colonel's presence again, when we walk past his house? After all, he is the uncle of my grandmother's great grandfather. And fog dispels the mist of ancestral memory.

The next day the sky is bright when we continue our walk through Utrecht. We stop at streetcorners with a story, we stand on squares with a past and we follow the town militia of 1785 and 1786.

CHAPTER VII

We start again at Lange Nieuwstraat 18.

There, in the morning of the last day of May 1785, an important looking person entered the grocer's shop of van Renswoude. The bell announced his presence. The grocer recognised him, van Dam, the town beadle. He asked for Mr. Ondaatje. The grocer showed him upstairs.

Our chronicler van Hardenbroek heard the story from the head bailiff of Utrecht himself, F.C.R. van Reede, one of the grandees of the province. His great grandfather had accompanied Prince William III on the glorious expedition which made William King of England. Old van Reede was showered with honors, estates, offices and money. His great grandson inherited the great castle of Amerongen on the Eastern border of the province of Utrecht. His rather grandiose portrait can still be admired on the spot where it has hung for two hundred years. The head bailiff was one of the ex-colonel's men. He was known by the titles which he had inherited from his fortunate ancestor, Baron of Antrim and Count of Athlone, Irish estates giving him a seat in the British House of Lords. The people in Utrecht called him "Milord," his fellow nobles "Athlone."

Van Hardenbroek described him as a haughty and hare-brained fellow. As head bailiff of the city of Utrecht, he had to maintain justice and prosecute offences. After the events of the 11th of March, he had been sniffing for culprits. Insurrection, treason, lese-majesty, any or all of these crimes have been committed. Milord is not a lawyer. For the technical details he relies on his experts. An old fashioned Regent does not need to know details. For that he can consult experts. That is what the professional classes are good for. A Regent's job is to keep a firm hand on things, to make sure that a gentleman remains on his cushion and the common man at his work.

The head bailiff had quickly come to the conclusion that the main culprit of March 11th had been a certain Pieter Philip Juriaan Ondaatje, a student without means, who had nothing to lose, born in the East and who had been a citizen only for two years: the profile of a troublemaker.

Let us put that fellow behind bars and set an example. But his experts raise legal objections, citing learned jurisprudence. The aldermen from whom he asks permission for "corporal apprehension" are real sticklers for legal niceties. He only gets permission to summon Ondaatje in person, not to arrest him.

Hence the town beadle that May morning in 1785, requesting permission to enter Mr. Ondaatje's room.

"Who having received the beadle in his room, asked him to take a seat; also if he wanted to partake of a cup of tea with which he himself at that moment was breakfasting; then, as he read out his summons, Ondaatje said to the beadle: "Pray read me the conclusion, because the form of this sort of summons is known to me," and after this had been done: "this manner of proceeding is more appropriate than that followed in Amsterdam, for here people still are given time to defend or excuse themselves; pray answer in my name that I shall appear."

I believe van Hardenbroek admired this cool and civilized behavior of the hotheaded troublemaker as did perhaps Athlone who told him the story himself. The proceedings in Amsterdam which Ondaatje mentioned to the beadle concerned Mr. Johan Christiaan Hespe, the son-in-law of worthy Adrianus Hoevenaar. Hespe had been accused of lese-majesty against the city of Amsterdam, committed in one of the issues of his "Political Wheelbarrowman." But in Amsterdam the law was not as lenient as in Utrecht, and Hespe had been put behind bars even before his case was heard. The whole Patriot press rose up in arms. Mrs. Hespe, who pursued the authorities with petition after petition, became a national hero. Hespe was finally released on paying a fine.

Christopher is taken aback. He had hoped that his great grand uncle would go from triumph to triumph. Will he after all end up behind bars?
We leave Ondaatje and the town beadle to finish their cup of tea and retrace our steps along the dignified Nieuwe Gracht.
"Do you see these 'For Sale' signs on a dozen of the most impressive houses?" I ask Christopher.
Christopher looks interested. "That is a great opportunity to buy. Let's look into it. I am thinking of establishing an Ondaatje Museum. Do you think people here would be interested if I would add some Ceylon stuff as well? "
I have to disappoint him. Although these houses had been put up for sale in March 1785, none had actually been sold. The "For Sale" signs were only a threat. What had happened?

You remember that nineteen Regents had, out of indignation, resigned from their posts a few days after the 11th of March. The people had dared to put pressure on them by appearing en masse around the Town Hall and frightening them into revoking the appointment of Mr. Jonathan Sichterman. These nineteen had decided to put some pressure on the people in their turn.
Shopkeepers, artisans, workmen, in fact most people in Utrecht depended on the patrician families for a living. The nineteen and their friends now put their houses up for sale and announced that they would move out of Utrecht for good. In this den of sedition an honest gentleman could no longer be sure of the quiet enjoyment of the fruits of his capital. Citizens who owed anything to these nineteen and their kin were demanded to repay their debts. Patronage was withdrawn from tradesmen and shopkeepers who were known to have Patriot sympathies.
Those affected started to have second thoughts. Was the voice of the people worth fighting for if the purse of the people was going to be hit so hard?
The Provincial States were also throwing in their weight and threatened to take action if Utrecht became ungovernable. They wrote that "the free Council Chambers had been converted into scenes of violence and tyranny instigated by some hotheaded and restless characters," and exhorted the head bailiff to investigate the matter.

The twenty-four and sixteen deputies declared openly that they never had any intention of insulting Council and offered their good services to pacify the nineteen Regents who had left their posts. They had the courage, however, to add that their offer of conciliation did not imply that Mr. Sichterman could be reappointed.

Five militia companies found these conciliatory tones unbecoming to the Majesty of the People and wrote to the twenty-four and the sixteen instructing them to appoint nineteen new councillors if the old ones persisted in their sulking absence. And lo and behold, at the next Council meeting all the nineteen were back in their seats.

Poor Jonathan Sichterman, after counting on his fingers, "I am in, I am out, I am in," told Council "include me out."

The majority of Council, back on the cushion and sensing a weakening of the opposition, was in the mood for revenge. It revoked its decision of the 11th of March, using as an excuse that it had been taken under duress. It issued a decree forbidding any assembly of people around the Town Hall during meetings of Council. It decreed that any decision taken henceforth by Council, while unlawful assemblies were being held outside, would ipso facto be null and void. As if this legal shield against its own cowardice were not sufficient, Council finally declared that all decisions taken on petitions during evening meetings would be invalid.

Who could hereafter be afraid of Pieter Ondaatje?

The democrats were in disarray. The whole Sichterman affair had obscured the main issue: the long awaited draft for the municipal section of the reformed Regerings Reglement.

Council had taken five months to deliberate and in March, when it was due to come with a proposal, the Sichterman storm had broken loose. It now had to address the main issue. It would have been so nice to accept the proposal of the Provincial States: appointment for life from a binding proposal made by Council itself and "some influence" from the citizens. However, the citizens expected Council to be a little more precise. Still on the table was Ondaatje's draft Regulation, signed by 1,215 citizens, giving very concrete shape to "some influence" in the body of the Meentemannen and in the cascading ballot system, all of which left no room for binding proposals based on cozy family arrangements. Council pondered on this matter for another four months.

Pieter Ondaatje was discouraged by the loss of the fighting spirit of his fellow democrats.

In April he tendered his resignation as one of the twenty-four and as officer of the town militia. His friend von Liebeherr resigned on the same day. The official chronicle of 1785 published their address of resignation in full.

Von Liebeherr invoked "the God of the Netherlands." He, too, had been accused of being an Oriental.

Pieter Ondaatje referred to his frank character: "I speak as I think. At present Utrecht counsels me to govern myself with extreme moderation. And because I am more master of my honesty and frankness than of my temper and zeal I know that in the long run it would be difficult for me to keep quiet." He explained that he could try to keep quiet as a private citizen but that it would go against his grain as a representative of the people if he had to acquiesce in the actions taken by Council since the return of the nineteen Regents. Ondaatje too invoked God, not the God of the Netherlands, but the God of Freedom.
The Almighty has many names. We choose the one which suits us best. No name can express it all.
Ondaatje concludes by stating his wish to live henceforth "as a forgotten citizen."
And as "a forgotten citizen," he signed one of the few letters which remain of his, no doubt, voluminous correspondence, a letter written shortly after the death and burial of his friend and fellow lodger Jacobus Bellamy, in March 1786.

For a full year Ondaatje tried to remain unobtrusive.
We can follow the shape of his life during that year from some exposed outlines: a reference here and there to his role as a stagehand and prompter in the continuing drama of Utrecht.
The diaries of Gijsbert Jan van Hardenbroek give glimpses of Ondaatje whom the writer in his lordly indifference to the spelling of commoners' names refers to as "Undati."
Did van Hardenbroek perhaps unconsciously hit upon the real family name?
We know that the first Ondaatje came from South India and was a famous doctor. When he was baptised in Colombo, he took a Dutch sounding name and a Portuguese sounding wife. Dutch sounding because the name Ondaatje is unique. No other family of that or of a similar name is known in the Netherlands. Could it have been a Dutch version of Undatee? Forgotten, as our "forgotten citizen."

That summer of 1785, a national conference of Freecorps met in Utrecht. They issued a fiercely democratic proclamation and declared that the criminal proceedings against Pieter Ondaatje were "a matter concerning the entire people of the Netherlands."
That was a potent declaration indeed. It made Pieter Ondaatje a national hero. The twenty-four had not forgotten him either. They continued to press Council and the Provincial States with petitions in favour of Ondaatje.
Finally the whole criminal procedure was quashed by Council.
Neither had the ex-colonel let him slip out of sight. Van Hardenbroek relates that at the end of the year 1785 the Pesters clan are seeing a lot of Undati and friends.

CHAPTER VII

How did that come to pass? If we want to guess, we have to go back to the aftermath of the "revenge of Council."

The anti-democratic resolutions and decrees of Council, reversing their decisions taken on the 11th of March, had a predictable but ironic effect. It drove the leaders of the democrats to the Stadhouder, the other pole of power. After all, the democrats had not supported Council in its first moves against the absolute powers of the Stadhouder to allow Council to take over those powers entirely for itself.

Although playing the forgotten citizen, Ondaatje was not capable of remaining a passive citizen. He wrote articles for newspapers and a series of pamphlets, published under the initials AOM with a typically eighteenth century title: "Letters of a gentleman of Utrecht to his friend in Amsterdam" and with the motto "Neither hesitate, nor despair." In those gentlemanly letters, he referred to a song then popular in Utrecht:

> If we must take the yoke
> We'd rather have one bloke
> We'd rather do the Will of one
> than bend to forty gentlemen.

The majority of Council, now dubbed "aristocrats," were warned that the citizens would turn to the Stadhouder, and that Council would be put back in the bag, unless Council listened to the Voice of the People.

And, in fact, strong moves were made to approach William V. Ondaatje and his friends von Liebeherr, de Nijs and Hoevenaar were seen in the Hague.

They even visited the daily parades of the garrison which William always inspected in person, hoping that he would notice them and establish contact. They wrote letters to the Hague, and saw the private secretary of the Prince.

Now Prince William got his chance to play the old game which every Stadhouder before him had been good at: playing the people off against the Regents. This time he did not even need to stoop to stuivers and genever, the people were coming of their own accord to eat out of his hand. Not the primitive and stupid rabble, this time, but – in Ondaatje's words – "the '85 men," enlightened, well-informed citizens.

But William's heart was with the aristocratic Regents. He did not reply to any of the letters sent to him by Utrecht's democrats. He ignored Pieter Ondaatje at the parades in the Hague. He did not grab this opportunity of turning adversity into victory. He lost his chance of demonstrating to the people that the Stadhouder was willing to defend their rights and liberties. He was not prepared to make one single concession to the democrats. His maxim remained: "Aut Caesar, Aut nihil," or in plain language which he preferred to use: "Either King, or shit."

Marx would conclude in line with the Stadhouder's plain language: William was fit for the dung heap of history.

Usually it is a long way from a palace to a dung heap.

The first step on this way was a surprise to William's friends and foes. William received an instruction from the States of Utrecht to take decisive action in his capacity as commander-general of the armed forces.

The little town of Amersfoort, northeast of Utrecht, had experienced similar convulsions as the city of Utrecht. But there the "aristocratic" majority in Council had not hesitated when confronted with Ondaatje-like opposition. In August 1785 it asked the Provincial States for armed protection. The States readily complied and "instructed" the Stadhouder to send troops which William did with exemplary speed.

That was the end of the political activities of the democrats in Amersfoort but the beginning of the troubles for the aristocrats elsewhere in the Republic and for William V, who now in the eyes of the peace-loving democratic citizens had shown himself to be a tyrant, although he had only done his duty as commander of the army by following the instructions of his sovereign, the States of Utrecht. But it might have been more politic of William if he had been as dilatory in this matter as he usually was when speed was in his interest.

Amersfoort confronted the democratic Patriots in the whole Dutch Republic with the reality of armed intervention in what so far had been a political struggle. The aristocrats had lost the last bit of trust of the thinking part of the nation, peace-loving and law-abiding in normal times, but now more and more prepared to condone the use of force in self-defense against armed attacks by the Stadhouder's troops.

The next step downhill for William was a personal defeat on this same field, the military, so near to his manly heart.

One month after Amersfoort, the States of the province of Holland issued direct orders to the military garrison of the Hague, publicly ignoring the Prince as its commander-general. This was more than William could take. He left the Residence in a pique with his whole family and settled in Nijmegen on the border of the Republic where on the other side of the Rhine lay territories of Prussia's great Frederic. Only some far-sighted pessimists in the Dutch Republic saw the portents. Already as early as 1784, Joan Derk van der Capellen tot den Pol had warned that Prussia might intervene in the Republic unless France would be prepared to defend the Dutch.

For the time being the Stadhouder sulked in self-imposed exile and the Patriots in the province of Holland steadily gained strength in most city councils.

Amsterdam steered an independent course, aimed at curbing the powers of the Stadhouder while preventing "democratic excesses" and fostering good relations with France to keep the English in their place.

A formal peace had been concluded with England but the Dutch did not trust the English. Henrik Danielszoon Hooft had written "the English are less reliable than the Turks or the barbarians."

Hooft knew the English from personal experience. In his youth he had travelled in Great Britain and Ireland and had been made an honorary citizen of Dublin.

CHAPTER VII

During the summer of 1785, the City Council of Utrecht finally adopted a new regulation for the appointment of councillors. It was not to the liking of the twenty-four and the militia.
All eight companies of the town militia appeared in full strength, but unarmed and assembled, not around, but near the Town Hall. In that way they respected the letter of the decree forbidding assemblies around the Town Hall during council meetings.
With remarkable flexibility, Council amended its draft regulation. It was now almost a copy of the original "Ondaatje draft." Pieter and his fellow democrats should have had reasons to be content. But they were not.
It was very well for Council to accept whatever recipe for the pudding the democrats were prescribing; the baking and eating was going to be what counted.

The majority of Council maintained that the pudding could only be eaten when the States of the province of Utrecht had incorporated Council's new municipal regulation into their new provincial Regerings Reglement. They claimed that they could only swear the oath on the new Regerings Reglement in its entirety, not on the municipal part of it alone. They were hoping that the other two Orders of the provincial States – the Elected and the Nobles – would derail the whole project. The democratic citizens of Utrecht realized very well that such a hope was not an illusion. The Elected were handpicked by Pesters and the majority was against any democratic changes; the Nobles had supported Council of Utrecht in gaining independence from the Stadhouder, but they had now become concerned that the democrats in Utrecht were going too far.

In December the companies of the town militia again assembled unarmed, in rain and sleet, outside the Town Hall where a council meeting was taking place. Adrianus Hoevenaar was allowed in with seven men and submitted a respectful ultimatum: Council must adopt, without further reservations or conditions the new municipal regulation and introduce it within three months, regardless of provincial approval.
Events unrolled similar to the two days in March when Ondaatje had been the driving force. This time he worked behind the scenes.
A second council meeting, in the evening of the first day of the December crisis was being forced upon Council, but most councillors remained at home, and no decision could be taken without a quorum. The crowd was growing.

When Burgomaster Loten, who had been compared to the postillion of Nicolaas Pesters, entered his coach with a colleague to go home, the mob tried to stop them from leaving. Loten's coachman knows how to handle the situation. He uses his whip both on the horses and the crowd. The horses rear, the people fall back and the coach sets off. The ex-colonel would have approved of such coachmanship.

The mob has Burgomaster Loten by the tail.
by J. BUYS and R. VINKELES

But at Burgomaster Loten's house, a group of angry people is waiting. When the burgomaster tries to ascend the steps to his front door, they grab him by his coattails and pull him back. "Back with you to the Town Hall!" they shout. Loten's son and servants appear in the door, grab him by his arms and pull him up while the crowd is pulling the burgomaster down. "Hold on! Hold on! The rascall shall not escape," the crowd shouts. The coattails tear and Burgomaster Loten tumbles over his doorstep into safety. The coach has managed to escape with the other Worship, whom nobody discovered because he had hidden himself under the bench.

CHAPTER VII

A new meeting next morning. Militia and crowd surround the Town Hall. This time the opposition resorts to passive resistance and civil disobedience.
A wishy-washy decision is being promulgated from the balcony on the first floor of the Town Hall. The crowd below shouts "Matters have to be decided now. No further delays!"
One of the conservative councillors, Otto Willem Falck, described the events hour by hour in a memorandum for his descendants. Although never printed, the manuscript is preserved in the city archives of Utrecht. This is what Falck wrote down immediately after the second day of the December episode:

> Another rabble-rousing young man who already had made himself a name by his threatening talks, demeaning to the authorities, in Council on the 6th and 11th of March 1785 – and who had become the subject of criminal proceedings – called Ondaatje, an Asiatic foreigner studying here, whose face expresses the clearest signs of his slavish descent, emerged full of passion from the Stadskelder Inn and shouted on the steps like a madman in a loud voice, after he had secured some silence by his gestures and exclamations: "Yesterday I prayed to God who will help me most certainly to assist you, good citizens! Therefore follow me! Let us show ourselves in the city hall, where your rights and privileges are being frustrated instead of being respected."

No councillor can leave the Town Hall. Whose patience is going to wear out first? Council has lost all credibility with the people. They have delayed and avoided the issue for too long.
One of the beadles appears in the Council room and warns that things begin to look ugly outside. "If your Worships cannot resolve to give in, you better make sure how you are going to get out, because things are going to end all topsy-turvy." It might not be the voice of the common people but at least the beadle's was the voice of common sense.
Two councillors, belonging to the democratic faction, ask Council if they should call in the two militia companies of which they are the commanders, to guarantee the security of Council and - if necessary – counter possible mob violence. By this offer they want to prevent Council from using, for a second time, the excuse of having had to make decisions under duress. They add, that if Council asks for protection, they will insist on a final decision during that meeting. Council knows how the militiamen are disposed and prefers an unarmed militia in front of the Town Hall over armed protectors inside.
At three in the afternoon, from the balcony above the big entrance to the Town Hall, the decision of Council is read out: the new city constitution has been adopted and will go into effect within three months after a mutual swearing-in between councillors and deputies of the citizens.
Although this decree gave in to every demand of the twenty-four and sixteen, some confusion arose amongst the crowd in front of the Town Hall. Did the people suspect a trick? Falck wrote:

> The people shouted, 'No, No' notwithstanding the fact that the aforesaid Ondaatje who was present in the crowd at first gave signs of approval with his head and with his walking stick and tried in vain to elicit general approbation. But then, when he

could make himself understood after having raised his hands and having requested silence, he asked the secretary who was still standing on the balcony: How, dear Sir, the citizens have not quite understood the last part of the publication. Pray, be so good to read it again.

Whereupon the secretary read the publication again and Ondaatje and some assistants, raising in time their hats, latched on to the last words with a loud exclamation of Hurrah! which was repeated by the crowd with a threefold Hurrah!

The Voice of the People needed some prompting.

The twenty-four and the sixteen, who had by now learned not to take any chances, did not believe Council on its word but insisted on an authenticated copy, on parchment, of the long awaited decision. Until this had been executed, no councillor was allowed to leave the Town Hall. When they finally received what they had been waiting for, in black and white and on parchment, did Ondaatje's people realize that they had "ordained" a new constitution, very much in the American way?

Falck did not mention in the memorandum for his descendants that one of the town beadles had helpfully suggested to smuggle him out of the Town Hall through a back door. In a parody of Ondaatje's famous words uttered in March of that same year Falck declared, "My way is not through a back door." But when he noticed the thick crowd barring the "Royal Entrance," he wisely followed the two burgomasters and escaped through the back door.

The people celebrated their victory until 10 o'clock in the evening, . Then the "knaves" bell of the Dom Tower called them to bed. A company of the militia reported for duty – in arms – against burglars and fire. But the Regents, that night, had other worries.

CHAPTER VIII

Jewels in His Head

The year 1783 was the starting point for Pieter Ondaatje in Utrecht.
Mankind went up in the air, ideas came down to earth, the English held the seas. The Dutch East Indies, Ceylon, all the Dutch trading posts on the coast of India, the Cape of Good Hope were cut off from the Dutch Republic.

A young man, three years older than Pieter Ondaatje, got stuck in Jaffna, the most northern town of Ceylon. He wanted to go to Colombo, but the sea was unsafe. The English had been picking off, one by one, all the towns on the coast of India where the Dutch flag was flown.
Now the Brits were swept off the sea by the French.
The young man had been caught in the middle. He was called Jacob Haafner, or Haffner as he spelled his name at that time.
His ancestors came from Colmar in the Elzas, the territory between France and the German States on the bank of the Rhine.
Jacob's family was important enough for Mozart to have dedicated a symphony and a serenade to a Haffner, K.V. 385 and K.V. 250.
Jacob's father had escaped from his home town because they had wanted to make him a monk and had married Jacob's mother in a small university city deep in Germany where he had gone to study medicine.
When Jacob was only a few years old, they had moved to Amsterdam. He considered himself a Dutchman. When he was eleven, his father took him along on a VOC ship to Batavia, the capital of the Dutch Indies. His father was the ship's doctor, but in the Cape colony the doctor himself fell ill and died. Jacob stayed at the Cape and later was moved around between Batavia and Amsterdam. He became an accomplished seaman, was taught drawing and bookkeeping and spoke Dutch, French, German, Latin and Portuguese. Later he learned English and various Indian languages.
When he was eighteen, he took up employment with the VOC in Negapatnam on the east coast of India, then an important Dutch trading post. The English were fighting and intriguing their way into India.
The Anglo-Dutch war of 1780 – 1784 gave the English the opportunity to grab the Dutch posts on the Indian coast. They also tried to invade Ceylon, which was saved for the Dutch by the French. India was lost to England.

CHAPTER VIII

In the summer of 1781, Jacob Haafner had been staying in one of the Dutch forts on the Indian coast. He had lent all his capital to the commander. It was the goodly sum of 1,000 star pagodas – the equivalent in Dutch money of ten years of the salary of a schoolmaster.

The commander had told him that he needed to pay his soldiers and that a VOC ship with money was due any day. The next day the English took the fort by surprise. Instead of being paid, the soldiers, with Jacob in tow, were being marched off to Madras, the British headquarters on the coast. Jacob Haafner was detained in Madras for over a year.

Haafner managed to escape and reached Ceylon after fights and storms at sea. A romantic note serves as an undertone. He travelled with a beautiful half-caste girl, Anna. The night before reaching Jaffna and Ceylon "all my decisions, all my plans, all my fear and precarious prospects; fatherland, friends, – I forgot all in the arms of Anna." This is how he described it twenty-four years later in the first of the three books which he would write about his life in India and his visit to Ceylon.

His second book, *Reize in eenen Palanquin*, deals with the period after the Anglo-Dutch war, when young Jacob was travelling as a merchant along the coast of East India, then called Coromandel.

For many years I had owned a copy of that book, "Travels in a Palanquin," until one day I started to read it. There was a work which in its freshness and directness surpassed any old travel book I had read. Something timeless attracted me and made me read on and forget the clock. I later found that an earlier literary critic had been as attracted as I was and had called Haafner's style "sweeping away." Haafner's violent likes and dislikes appeal, not to reason or common sense, but to feelings of magnanimity and compassion.

His travel books have been called high marks of early romantic art. They were translated into German, French and Danish and even into English, though Haafner had reserved his deepest scorn for the English. His furious indictments of English behavior in the East, backed up by factual observations, must have been uncomfortable for English readers.

Not that he was uncritical of the Dutch. He was more modern than most nineteenth century critics of colonialism. Clearly and repeatedly he states that the Europeans should leave the East altogether.

He has the greatest respect and affection for the Indians and Ceylonese. A quarter of a century after he had left Asia for good, he writes with nostalgia how much he would have loved to remain there for the rest of his life. During his travels he is proud to be held for a local half-caste. He walks in Ceylon through jungles and marshes bare-foot, but keeps attached to his hat; he speaks the local language with relish and loves a local dancing girl, one of the frankest and most suggestive love stories of the eighteenth century.

Why had I never heard of him before? Why were his books out of print since the middle of the last century?

Some time ago an antiquarian bookseller offered me the first edition of Haafner's travel books, uniformly bound and rare.
I read everything in one go. The last book which he completed on his deathbed in 1809 contains the story of a tour through Ceylon on foot. I decided I would let myself be carried away by Haafner for at least a part of that tour.

When Christopher and I were planning our journey, I sent him the title vignette of Haafner's "Travels in a Palanquin" and suggested that we would travel in the same manner at least for the Ceylonese part of it. In Holland, this mode of

conveyance would draw too much unwelcome attention; we would use more indigenous Dutch means of transportation in Utrecht and in Amsterdam.
We were planning to make our journey with one foot in the present and one in the past. Our intention was to follow the tracks of our own forefathers, the old Amsterdam burgomaster and the young student from Ceylon. Lacking a magic carpet, a palanquin might after all not be such a bad idea.
Would we find traces of their lives if we would walk in their tracks? Would the tracks of Hooft and Ondaatje cross each other? Would they cross Haafner's tracks? Which other tracks would we find?
In the end we did a lot of walking and found a network of tracks so marvellously interconnected that it seemed as if a great choreographer had been at work.

CHAPTER VIII

When Haafner had arrived with his Anna in Jaffna, he remained there for some months. "My days passed away, like the current of a clear brook among borders of flowers."

He met fellow refugees from Negapatnam and enjoyed nature walks with Anna. Did he ever go to the imposing Dutch Reformed Church? I am sure he did. The minister was Dominee Willem Juriaan Ondaatje who preached in Dutch, Tamil and Portuguese, all languages which Jacob Haafner spoke. The Dominee was the father of a promising young man who was studying in Utrecht.

Did he meet this Dominee Ondaatje's sister and her husband, the famous Reverend Philippus de Melho, now retired, who devoted his time to poetry in Tamil and to translations of Dutch religious works into that language?

In the north, in Jaffna and along the east coast of the island, Tamil was the main language. The people had come from South India many centuries ago in various waves of immigration. Even Muslims had settled there, called Moors, who spoke Tamil.

In the interior and along the west and south coasts, the people were Sinhalese and spoke Sinhala, an Indo-European language. Their ancestors had come from northern India and prided themselves on their Indo-Aryan origin.

The Tamils were descended from the original Indian people, the Dravidians, and looked smaller and darker than the north Indian settlers.

In Colombo both Tamil and Sinhalese were spoken and many more languages. Colombo was a real melting pot of old settlers and new immigrants.

The seas were unsafe. The English were prying on Ceylon. They had taken and lost Trincomalee, the best natural harbour along the whole east coast of the Indian subcontinent. Haafner does not need much encouragement to decide to travel over land.

An old friend wants to go to Colombo to apply for the job of cooper at the VOC shipyards. They find a second travel companion, a former soldier, who had lost his hearing at the battle of Rosbach, due to the cannon of Frederic the Great. "He was deaf and almost always drunk. Otherwise he was a good fellow."

On top of that he was a baker by profession.

A Swiss who pretends he is on a diplomatic mission completes the group.

They set out with twelve bearers, food, flares to scare off elephants, cymbals for the same purpose, and a violin on which the Swiss plays tunes to which the stone-deaf baker dances. Their bearers carry enough spirits to keep up his spirit. If he does not dance or sleep and snore, the baker is armed with a long hussar saber "which struck upon the ground with every step he took." The cooper is trigger-happy and shoots at everything that moves to the dismay of Jacob who is a tender-hearted naturalist. Since the outbreak of the war, two and a half years earlier, no elephants had been trapped because the barges in which they were transported to India could not cross to the mainland without danger of an enemy attack. The countryside is infested with wild elephants which devastate whatever fields and villages there are on the coast. The interior is desolate. Nearly every night the travellers are in danger of being obliterated by herds of stampeding elephants. Most nights they camp behind watchfires.

Haafner devotes some lyrical descriptions to the forests of Ceylon.

> I have travelled in many forests, and traversed many woods in various countries; but never have I seen one that could, in any degree, be compared to those of Ceylon. Where the sun shoots his burning rays, only a trembling and coloured light could be perceived. Trees, almost as old as the world, spread a refreshing coolness, and proudly exalting themselves on high, extend their branches far and wide in the air. Others, loaded with wild fruit, protect aromatic plants that grow in the shade, and fill the atmosphere with a balmy and refreshing shade. Butterflies, of the most splendid and glowing colours, wander among the trembling leaves, or pursue one another in sport. Here and there are seen through the trees, as in perspective, troops of deer, elk, and antelopes of all sorts, and sometimes bears and wild swine. Game swarms on all sides; hares, partridges, wild fowl; while the cooing of pigeons, and other birds of that species, continually resounds through the forest. Apes of various sorts skip from branch to branch, and have afforded us much amusement by a thousand ridiculous leaps and grimaces. In short, these enchanted forests had, for me, so many attractions, that whenever I recall them to mind, I feel an irresistible longing to see them again. How passionately I desire to wander once more under their delightful shades, and again to listen to the sweet and melodious voices of the plumed inhabitants.

But to return to our journey.

Their guide had been an elephant hunter and knew most paths across the island. He offered to lead them into the highlands which had always remained closed to Europeans. The interior was cut off from the outer world by mountains ranged more or less in a circle around the highland interior, like the ramparts around a walled city. The role of an outer moat was fulfilled by the thick jungle which stretched almost to the coast. Only around Colombo, Galle and a few other coastal towns had the jungle been cut back for fields, plantations and villages. Some large rivers which sprung from the highlands had made breaches in these defensive mountain walls. They were not navigable; an impenetrable growth was left along the banks. These waters were gathering places for elephants, leopards and wild buffalo, terrifying anyone who might want to travel into the interior. Between the coast near Colombo and the highlands around Kandy there were mountain roads or rather paths, as the Sinhalese made sure no road would be wider than necessary for one man to pass. These paths were tortuous and easy to close off by toppling down rocks and trees.

Haafner describes the paths which they follow: "one man wide, with a thorn hedge on both sides, double the height of a man, steep and perpendicular and so close and even that they might have been planted by the hand of a man and clipped and kept smooth by an experienced gardener." They were probably planted on purpose. We know that the Kandyans went to great length to add thorn hedges, interrupted at strategic places by thorn gates, to the already formidable natural defenses of their inner territories. Ceylon has a variety of thorn bushes of the acacia and other sorts with needle-sharp, inches long spikes, some of them in the form of crowfeet so that when strewn over the ground always one spike will face upwards.

CHAPTER VIII

Haafner had boots but halfway they wore out and he continues barefoot, complaining more of blood suckers than of sore feet.

They run into bears, the vicious sloth bear of Ceylon, or rather Haafner runs over a bear. The animal rushed out of one of these high clipped hedges just in front of him while the party was proceeding "like a flock of wild geese" with Haafner at the head. The bear "stood directly before me, and, apparently, undecided whether to attack me or turn back, prevented me from retreating, and so suddenly did this take place, that before I was aware, I had tumbled over his broad back, and fallen to the ground on the other side."

While he is trying to get up the bear bends over him " with paws lifted up, growling and ready to fall upon me. I gave up my soul to God and waited for death with closed eyes. At this decisive moment I heard something whistling past my ears and at the same time a report took place which frightened the bear to such a degree that, instead of attacking me, he raised a frightful howl, and fled through the same opening in the forest by which he had come."

One of his companions had fired his pistol. Haafner observes ruefully that the ball could have split his head as thoroughly as the paw of the bear. "It was fortunate that the shot did not strike the bear, as in that event he would have torn me in pieces either in his agony or fall."

Some days later he is pursued by a wild buffalo. He runs for his life but "the furious beast was now close upon me; already I was affected by his breath;" in fact too close for Jacob to jump aside, "I threw myself on the ground at full length, and the next moment the furious beast ran over me at full speed. What a narrow escape I had made! His hindfeet were scarcely a span distant from my head. . . ." As soon as the buffalo had passed, Haafner creeps under the nearest thicket from which he is extricated by his friends "and they were quite astonished how it had been possible for me to penetrate so far into these thorns."

They hardly see human beings on their journey. Only when they reach the coast do they meet some solitary Dutchmen guarding the small forts which the VOC maintained between Colombo and Jaffna. A Brahmin gives them hospitality at a Hindu shrine and offers to cure the baker from his deafness by some charm and sacred oil to be dripped into his ears, but they spurn the offer thinking it is not Christian to cooperate with such mumbo jumbo. Poor baker, but he probably did not catch the point.
To Haafner's astonishment, however, their guide is able to cast a spell on the crocodiles when they have to wade through a crocodile-infested river. The bearers are all anointed on their foreheads with a few drops of a prepared pilisuniam or charm. The four Europeans refuse "because we considered this superstitious ceremony as wholly useless, and altogether without effect upon the jaws of the ravenous monsters." To show them that the charm works the guide throws into the river six small balls kneaded from sand and the charmed liquid and takes five bearers over "without the crocodiles making the least motion of attacking, though we could plainly see the snouts above the water of several that were swimming here and there, not ten yards distant."Then all the others enter the water followed by the guide who has instructed each of the charmless Europeans to hold the one in front of him by the shoulder with the left hand and not to lose hold of one another, "otherwise he could not answer for any accidents that might happen." Haafner says that they held their hunting knives in their other hand" by way of precaution. This, however, was unnecessary as the crocodiles did not seem to look or at least they paid no attention to us." The ungrateful cooper, no sooner safely arrived on the other side, wants to shoot at the crocodiles, or perhaps he just wants to stress the fact that he is a Christian. The bearers all join together begging him to desist, otherwise their comrade who had prepared the charm would certainly meet with some misfortune. Common sense – or Christian feelings – prevails.

After some weeks of travel in this entertaining manner, they arrive in Colombo. Haafner describes the city as a pleasant civilized place with liquor shops, gaming and coffee houses "in the Dutch manner" where people amuse themselves at billiards, bowls, chess and other games and with large avenues of high and umbrageous trees and spacious buildings. He writes highly of the Governor, "a native of Ceylon, a man of much judgement and understanding."

CHAPTER VIII

That Governor was Iman Willem Falck, of an old Danish noble family, whose ancestors had taken service in the army of the Dutch Republic and with the VOC. His mother belonged to a Dutch family and was born in the Dutch East Indies. Her father had been Governor of Malacca, present day Malaysia, North of Singapore, then a VOC trading post.

Rumors had it that Iman Falck had oriental blood. He was swarthy and his nickname was "the Black Crow." His father had been Prosecutor General – Fiscaal – of Ceylon and lies buried in Jaffna in the Grote Kerk where Dominee Willem Juriaan Ondaatje had been preaching for so many years. Iman Falck and Willem Ondaatje were of the same age and had travelled to Europe in the same ship to study at Dutch universities. When Iman came back and had risen to the highest position on the island, he had helped Dominee Willem Ondaatje to reorganize the Dutch Seminary in Colombo, where Ondaatje had become rector. Governor Falck had also supported Dominee Ondaatje to send his fifteen year old son Pieter to Holland to complete his schooling at the Latin and Greek school in Amsterdam.

Falck was the longest serving and most effective Governor Dutch Ceylon ever had. Two years after Haafner's visit, he was dead and buried in the old fort of Colombo.

His first cousin was that conservative member of the town council of Utrecht, Otto Willem Falck, who had described Pieter Ondaatje during the December days of 1785 in Utrecht as an "Asiatic foreigner of slavish descent." A year later, Otto Willem Falck would express himself in more complimentary terms and would have less reason to regret that his cousin, the governor of Ceylon, had helped this Asiatic foreigner to come to Utrecht.

In one of those coffee houses in the Dutch manner, Jacob Haafner meets a Portuguese called Manuel de Cruz. They become friends and the Portuguese tells him that one of his forefathers had taken part in one of the Portuguese raids on Kandy – 150 or 200 years ago – and had carried off a large iron chest filled with jewels and gold, looted from the Royal Palace. Before he could reach the coast, he had to hide his loot in a cave in the mountains, but Manuel's father had told him before he died where to find this chest. The Portuguese had ventured into the mountains of Bocaul and had found the chest but could not open it nor carry it away alone. He begs Jacob to help him recover the treasure and promises him half of it. This appeals to Jacob's love of the adventurous. He is also attracted by the prospect of improving his material position.

They proceed to Chilaw on the coast north of Colombo, buy provisions, a rope, files and a crowbar to open the iron chest.

The remainder of Haafner's book on Ceylon is taken up by the story of their treasure-hunt through jungle and mountains.

Every day of the two weeks of this expedition is described in detail, the hours they walked, the distances they covered, the geographical features they observed and the terrifying confrontations with the wilderness. No more lyrical or romantic outpourings. Just a catalogue of horrors.

I do not think that anything similar has been described so grippingly before the nineteenth century classics of exploration.

I wanted to follow Haafner and Manuel de Cruz. Thoughts of material improvement were far from me. No files or crowbars would be needed. My highest ambition was to reconstruct Haafner's journey to the mountains of Bocaul. The most visible landmark would be the spot where Haafner was blocked on his way into those mountains. The description which he gives of that spot is very precise: a vertical, sixty foot high cliff, "as smooth as a wall," jutting out from the jungle and overhanging a deep ravine, canal or dry riverbed with steep banks and solidly filled up with impenetrable brushwood, which had prevented the adventurers from reaching the mountains on the other side. Studying Haafner's description I reckoned that such a formidable natural barrier must still be recognizable in today's landscape. It seemed impossible that it could have disappeared in a mere 200 years.

While in Canada, I started a correspondence with Ismeth Raheem, a Colombo architect, naturalist, historian and polymath. Christopher had asked Ismeth to design a guest bungalow in one of Sri Lanka's wildlife parks.
Our first week on the island was spent among the elephants and waterbirds of Yala, with the Ondaatje bungalow as our base. The beautiful structure, inspired by Dutch-Ceylonese architecture, was donated by Christopher to the Sri Lanka wildlife department. While we were there a short ceremony confirmed the transfer. The foreman chanted a Buddhist prayer and invited Christopher to smash a coconut on the pavement of the verandah, the same coconut which had been hanging in a small improvised shrine in a Cohomba tree on the edge of the lake in front of the bungalow. Every night the workmen had lit a small oil lamp under the coconut which gave it a warm yellow look against the stem of the tree under the darkness of the crown. The golden glowing light was repeated many miles away by a colder, more starlike light on a hill behind the dark surface of the lake: the hill-temple of Kataragama, Sri Lanka's earliest protector. For thousands of years people have gone there on pilgrimage, Hindus, Buddhists and Christians.
Two small lights, one in the front and one in the back of the sky-filled stage, where night and day, the moon, the stars, the sun, the clouds and the rain are both the actors and the scenery in a play which had its opening night at the beginning of time.

During the daytime, Ismeth took us on birdwatching trips. All the while we were discussing Haafner. At lunch we would study Ordinance Survey Maps and every word of Haafner's description. After counting curlew-sandpipers which breed in Northern Siberia, we counted Haafner's miles and found that they did not match with the distances indicated on the maps until we discovered that the Dutch mile of Haafner's days was three and a half times longer than the English mile.

CHAPTER VIII

Ismeth Raheem and the author studying Haafner's journey.

From the guides of Yala Wildlife Park, we learned the reality of the metaphor of "following the tracks of our ancestors" when they tracked down elephants and other relatives according to Darwin, and made Christopher pursue leopards for days on end, the leopards for which he feels such a fascination.
When Christopher and I finally set out in Haafner's footsteps we were prepared. We had marked and discussed over dinner and while travelling through Sri Lanka's highlands and lowlands every step as described by Haafner, every incident. When we had lunch in the trophy-stuffed Hill Club in Nuwara Eliya, still the island's tea planter's center, we discussed Haafner's adventures with leopards. When we stood in front of the twenty-foot Buddha statues in the Rock Temple of Polonaruwa we talked about Haafner's sixty-foot perpendicular cliff; when we entered the caves of Dambulla with the 100 Buddha's, we speculated about the jewel chest of Manuel de Cruz. But when we climbed Adam's Peak we talked about Adam and Buddha and we tried to measure the footprint, not to tread in it.

Early one morning we set off from Chilaw, a cheerful town north of Colombo full of crows and fishermen. We were looking for a river which had dissolved since Haafner's days into man-made irrigation reservoirs and canals. We tracked

Chilaw full of crows and fishermen.

the river down to a lake – called tank in this part of the world after the Portuguese word tanque. It was covered with flowering lotus plants. Pheasant-tailed Jacanas, with spidery feet and toes nearly as long as their tails, ran on top of the floating lotuses as if they were waterskiing in jerks. Snow-white ibises and shining black cormorants were taking it easier.

The nasal sound of an unharmonious wind instrument and the muffled, monotonous tom toms of a drum drew us to the dilapidated compound of a Hindu temple. We had been looking for Haafner's Munasseram river which nobody knew and no map shows. This was the Munasseram Temple. We were not far off.

Past stone statues, festooned with flower garlands, some wrapped in yellow and red clothes, and a lingam dripping with oil, giving it a semblance of throbbing life, we found our way into the inner sanctum where musicians were calling, streaked with white ashes, charms hanging from their neck. Three Brahmin priests were changing the dress and the garlands on a statue, burning incense and leaves and boughs. A few sareed women were worshipping. In the corner sat an Englishman with the face of a Saint Bernard hound, eyes focused on eternity. A bankrupt stockbroker on his last high?

We found the remaining part of Haafner's Munasseram river. He and his Portuguese companion were so intent on avoiding the crocodiles when wading through the river that they nearly walked into a leopard. We had no charms or sandballs to lock the jaws of the ravenous monsters, but found a palmtree trunk to cross over. The local people we met confirmed that the river is still infested with crocodiles.

Thereafter Haafner and friend followed the Chilaw river, now called the Deduru Oya. We reached the river at about the place where they also must have joined it. The bed was half dried out. Large banks of yellow sand and puddles and streamlets with clear water made us think of picnics and swimming parties.

Our two predecessors followed the river for two days and covered forty-two English miles by their estimate. They saw no sign of human life. On both sides of the river Haafner noticed beautiful forests.

At the Chilaw river, now called the Deduru Oya, Haafner in hand.

We found the area in total cultivation. No natural forest was left except along the riverbanks. But the Sri Lankan farmer makes a light impression on the soil, and trees are used for food and shade, even worshipped. Forest clearing has not had the same effect as in so many Western countries. You feel as if the people have temporarily moved in under the trees, as if they have come for an outing only, ready to leave.

We did not follow the river all the way. We took a shortcut and rejoined the Deduru Oya further up-stream where an irrigation canal had been dug parallel to the river, with a dike on one side called a "bund." We walked along the bund, close and parallel to Haafner's track, for the whole afternoon. That walk brought us back in time, not in Haafner's primeval wilderness, but in a Ceylonese version of a Thomas Hardy rural novel.

Travelling peddlers with oxcarts laden with pottery, farmers going to their fields, children on their way home from school, women wading through the canal, straight as ramrods, with heavy burdens on their heads, and bathers everywhere. Christopher has a fixation for bathers and takes photographs wherever he spots them. When I finally jumped in, he was so absorbed in photographing the event that he had no time to make a splash himself.

We followed the canal until we reached the Deduru Oya, just upstream from a modern barrage. The river here was a broad expanse of water. The sky was covered with thunder clouds. To the east, in the distance, we saw mountains. Here Haafner and his companion camped the second night. His description fits perfectly with our modern map and with our own findings.

"At about five in the evening we came to the place where the river divides itself into two branches, one of which takes its course to the northeast, and the other, which is larger, towards the southeast. From this place we saw, very plainly, the tops of the mountains of Bocaul, behind an immeasurable forest."

That night they were disturbed by a "tiger," in fact a leopard, pursuing a deer straight across their camp. The tiger looked at them for some time and then fled "howling " into the forest.

CHAPTER VIII

We did not camp on the river and our night was not disturbed by tigers. We spent the night in Kurnegala, just outside Haafner's territory where Ismet Raheem joined us.

I had not been able to locate the Bocaul mountains before our tour. Nobody in Sri Lanka seemed to know this name. I had discussed the issue at length with Ismeth, who is an expert on the topography of Dutch Ceylon. He did not know either.
Haafner wrote that he had a map. In my opinion he must have used the map of Ceylon published by Isaac Tirion of Amsterdam in 1754. A new map was published in 1766, when a war between the VOC and Kandy had made it necessary to delineate the boundary between Dutch and Kandyan territory. That map does not give names of mountains or details of the interior. The next revision dates from 1786, three years after Haafner's voyage, and could not have been used by him.
"Berg Bocaul," Bocaul Mountain, is clearly marked on the Tirion map as the source of the Chilaw river. A comparison with a modern map, however, shows the Tirion map is incorrect in many ways.

When Ismeth met us at the Kurnegala resthouse the first thing he said was: "I have found your Bocaul Mountain." He produced an old folio book. It was called: *An historical relation of the island Ceylon in the East-Indies, together with an account of the detaining in captivity of the Author and divers other Englishmen now living there, and of the Author's miraculous Escape,* written by Robert Knox, "a captive there near twenty years."
The book was published in 1681.
"A hundred years before your Haafner was trying to get into the interior, this Knox was desperately trying to get out," said Ismeth. "He succeeded in the nineteenth year of his captivity and gives us in his book a description of the route he took and the villages and roadmarks. One of the first places he mentions is the Bocawl Mountain. Your Bocaul!"
We sat down and studied Knox' text.

Chapter IX
How the Author began his Escape, and got onward of his Way about an Hundred miles, having often gone this Way to seek for Liberty, but could not yet find it.
We again set forth to try what Success God Almighty would now give us. In the Year MDCLXXIX on the Two and twentieth of September. . . . the Moon being seven and twenty days old.
Which we had so contrived, that we might have a light Moon to see the better to run away. . . .
We went down at the Hill Bocawl, where there was now no Watch, and but seldom is any. This hill of Bocawl is so high and steepe that very few people goeth that way. It hath six assents and a good space of smooth ground betweene each one; it

windeth very croocket, that one unacquainted would often thinke himselfe at the top as he is goeing up, and noe water all the way, which is often requisite especially in ascending mountains. It is all great woods as all the other hills, but noe enymie ever ascended this way.

From Knox' description, it is easy to find the exact present-day location and all later commentators of Knox have pinned the Bocawl hill on the map under its modern name of Bokavala. It is close to Kandy, far in the interior and impossible to see from the Deduru Oya east of Chilaw.

But Haafner speaks not of a Bocaul Hill but of the Bocaul Mountains. Could the whole mountain range to which the Bocawl Hill belongs have carried that name? Haafner seems to believe so. Furthermore, he writes that the Bocaul mountains run more or less north-south.

On the Tirion map of 1754, a range under that name is shown due east of Chilaw. In actual fact, Bokavala, and the range of which that hill forms part, is at least fifty miles further away and behind other hills and mountains, which one had to cross first, coming from Chilaw and the coast. The mountains which Haafner did see, therefore, could not have been the range with the Bokavala hill.

There was no one around whom Haafner could have asked for the name of the mountain range which he did see. So he gave it the name which he found on the Tirion map, Bocaul.

That map, by the way, gave a totally wrong picture of the course of the Chilaw river – or Dedura Oya. Haafner's description coincides with its actual course shown on modern maps.

Although he gave the mountains which he had seen from his camp on the second night the wrong name, he did in fact see mountains "very plainly behind an immeasurable forest." Christopher and I, too, had seen mountains very plainly behind an immeasurable forest from that same place.

We picked up Haafner's tracks again the next day close to the foot of those mountains. We hereby skipped three days which for Haafner had been filled with toil and trouble: hours of struggling through fine deep sand; an attack by wild boar in that "immeasurable forest;" a mosquito-infested marsh; an attack by a bear which they had to kill, and by red ants which stung them; a struggle through creeping ivy full of sharp thorns, the fruit of which, however, was delicious to eat. They camped near a watering hole and the whole night had to keep leopards and jackals at bay. They shot a leopard but were too tired and weary to go and inspect him. All the time they believed the mountains of Bocaul to be ten to fifteen miles away. They wandered about in thornbush thickets "on the tops of which it seemed less difficult to walk, than to pass through."

They spent the night in a tree after having evacuated a leopard from its branches. "We smoked our segars with a certain sort of satisfaction." But Jacob was less

CHAPTER VIII

pleased when he woke up with a shock from his ropebed in the tree when a tepid liquid was hitting his face: "Monkey piss."

The next day the mountains came closer and closer "when we suddenly found our progress obstructed by a canal, or ditch, upwards of thirty feet wide and, to all appearances, very deep, which lay directly across our path, and stretched to the right and left, as far as the eye could reach." The banks on both sides were high, rough and almost perpendicular, the canal was filled solidly with "weeds, bushes, and brambles." An impenetrable mass of underwood of every description.

After some fruitless efforts to follow the canal in a northerly direction, they returned and followed it southwards. Manuel offered to cross over by cutting himself a way through the undergrowth. Then he would fasten the rope they were carrying with them to a tree on the other side to enable Jacob and the baggage to cross over along the ropebridge. He disappeared into the bushy abyss. "All at once I observed an unusual movement among the bushes, accompanied with piercing cries and horrible yells of my poor companion, which I mechanically repeated." Jacob fired his pistols in the air, beat upon the copper cooking plates, but the rest was silence. "I burst out into loud lamentations and called upon my companion by the tenderest names." Jacob ventured several paces into the opening but gave up. What should he do?

He decided not to return to Chilaw but to follow the canal to its source which he believed to lie in the mountains. By then he was convinced the canal was a dried-up riverbed. After a horrible night in thunder and lightning, shattered by the loss of his friend, he continued along the edge of the canal until the mountains were only three miles away. The canal came closer and closer to the mountains. "Their bare tops seemed to reach the clouds."

Another night in rain and wind with a visit from a horned spider. The next day the jungle closed in on the canal, and the moment Haafner thought he would finally reach the mountains, his path was blocked by a cliff sixty feet high, steep and smooth like a wall, rising perpendicularly from the abyss. He could not get by on that side. After hesitating for a while, he decided to circumvent this obstacle by trying to get through the jungle on the other side. He had only ventured a few yards into the thick undergrowth when he withdrew in terror pursued by a giant python, a pamboeraja seventy feet long and twice as thick as a man. In desperation Jacob jumped five feet up and five feet sideways against the cliff, caught a ridge with his hands and managed to pull himself up. Gun and rice were left behind. The pamboeraja devoured the rice, goatskin bag and all, and shuffled back into the jungle, leaving Jacob high and dry on the cliff. Talented draughtsman that he was, he later made an action drawing of the scene, engraved and published in his book.

Terrible days followed in the mountains, bare and rocky. Voices of ghosts disturbed him at night. He went east most of the time. He climbed a "steep mountain wholly destitute of vegetation," all the while keeping the canal deep down. His menu consisted of the odd serpent or bird which he managed to kill with stones; he drank rainwater from rockpools. At the end of his tether he

found some "segars" which had slipped into the lining of his coat and smoked them with relish. His tinderbox had not been swallowed by the pamboeraja. Finally, prepared to die, he saw a way into the canal, caught an Oedoembo or Teelgoin, a large lizard with tender meat considered extremely wholesome even by modern Sri Lankans, ate it, knelt down, thanked "the Almighty for his goodness in having thus far preserved me from perishing of hunger" and resolved to "persevere to the last extremity."

The next day he managed to cross the canal, ran into the forest and stumbled upon a party of Sinhalese on their way from Kandy to the coast. He swooned. They revived him with herbal medicine and to his great surprise he discovered the headman to be an old acquaintance from his earlier journey with his joyful companions. All is well that ends well. Jacob ends : "I have drawn this conclusion. Never to lose courage in any danger, or to despair in any difficulty, however great."

It is a moving story, even in the rather stiff translation for the London edition of Sir Richard Phillips & Co of 1821.

In Dutch we say, "a story which you are unable to read to the end with dry eyes."

CHAPTER VIII

Christopher, Ismeth and I have just crossed the Kimbulawana Oya, Sinhala for crocodile river, a tributary to the Deduru Oya. To the east are low hills, Haafner's Bocaul mountains; the crocodile river forms a loop at the foot of these hills. The land within the loop is open, rather sandy and intensively cultivated. The river provides enough water to irrigate the fields. We are due east of Haafner's fork in the Deduru Oya whence he set off in an easterly direction towards the mountains. These hills do not deserve the name of mountains. Further to the south, in the direction of Kurunegala, they rise somewhat higher. We allow Haafner some margin of error. He writes that he used a small compass; perhaps it was deflected by the iron files and crowbar. But in summer in Ceylon, it is not difficult for an early riser to find where the east is.

We move in a southeasterly direction towards the higher hills. We are still within the loop of the crocodile river. The hills are a few miles away. We study the landscape. Where is the canal, thirty feet wide, with steep banks, filled with such thick undergrowth that two intrepid adventurers could not cross over? A canal, furthermore, which continued for many hours walking to the north and for days to the south and then turned due east and into the mountains.

No indentation of this nature can be found in the whole area except the crocodile river itself.

Haafner described the canal as a dried-up riverbed. He observed that the undergrowth was so uncommonly thick because of the muddy and fertile soil of the riverbed.

Did someone, the King of Kandy, dam up the river further upstream and turn the bed into a natural defense? Haafner writes that he continued until the very head of the canal. He makes no mention of any lake or barrage, although he cannot have missed much of the course even when climbing the mountains. If we had studied our modern map only, I would have said that the crocodile river – in a dried-up state – would be a plausible candidate for Haafner's canal. But when we bathed our feet, cautiously, in the crocodile river we were reminded more of Smetana's broad "Moldau" river than of Schubert's rocky "Trout" stream. The crocodile river is not narrow and deep, the banks are nowhere steep, the bed is sandy and gravelly. Even in a dried and choked-up state there must have been many places where a passage was easy for travellers who had traversed thickets where you could walk "over the bushes" with less difficulty than through them.

We decided to follow the river all the way upstream and find the sixty-foot steep cliff which blocked Haafner's way and prevented him from continuing along the canal's bank.

The end of the day found us roaming around in an overgrown and somewhat dilapidated plantation.

Behind the company school, children were bathing in the crocodile river, here reduced to no more than a lizard's brook. On our way we had not found a trace of any rockface which could meet Jacob's description.

Christopher started to take pictures of the bathers. I wanted to take a picture of Christopher being pursued by an imaginary pamboeraja, but could not convince him to adopt Jacob Haafner's posture in which he drew himself against the rockface. Ismeth as a naturalist did not believe that a python would ever pursue a man and be "ready to swallow " him. Pythons usually do not go after their prey but lie in wait, and then strangle it by surprise. Even less plausible is Jacob's observation that it devoured his rice goatskin bag and all unless the python took the rice-bag for a live goat.

Sadder but wiser, we returned. More evenings were spent discussing various theories. Haafner, Knox and maps, old and new, were compared again and we decided to give Haafner the benefit of the doubt.

He was not known as an inventor of stories. His works are at the moment being reissued in the Netherlands. So far, all his adventures on the Cape and in India have been found based on reality.

But the treasure hunt in Ceylon?

When you read it critically, the story becomes more fantastic and less convincing the further away they travel from the coast. Although Haafner took notes, kept a diary and made sketches while he was travelling, he wrote his books much later, in the last years of his life.

The passage of time does not diminish the directness and freshness of his stories. But might he have fallen for the temptation to exaggerate the story of the treasure hunt? Could he have started out in actual fact with his Portuguese friend exactly as described until they reached the fork in the Deduru Oya on the night of the second day? The map of 1754 does not give any of the details which Jacob correctly described, such as the slight bend to the North and the fork, features he could not have gathered from that map but only from having been there himself. After the fork, however, things become unrecognizable. The crocodile river is never mentioned, unless it is the canal, but that is unlikely as we discovered by testing the water ourselves. Did the Portuguese lose his life somewhere after the second day? Did the crocodiles devour him when they were crossing the crocodile river without the charm of a local guide? And did Jacob perhaps think twenty-four years later that a story which ends with a fatal accident and no treasure would be a disillusion and did he, therefore, gild the lily somewhat near the end?

Did Haafner, in reality, return the way they came which is the most likely thing to do? Or did he continue due east which was not so difficult because the jungle there would have been less dense and the friendly hills would have given him some landmarks to go by? He knew he would eventually hit the road from Kandy to the north, the same road which Robert Knox had walked with his companion a hundred years earlier on his way out. That road is on the 1754 map. In fact, Knox put it on the map.

In Knox's day, the interior was heavily guarded and the King, Raja Sinha II, who made his appearance in Chapter I, did not only collect animals for his private zoo but hostages as well.

In any case, Jacob Haafner turned up in Jaffna again, lost his Anna, sailed back to the coast of Coromandel opposite Ceylon, became a travelling trader and made his unforgettable journey in a palanquin. He retired to the Dutch Republic with a nice capital and lost it all.

He later tried to recover the thousand star-pagodas which he had advanced to the VOC, and submitted one petition after the other to the committee which had replaced the Lords XVII. Haafner lost his case. Penury was around the corner. It was then he decided to take up the pen and make some money by writing his memoirs. If he had kept his capital or recovered his 1,000 pagodas, he would have had no need to write.

"Sweet are the uses of adversity which like the toad, ugly and venomous, wears yet a precious jewel in his head."

Shakespeare would have been pleased to know that on Ceylon the cobra is believed to carry a jewel in his head. A toad or a cobra, as you like it.

Out of pamboerajas and crocodiles, Haafner did extricate precious jewels: stories which sweep us away.

CHAPTER IX

The Cautious Coup

Burgomaster Loten who lost his coat on that eventful December evening in Utrecht did not like Ondaatje, although his coach, the ex-colonel, was courting the rabble-rousers. Loten had lost more than his coat, he had lost his dignity. Van Hardenbroek relates that someone went to see Burgomaster Loten that same evening and found him "more angry and irritated than hurt." The doctor did not even have to come to bleed him, as he had to do with another councillor for whom the emotions had been too much.

No doubt Loten's seventy-five year old brother came to see him too. Did he tell him that it was all his own fault? Why did Burgomaster Loten not have the courage to refuse calling these evening meetings? He should know by now what would be the outcome.

Loten's brother had dealt with more dangerous adversaries in his younger years.

At twenty-one he had sailed to the East Indies and made a splendid career in the VOC; prosecutor-general in the Moluccas, Governor over that difficult archipelago, known for its fierce fighters, then Governor of Ceylon from 1752 to 1757. In 1758, he had returned to the Republic as Admiral of the return fleet, the golden handshake of the VOC.

He lived in a large house on one of the canals of Utrecht amidst his collection of treasures from the East; colonial furniture, Chinese porcelain, Indian silver, objects of natural history.

He was an amateur painter himself. Some of his drawings of fish and landscapes have been preserved. He had his portrait painted by Sir Joshua Reynolds, but it has disappeared.

Highly praised was the collection of watercolors and drawings of plants, animals and landscapes which Loten had built up as Governor of Ceylon.

There he had discovered a young man with a Dutch name and Sinhalese features "the untaught Christian Sinhalese," a natural artist, called Pieter de Bevere. His grandfather had been a Dutch officer and ambassador to the court of Kandy. Loten employed Pieter who spent some years drawing and painting birds and mammals, insects, fruits, flowers and plants.

Loten kept his collection in a large brass box in the house where he finally settled in Utrecht.

CHAPTER IX

Governor Loten fishing on the river at Negombo, Ceylon, 1754.
by PIETER DE BEVERE.

During his stay in Ceylon, Loten's wife had died, only ten days after their grandson. I discovered their names and dates on tombstones in the Wolvendaal church in Colombo.
Loten remarried ten years later when he was living in England. The English appreciated his contributions to natural history and had made him a Fellow of the Royal Society in 1760. After his death, they erected a large monument for Joan Gideon Loten in Westminster Abbey. As far as I know, there is only one other Dutchman honored in that hall of English worthies: the King-Stadhouder, William III.

Did Pieter Ondaatje in his more quiet student days go and pay his respects to the ex-governor of his native island who knew his family?
I can see him listening to the reminiscences of the septuagenarian "naturalist" Governor and looking over with him the watercolors taken one by one from the brass box and spread out on a table in the tempered light which passes through the high windows of the house on the narrow canal. Finely traced and delicately colored birds and beasts, faintly hieratical against a background of elegantly composed branches, leaves and flowers like eighteenth century wallpaper. Each sheet carries a personal description in Loten's own hand.

At the back of the drawing of an owl: "Owl – if an owl can be called a beauty this one has a right to it."
Under a squirrel: "it lived long and cheerfully with me."
On the drawing of a tiny deer, now called mouse-deer in Ceylon, of the size of a hare, Loten writes:

> *Knox called it Meminna. Length 1 ft, 7 thumbs; it weighed 5 lbs and 2 ounces, was a male, on the East coast of Java. I kept many but could not keep them alive for more than three to four months mostly on Bidara apples. There they turn out even smaller than this one in Colombo, drawn after life and feeding on Potatoe leaves. I have eaten them many times, roasted whole and served in a moderate dish; the taste is that of a tender heather rabbit or a young Feasant. Have not been able to discover them on Celebes. The Malays on the Western islands somewhat N.W. of Maccassar have shown me small antlers which they always carry with them as objects of curiosity and magic power and told me that these were sometimes found on the males.*

These are not the comments of a pedantic collector but of a warmhearted man admiring the wonders of creation. Did he observe young Pieter Ondaatje in the same spirit: a specimen of the inhabitants of his beloved Ceylon adapting to the froggy Netherlands?

The next three months Burgomaster Loten stayed home, "indisposed" and felt "An aged man is but a paltry thing, a tattered coat upon a stick."

CHAPTER IX

In the meantime the two other Orders of the States of Utrecht had made it clear that they would not incorporate into the provincial Regerings Reglement the new municipal regulation as adopted by Council in December under pressure from the democrats.

Floods of petitions, decrees, counter petitions, committees and bad faith ensued.

March 20 approached, the last day of the three month period allowed to Council by the democrats for putting into effect the new municipal regulation – with or without the blessing of the Provincial States. Council, on the 6th of March, finally retracted its previous decree, again alleging that it had been extracted under duress.

More force would be necessary than the pulling of a Regent's coat. More than bare hands. Naked arms will be presented but no more coats will be torn. The final pull will be given in an orderly, even stylish fashion, to the amazement of posterity.

If you have to make a revolution, do it gently.

The other side – the "aristocrats" – now drifting towards the Stadhouder's party out of fear of the democrats, had not been adverse to the use of force. The military occupation of Amersfoort had given evidence of that. It had removed the last hesitation on the side of the democrats to resort to stronger pressure, if need be with arms in hand.

Two companies of the militia appeared in the early morning of March 20 and ceremoniously mounted guard around the Town Hall, with the approval of Council. This time they carried their sabers and muskets. The other companies gathered at their official assembly points in town. There were few passers-by who stopped to watch. The weather was miserable with snow and a cold wind; "April showers" in Dutch are called "March squalls."

Thirteen councillors were prepared to accept the new regulation, fourteen voted against; many of the "aristocrats" had not dared to appear.

While a committee of Council consulted with the deputies of citizens and militia, the members of Council were asked to remain in session. An exception was allowed for ex-burgomaster Cypriaan Berger who had asked leave to go home. He was eighty-five years old; the meeting had already lasted for more than four hours. The militiamen presented arms to the old man. He had voted with the democrats, and not out of fear. It turned out to be his last council meeting. He died later that year. He had been a councillor for fifty-one years. The rest of the detained councillors were getting hungry. A picnic lunch was brought in: white bread, raisin buns, cakes and five or six bottles of wine. The twenty-six remaining council members could not have gathered much Dutch courage from that lunch.

Finally, at 9 in the evening, after eleven hours of deliberations, a compromise was reached whereby some faces were saved. Twelve councillors remained. Fourteen members of Council left the Town Hall in peace.

Council of Utrecht swears obedience to the new Regulation, March 20, 1786.

A deputation from the citizens and the militia was invited into the council chamber and the twelve remaining councillors pledged that as from the twelfth of October, the traditional date for the annual renewal of Council, they would continue their functions under the new regulation.
Thereafter the company on duty at the Town Hall was called to the entrance hall. The secretary of Council, Mr. Isaac Falck, read a declaration, and officers and men all swore to comply with the new municipal regulation. Isaac Falck was an uncle of councillor Otto Willem Falck and had democratic sympathies. A deputation from the twelve democratic councillors and secretary Falck now walked to the Neude where all the other companies had been assembled. Torches illuminated the square; close to 2,000 uniformed and armed men were lined up company-wise with drums beating and colors flying. They were all asked if they were prepared to swear obedience to the new regulation, and all,

CHAPTER IX

The Militia of Utrecht swears obedience to the new Regulation, March 20, 1786.

excepting a few officers, lifted up their right hand with two fingers outstretched and swore obedience, invoking God's help.

Arms had protected the authorities of Utrecht. Fear of arms had made some of Council give in. But there had been no need to actually use the ultima ratio regum. Not a shot had been fired. And in this case the final argument had been with the people, not with the Regents.
But the sword remained hanging over the city.
The militia was purged of any officers who were unwilling to swear obedience to the new regulation. Pieter Ondaatje allowed the world to remember him again and was appointed commander of his old company, "the Black Boys," with his friend von Liebeherr as lieutenant-captain.

The Provincial States continued to assemble according to tradition in the City of Utrecht. A close watch was kept on their deliberations. The watches at the city gates were doubled. On the Dom Tower, Freecorps soldiers observed the countryside by day for any suspicious movements of troops.

The city lived under a shadow regime for some months.
Council had been left in place. It continued business as usual and the majority stonewalled all attempts to prepare for the twelfth of October.
The stream of petitions, replies, decisions and procrastination continued in the same steady way as before, like those many broad and unexciting rivers which cross the central provinces of the Netherlands on their last stretch from the mountains to the sea.
In the three and a half years which it did take to introduce democratic reforms in Utrecht, the citizens submitted some 100 formal petitions.
The reforms were certainly revolutionary; a revolution, however, by steps and with a deliberately delayed effective date.
The final word was with the sword, albeit used ceremoniously only.

For four months the twenty-four and the sixteen had tried to get Council to administer the oath to the committee of Meentemannen who had been elected by the citizens according to the new regulation, and who were to be the linchpin of the new municipal democracy. When it became clear that Council would keep its head down, the militia decided to take the lead and bring things to a head.
On August 2, on the Neude Square, the Meentemannen were solemnly sworn in by the Commander-in-Chief of the militia, surrounded by the eight companies and the democratic councillors.
Thereafter each commander proposed to his company to deprive all councillors of their posts who had not sworn the oath on the twentieth of March. This proposal was unanimously accepted by all companies.
This was the second truly revolutionary act in the three years of struggle for democracy. The citizens, or the People if you wish, had "forsworn" their Regents, had deposed them as they had done some two hundred years earlier with the King of Spain.
But the revolutionaries remained practical, even conciliatory Dutchmen. They left those council members in place, at least until October 12, who served on city committees, even if they had refused to take the oath of the twentieth of March.
Fifteen new members of Council were selected by the cascading ballot system prescribed by the new municipal regulation.
Early in the morning of August 28 the citizens were awakened up by cannon fire from the city walls and gates. A new manifestation was being organized on the Neude square. This time a band had been engaged to give a cheerful note to the festivities. All companies lined up in a circle around a dais with an enormous table covered with green cloth and surrounded by fifteen chairs.
The fifteen newly elected members of Council were being escorted through town, while cannon roared at appropriate intervals to impress the martial aspect of the day upon the crowd. After having made various rounds and having been surrounded by various circles of militia officers and deputies old and new, the

CHAPTER IX

The "Meentemannen", the representatives of the citizens, are solemnly sworn in on the Neude square, in Utrecht, August 2, 1786.

ritual dances were concluded by solemn declarations and oaths and a final procession to the Town Hall.

Utrecht had a democratic government, closer to a true representation of the people than any other government in Western Europe.

One of the spectators that day was John Adams, now Minister of the United States of America at the Court of St. James. Three years earlier he had seen the restoration of liberty symbolized on a dinner table in Amsterdam. Now he witnessed the very act of the restoration of liberty on a square in Utrecht.

He wrote to Thomas Jefferson: "In no Instance, of ancient or modern History, have the People ever asserted more unequivocally their own inherent and unalienable Sovereignty."

One hundred and fifty-nine years later American troops, together with their allies, would be honored with music and parades on that same Neude square and along those same streets and canals of Utrecht, for having helped the Dutch people to assert again their inherent and unalienable sovereignty.

Shortly after these August days of 1786, a national conference of Dutch Freecorps was held, in Utrecht as it so happened. By coincidence, an assembly of National Regents was meeting at the same time in Amsterdam.

The first time that Patriot Regents from all over the Republic had met together with the aim of coordinating their policy had been at the occasion of the dinner at the Shrimp Doelen in April 1783. They had met at Father Hooft's house where they had decided to hold regular meetings from then on. Joan Derk van der Capellen had been one of the founding fathers, together with Father Hooft, of this first truly national Patriot organization.

The national conference of Freecorps and the assembly of National Regents, impressed by the August events in Utrecht, issued a joint statement, under the name of "Act of Association." They declared their adherence to "The true republican form of government in our commonwealth, namely by representation of the people, as based on the constitution and freedom charters of the individual provinces, cities and members of state, and confirmed by the Union of Utrecht." Representative democracy but strictly confined within the "Gothic Ruin." Had not of old the members of state been deemed to represent the people? What was new here?
The joint manifesto allowed, in line with the spirit of a return to the old constitution, "a limited role for a hereditary Stadhouder from the House of Orange." It rejected "absolute government and unrestricted family-rule, insofar as that would run counter to the old freedom charters."
The manifesto further proscribed any form of government which would "smother the reasonable and respectful voice of the people."
This was as far as the Patriot Regents were prepared to go, but far enough to spell the end of their self-appointed oligarchies. Father Hooft, who headed the delegation of Amsterdam Regents, and two of his Hooft nephews, also present, were of their own accord giving up the system which had preserved their families in power for two hundred years.

After the August days in Utrecht, a few windows of houses and shops of Orangemen in that city were smashed. But these sounds of an unreasonable and disrespectful voice of the people were quickly supressed and the damage reimbursed.
Foreign historians are amazed by the gentle and civilized character of the Dutch democratic revolution of the eighteenth century. Even Dutch historians praise, somewhat self-congratulatory, the un-bloody nature of this revolution, or rather of these revolutions, because similar changes of government took place in smaller cities in the province of Utrecht and in the town of Haarlem in Holland. I suspect that the unacceptable face of revolutions would not have remained confined to some window-smashing if things would have run their course, as

they did in France five years later. Nothing in Utrecht's new system provided for the checks and balances which Montesquieu had recommended and which the new American constitutions had tried to put in place. All the might of city government still rested with one body only, City Council, from which emanated the legislative, executive and the judiciary powers. Besides, councillors were appointed for life. What would happen when Council's will clashed with the will of the Meentemannen who were supposed to check Council? The new system was based on an Enlightened belief in the basic goodness of human nature. It neglected the time-proven Calvinistic working hypothesis that man is wicked and inclined to all evil.

The little we know of real experience with Utrecht's one year experiment in democracy shows that the people quickly tired of the time-consuming task of exercising their Majesty. Soon instead of five thousand voices, only a few, and always the same, were heard, and they became less reasonable under the increasing pressure from outside.

If John Adams had come back a few months later, he would have found that the new system did not have "the right mixture," a mixture, already recommended by Aristotle, between monarchy, aristocracy and democracy.

Sovereignty of the people without the right mixture had led to disasters before. When it had come to drafting constitutions, Adams' Puritan background had saved him from putting all his trust in the nature of human beings, at least not when they acted as political animals.

The provincial states which from time immemorial had assembled in the city of Utrecht moved their meetings to Amersfoort, freshly subdued by the Stadhouder's troops. A week later, two small towns in the adjacent province of Gelderland, Hattum and Elburg, were occupied by order of the Stadhouder. This time the occupation was against the wishes of the councils of the unlucky towns, and not so gentle and civilized. The troops, consisting of German mercenaries, indulged in plunder and destruction.

The Stadhouder could excuse himself by pointing to the orders which he had received from his sovereign, the States of the province of Gelderland, but he knew very well that the States had acted against the provincial constitution by interferring in the internal affairs of cities against the wishes of those cities' own councils. The other provinces with Patriot sympathies rose up in arms.

Freecorps and town militia were put on the alert. The flow of pamphlets went over the rapids, the Republic was swept into civil war.

Pieter Ondaatje contributed to the defensive measures taken in Utrecht. Although he was preparing his doctoral thesis on civil and canon law, real cannon now loomed foremost in his mind.

The Patriot Regents of Amsterdam made an effort to heal the rift between the City and the States of Utrecht. Van Hardenbroek relates that at a dinner

Balthasar Elias Abbema, one of the Regents sent by Amsterdam to make peace, fell out with Pieter Ondaatje, who had qualified that Regent's brother, one of the deposed councillors of Utrecht, as a "scoundrel." The would-be peacemaker threw a plate in the direction of Ondaatje which hit him "in such a way that he broke his head as a result." After which incident the dinner ended without dessert for the two gentlemen.

A few years later in France this sort of quarrel usually ended with someone having his head not merely broken but completely severed from the body.

Ondaatje was hit by a dinner plate, the ex-colonel, this time called "the old gentleman" by van Hardenbroek, who detested the whole Pesters clan, was molested by the mob in Utrecht. But the new city government maintained order and organized the city's defenses.

The common citizens were helping to reinforce the city walls. Pleasure pavilions built on the ramparts were replaced by artillery batteries and stockades. However, a civilized atmosphere prevailed.

One of the deposed councillors who had been requested to continue their work was Otto Willem Falck, that cousin of Governor Iman Falck of Ceylon, from whose diary I have quoted earlier. He had moved his valuables, including his family, to a country house near Zeist, but was asked to return to Utrecht to officiate on the bench as alderman.

Once inside the city gates he was told not to leave again. His presence was necessary for a proper administration of justice.

In his "memoirs" he referred to this period as his "exile." After a few days he received a letter from his wife imploring him to leave the city, "for God's sake" as quickly as possible because of the rumored approach of troops. He disguised himself as a groom and left the city on foot at six o'clock in the evening. He was already some distance away from the gates when he was arrested by two militiamen who recognised him. Falck knew them too, one was his own watchmaker, the other a cobbler. They addressed him impudently: "You know that you are not allowed to leave the city. What the blazes! Thus disguised. Call the guard. Come with us. Now that you know that troops are coming you want to waggle your ass out of the whole business and put our heads at stake. Do you want to betray us citizens like that?"

Falck wrote that he was very upset but that God gave him strength to remain patient. They took him back to the city gate where he was detained for a while, until visited by two officers of the guard, one of whom was Ondaatje.

They "requested" Falck to accompany them to the principal guard at the Town Hall in a coach surrounded by militiamen on foot, with drawn sabers. This obviously drew the attention of the mob, whose expressions, in Mr. Falck's words "were too bad to insert here."

"Even Mr. Ondaatje" – this is the first time Falck promotes Ondaatje to the rank of Mr. – "seemed to have no influence over the men."

CHAPTER IX

It must have been quite a strange sight: a coach at walking pace, transporting two officers and an elderly groom flanked by soldiers with drawn sabers and a raging mob shaking their fists and insulting the portly groom in the coach.

When they arrived at the Town Hall, Falck was "graciously" received. "Mr. Ondaatje was particularly helpful to me," and even went with a letter to the burgomaster in which Falck tried to explain his desertion and at the same time tendered his resignation as alderman. The revolutionaries were kind and respectful enough to call a council meeting that same evening at ten o'clock, to discuss Falck's case. In the meantime his valet was ordered to come with a more becoming suit of clothes and Falck could again assume the airs of a Regent, be it of a resigning Regent.

Otto Willem was offered a dinner and wine and was visited by two members of Council who explained to him that Council could not allow any authorities to leave the city as the citizens were suspicious that the magistrates might collude with the approaching enemy troops. They suggested that he put up some security for his promise to remain in town.

At midnight a notary public appeared and a deed was drawn up in which Falck offered one of his houses as a bond for further good behavior. Then Falck was a free man again, at least within the city walls. They all accompanied him to the door and took their leave most gently.

"Especially excelled herein again the treatment I received from Mr. Ondaatje, who could not refrain from communicating to the guards on duty that Council was fully satisfied with my declaration, expecting that the militiamen in their turn would now be satisfied, guaranteeing my good faith towards the militia and admonishing them to be polite to me and not to do me any injustice in the future, neither by word, nor by deed. On which a general approval was shown in the exclamation of "Hurrah for Mr. Falck."

Those who politely accompanied Falck home were invited in for a glass of wine. Falck fulfilled his duties until June 1787. He was relieved that his attempt to escape was not mentioned in the newspapers and that the citizens did not show any contempt. "Which I have to ascribe to my having asked Mr. Ondaatje to help therein who has been very valuable to me and who promised me his assistance in that matter."

Was this the same Ondaatje whom Falck had described a year earlier as a rabble-rouser whose "face expressed the clearest signs of his slavish descent?" One of the two must have become a different person.

CHAPTER X

The Pear Is Ripe

In the summer of 1786 the story of Utrecht flows into the mainstream of Dutch history. In its waters, troubled by impending civil war, France, England and Prussia are throwing out their fishing lines.
France supports the Dutch Patriots.
World-wise wary Frederic the Great is dead and can no longer restrain his niece and her stubborn and indecisive husband.
England has sent its most cunning diplomat to the Republic, Sir James Harris, later Earl of Malmesbury.

England had for centuries aimed at a balance of power in Europe. The "renversement des alliances" of 1756 had tilted the scales against Britain. In that year Austria and France, age-old enemies, had become allies. To seal this knot the future Louis XVI had married Marie-Antoinette, the daughter of the formidable Austrian Empress. The alliance would be dissolved in blood, the marriage too.
Russia had joined France and Austria.
In 1786 England's only ally was Prussia.
In the past the English and the Dutch had put up a united front against the aggressive French. Now growing competition at sea and in the colonies had driven a wedge between England and the Dutch Republic.

The Dutch Patriots were in favor of a formal alliance with France. This the English cabinet tried to prevent. It therefore backed the party which opposed the Patriots, the Stadhouder and his men. After the outbreak of the Anglo-Dutch War of 1780 – 1784, this English support contributed to the rising unpopularity of Prince William V in the Netherlands.
When the Dutch Republic finally concluded a formal treaty of friendship with France in 1786, the British Ambassador received instructions to play the dog in the manger and to prevent the Dutch from consumating their French alliance. The more Harris could fan the fires of civil unrest in the Netherlands and weaken the new French ally, the better. From his correspondence with London, we get the impression that he relished his role.

Prussia was as much concerned with a balance of power in Europe as England.

CHAPTER X

Friedrich II, named Frederic the Great, King of Prussia [1712–1786].
by FR. RAMBERG.

After the aggressive wars of his youth, which had added large territories to the Prussian State, Frederic the Great in his later years had managed to keep his gains by cautious diplomacy.

He had died in the summer of 1786; the son of his brother succeeded him as Frederick William II. He was the brother of Princess Wilhelmine, the Stadhouder's wife.

Since her marriage, she had been corresponding with her uncle, Frederic the Great, giving him information about court matters, politics and military affairs in the Dutch Republic. Whenever she urged him to support her weak and losing husband, the King used to reply that he should follow the path of conciliation and compromise, to which the Stadhouder seemed incapable by nature.

Sir James Harris had visited Frederic the Great in Potsdam in 1785 to propose a joint intervention in the Republic. The King had taken him to a globe and explained a thing or two about the realities of power in Europe. An ill-tempered overture by England and Prussia would have to face the music of an orchestra in which France would play the strings, Austria the brass and Russia the bass. Speaking about the Dutch Republic, the King had said: "La poire n'est pas encore mûre," "the pear is not yet ripe."

Frederic knew what he was talking about. Not only did he cultivate pears, and even figs, along the terraces of Sans Souci, where they are still growing today, he himself had paid a visit to the Dutch Republic, incognito and in disguise, some thirty years earlier. Czar Peter the Great of Russia had done the same before him, not only travelling but even working in Holland as an apprentice shipwright.

Great Frederic had taken a military engineer with him. The King had visited a picture gallery in Amsterdam and a famous garden on the river Vecht. In the trekschuit to Utrecht Frederic had befriended a young Swiss private tutor, who has left us a description of being accosted by a foreign, rather authoritarian gentleman with a black wig and a cinnamon-colored coat, all dusty with snuff, who in a gruff manner brought the conversation on the following topics: human happiness, the Dutch, Creation, good and evil in the world, and the best form of government.

In the "Trekschuit".
by S. FOKKE.

CHAPTER X

The young Swiss maintained candidly that a monarchy is the best form of government "if the King is just and enlightened." Whereupon the stranger had sighed, "where will you find kings of that sort," and went into a sally upon kings. When they had reached Utrecht, they parted, the snuffy gentleman having obtained the address of the young Swiss who shortly afterwards received a letter from the King of Prussia reminding him of the pleasant reflections on the backwaters of Utrecht and inviting him to become Court Lecturer at Berlin which the Swiss accepted. He remained there for twenty years.
From visiting picture galleries and country gardens and travelling in trekschuiten, the King and his engineer had come to the conclusion that Holland could deny access by inundation to anyone attempting to enter the Dutch garden to steal forbidden fruit.

Princess Wilhelmine took heart again when her own brother became King. Surely he would help her husband, who was now at a very low point.
But her own brother, too counselled caution and compromise.
An autocrat in his own states, the King suggested that his brother-in-law should grant graciously what he was no longer capable to withhold: reforms and a reasonable influence of the citizens in the government of their cities.
The tones of the funeral music for Great Frederic had hardly died away when the cannonade against the townlets of Hattum (500 inhabitants) and Elburg (1,200 souls) opened the civil war in the Dutch provinces.
The Province of Holland resolved to withdraw from the federal army, commanded by the Stadhouder, all regiments paid by Holland, 28,000 men, over half the total strength. Holland furthermore suspended the Stadhouder as Commander General of its troops. These were now stationed in a chain along Holland's borders with Utrecht, and were called the Military Cordon. An attack from troops still loyal to the Stadhouder was expected from the direction east of Utrecht. The command over the Military Cordon was vested in an unimaginative old general, to the chagrin of the rising military star of the Patriot movement, who commanded a regiment of his own, Frederic of Salm-Kyrburg.

He was a princeling from a small state on the borders of the Rhine, ruled since times almost immemorial by the Salm family.
In the early Middle Ages the vast Salm territories had been held in one hand, but over the centuries different branches of the family had received ever smaller pieces. Now there was a patch-work of counties and principalities, all ruled by Salms of different shades. In line with the family name of these riverlords – salmon – the head of one branch carried the hereditary title of Wild-und Rheingraf (Game-and Rhine Count).
Prince Frederick III von Salm-Kyrburg, known in his role of Patriot general as "the Rhine Count," held a high rank in the French army. His ambition was to ingratiate himself with one of the parties in the Dutch Republic and, who knows, become the Washington of Holland. The Patriots seemed the most likely takers of his military talents. The new city fathers of Utrecht had elevated him to the

The "Rhine Count", Prince Frederic III von Salm-Kyrburg [1745–1794].
by J. C. MERTENS.

rank of Commander of their armed forces. He was biding his time to become the Generalissimo of the entire Patriot army.
The Rhine Count was ultimately responsible to a Defense Committee of the States of Holland seated in Woerden, a small town on the border with Utrecht. One of the members of this Committee was Pieter Vreede, that cloth manufacturer who had composed Patriot music at the Regents dinner in the Shrimp Doelen in Amsterdam, in 1783. His key was now notedly more martial.

The situation even in the predominantly Patriot province of Holland was far from black and white. The Stadhouder could still have achieved an honorable compromise had he tried. But he did not want to try. Neither did he have enough courage to place himself openly at the head of a counter-revolution. He could still count on his traditional adherents: the mob, most clergymen and the reactionary faction of the Regents in the various provinces of the Republic.
When Holland deprived the Stadhouder of all federal troops in Holland's pay, Harris persuaded him to incite their officers and men to desert to the Orange side. A large number, confused because their original oath of allegiance had been to both the States of Holland and to the Stadhouder, went over to the

CHAPTER X

Stadhouder, who was able to continue their pay thanks to ample English subsidies.

Amsterdam was still the linchpin of the Dutch Republic, although other cities, smaller but jealous of their independence, seemed to forget.
The patrician families of Amsterdam composed their Council and elected their burgomasters without any outside influence, neither from the Stadhouder and certainly not from the people. They were far from enamored by the victory of democracy in Utrecht.
Some of the younger Regents realised that if they wanted to preserve their positions they had better change. But young Regents had little influence. The burgomasters were the ones who set the tune. And burgomasters were advanced in years by the time they took their turn according to the roster established long ago.

On February 1, 1787, Henrik Hooft Danielszoon became first burgomaster again. He had been burgomaster and first burgomaster many times before and was by now seventy years old. His colleagues were Willem Gerrit Dedel Salomonszoon and Marten Adriaan Beels.

The Dedels were the only Dutch who could claim a Pope in the family. Adriaan Floriszoon d'Edel of Utrecht had been elected Pope in 1522 under the name of Hadrian VI. In Calvinist Holland, this was less of a recommendation than a long history of membership in a municipal regency. The Dedels qualified on this account, too.
Dedel and Beels belonged to the conservative faction of Council. People called them "aristocrats." The majority of Council in Amsterdam could be qualified as such. Rendorp, Huydecoper and that ilk were not enamored by democratic ideas which would allow the people a real say in government. If you wanted a say, you had to earn yourself a place by money or marriage, and that took a generation or two.

In 1786, many of the aims of the Amsterdam Regents had been achieved: the Town Hall had again, as in the Golden Age, become a branch office of the Exchange, peace with England and an alliance with France had been concluded; and the Stadhouder had been reduced to impotency. They did not want these results to be hijacked by the Ondaatjes of this world. Hespe had been put in his place in 1785; the citizens of Amsterdam were quiet.
Unfortunately some renegade Regents were disturbing this peace. Bicker and Abbema, well, they were young hotheads who followed the fashion of the day. But old Henrik Hooft, he should know better.
After all, there were no more typical patricians in Amsterdam than the Hoofts. They had produced more burgomasters than any other family and a prince of poets as well: Pieter Corneliszoon Hooft, chief magistrate of the Muiden district and governor of Muiderslot castle, where he hosted the cream of Holland's

Golden Age, and wrote his poems, histories and plays. He and his friend Vondel are considered the fathers of Dutch literature.

How could a scion of a family which had provided founding fathers to Holland's aristocratic republicanism and "doges" to the Venice of the North embrace those populist ideas?

It was not a case of "if you cannot beat them, join them." Henrik Hooft had been a democrat a long time before the troubles. He was unconventionally softhearted about the slaves on his Surinam plantations, which he forbade to be sold separately from the land. Some people said he was muddle-headed and relied on an avuncular behavior to reap cheap popularity. The chronicler van Hardenbroek relates a conversation with Abraham Calkoen, head bailiff of Amsterdam who called Burgomaster Hooft "a fool," who impressed people by "a deep voice and a multitude of incoherent words." When I read this passage for the first time, I could not resist repeating Calkoen's words to my wife, Eliane Calkoen.

A fact was that Hooft had been a friend of Joan Derk van der Capellen and his ideas long before those became popular and had been repeatedly ahead of his times in business decisions, by which he had managed to add considerably to his already large inherited fortune.

The fourth burgomaster was called Pieter Clifford. He was old and ill; not once during his whole year in office did he show up in the Town Hall.

One could expect every member of the ruling oligarchy of Amsterdam to be in favor of curtailing the powers of the Stadhouder. But few wanted any drastic changes in the constitution of their City or of the Republic.

Henrik Hooft and his friends had been responsible for the publication of a well-written manifest for the restoration of the original constitution: back to the Founding Fathers and the Golden Age. The author was a poor hack-writer whom Hooft had befriended and invited to his modest farmhouse out of town.

Over 400 patricians in Amsterdam had country houses. Burgomaster Clifford's father, half a century ago, had engaged the Swede Karl Linnaeus, the most famous botanist of his time, to become the head gardener of his grand "Harten Kamp." There Linnaeus had studied and enlarged the botanical collection which he thought was the finest in the world and which he had honored in his monumental publication of the "Hortus Cliffortianus."

It was the age of botanical discoveries and plant collections. For most owners it meant spending money, employing garden architects, plant collectors and armies of gardeners. When everything was laid out and ready for display, they would invite guests and let them admire their gardens, parks and plants. The ladies might cut some flowers, but none of the owners would ever soil their hands.

Hooft, however, was not interested in show gardens. He had inherited some farmland from his mother's ancestors, the Reaels. His great grandfather Reael had been a founder of the VOC and had invested a part of his Indian fortune in land. On one of those farms Henrik Hooft had a cottage for himself which he called his "hovel." He had been a widower since his thirty-second year. His tastes were modest. He did not entertain outside his canal palace on the Herengracht in Amsterdam. When he retired to his hovel, he would work in the garden like any cottager or small farmer. His contemporaries were struck by the rustic simplicity of the grand patrician burgomaster.

His elevation to the "magnificat," as the first burgomaster's position was called in Amsterdam, will not leave him much time for gardening in 1787. His presence will be claimed by the Town Hall, that regal creation built in the early years of the Golden Age to harbor the merchant-princes of republican Amsterdam. In the first years of the modern age, it would be turned into a mock Royal Palace by the first King forced upon the Dutch by the Imperial fancy of a Corsican adventurer, while the merchant-princes would retire to their truly regal residences in the country.

Within a fortnight a deputation from 3,115 citizens is civilly received in the Burgomaster's Chamber. The scene is reminiscent of Ondaatje appearing before the Council of Utrecht in 1784. Here, too, the deputation "is invited to sit down on chairs pulled up especially for them."

What does this deputation request?

"A wholesome and constitutional union between the citizens and their representatives against growing powers of the Stadhouder," aimed at "peace and quiet which will assure the citizens of a permanent tranquillity and everlasting happiness." Not a very revolutionary demand, it seemed. The petition, however, referred to a memorandum, submitted by Council itself to the Stadhouder in 1781, maintaining as a self-evident maxim the right of the people to have a say in their own government.

There was the ugly and venomous tail.

Burgomaster Hooft told the deputation that the subject had already been put on the agenda of the next council meeting.

Within a week, a far more substantial issue needed immediate action. The commander of the Amsterdam Freecorps with sixty officers appeared in the Town Hall on the Dam.

In the States of Holland a proposal had been made to garrison the Rhine Count in the Hague. This would result in the virtual occupation of the seat of the States General by the Patriot forces of Holland.

The outcome depended on the vote of Amsterdam. The deputation urged Council to vote in favor of the proposal.

The aristocratic faction in Council made a counter-move and proposed to dismiss the Rhine Count altogether and cut the subsidies of Amsterdam towards maintaining the Military Cordon. Council would vote in its meeting on Monday, February 26, 1787.

That Monday large crowds gather in front of the Town Hall. They press around Burgomaster Hooft when he arrives and ask him to defend their cause. Hooft shakes hands all round – "with head uncovered," as the newspapers report with appreciation – and says: "I will do my utmost. If necessary I will sacrifice my head for you." Hooft, spelled "hoofd" in Dutch but pronounced the same, means head.

The crowd replies with a threefold "Hurrah" and follows "the beloved gentleman" to the Burgomasters' Chamber where an official address from the Freecorps and the citizens is read to the three burgomasters present.

Hooft says that he supports the address and proclaims: "For my part I declare that the cause of the citizens is my cause and that I will risk my head and my fortune for it. I am not interested in my own honor or exaltation. When I am in the countryside removing with my own hand the weeds from the soil, then I am not depending on anyone except on the Almighty. For Him alone I kneel down.

Fatherly negotiations between Burgomaster Henrik Hooft and citizens of Amsterdam, Febuary 26, 1787.

CHAPTER X

Cheering of Burgomaster Henrik Hooft by citizens "of reflection", Febuary 26, 1787.

Whatever may happen, I entrust my safety to the people here of which I am the father and they are my children and to these brave men who honor us by appearing."
The reporter tells us that the voices of all officers are raised and the chamber resounds "The last drop of our blood for honest Father Hooft!"
Council, after long deliberations, decides in favor of the wishes of the Freecorps and the democratic faction. But the large crowd gathered in the Citizen's Hall of the Town Hall is confused. Father Hooft appears. He climbs on a chair and delivers a "fatherly speech" to the multitude.
Hooft calls an evening meeting that same day. In Council, Burgomaster Dedel protests against Hooft's behavior of that morning. Hooft had more or less accused his colleagues of obstruction and had thereby exposed them to the risk of being sacrificed to the wrath of an ill-guided and excited mob. Hooft did not reply.

Burgomasters Dedel and Beels harassed by the people.
by D. F. JAMIN.

Council's decision, in conformity with the will of the people, is confirmed: the Rhine Count will not be dismissed. The decree is read from a window of the Town Hall to a large crowd assembled on the Dam square.
General rejoicing and "Hurrah" shouting. Father Hooft in his coach is cheered and escorted to his house by the joyful crowd.
Dedel and Beels are advised not to leave the Town Hall through the front entrance. Dedel replies, "A burgomaster of Amsterdam leaves the Town Hall in the same way as he has come, by the front steps." Together with Beels he walks down the "Royal Entrance" and has to endure the insults of an angry crowd. One newspaper reports that some people shouted "Hats on" to bystanders who were automatically raising their hands to their hats to pay their customary and ingrained respect to a passing burgomaster.

The "aristocratic" faction in an attempt to outmanoeuver the democrats send ex-bailiff Calkoen to Nijmegen to compromise with the Stadhouder.
His mission to the Stadhouder is discovered.
"Treason" cries every true citizen of Amsterdam. "They want to sell us to the Prince." Even the Bijltjes – little axes – the workmen of the shipyards who by tradition are passionate Orangemen decline the honor to be put in the vanguard of an armed coup planned by the aristocratic faction. Prince William, true to

nature, lets the opportunity pass by. In Amsterdam 16,000 sign a pro-Patriot declaration.

At the end of April, the Freecorps and militia of Amsterdam decide to simply remove a few anti-Patriot councillors. No complications as in Utrecht; no need to introduce a new city constitution at the same time as new councillors. The coup in Amsterdam is not as original as the one in Utrecht. It is a typical palace coup; under armed pressure some men are removed and others put in their places, the rest of the machinery of government is left undisturbed.
Nightly meetings in clubs, the calling-up of armed men under the cover of darkness, the selection of the right mob to impersonate the Voice of the People, and a visit – at three in the morning – to the house of Burgomaster Hooft to ask for his fatherly blessing.
The scene is captured for posterity. Father Hooft, tall and thin, in the black clothes of a burgomaster, not lookinq at all as if he had just been woken up, more as if he is about to open a ball.

Burgomaster Henrik Hooft consulted at night in his house by a deputation of the citizens.

In the morning armed companies march to the Town Hall and close off the Dam square. The crowd is kept in hand. Inside Burgomasters Dedel and Beels and some councillors are solemnly removed. Some others, unremoved, propose a perfunctory motion, the removed Regents take their leave, draw up a protest duly attested by notarial deed, and life resumes its course.

The city of Rotterdam follows suit.
The States of Holland now have a clear Patriot majority.

The weeding to which Father Hooft had referred earlier in connection with his own garden had been undertaken metaphorically by his Patriot gardeners. A print with a poem was actually published showing uniformed wheelbarrowmen carting away the heads of the removed councillors of Amsterdam and Rotterdam while Father Hooft's bust in the cleansed garden of Amsterdam is crowned under a heavenly cloud. The Dutch confine their beheadings to paper and print and have their coups attested by notarial deed.

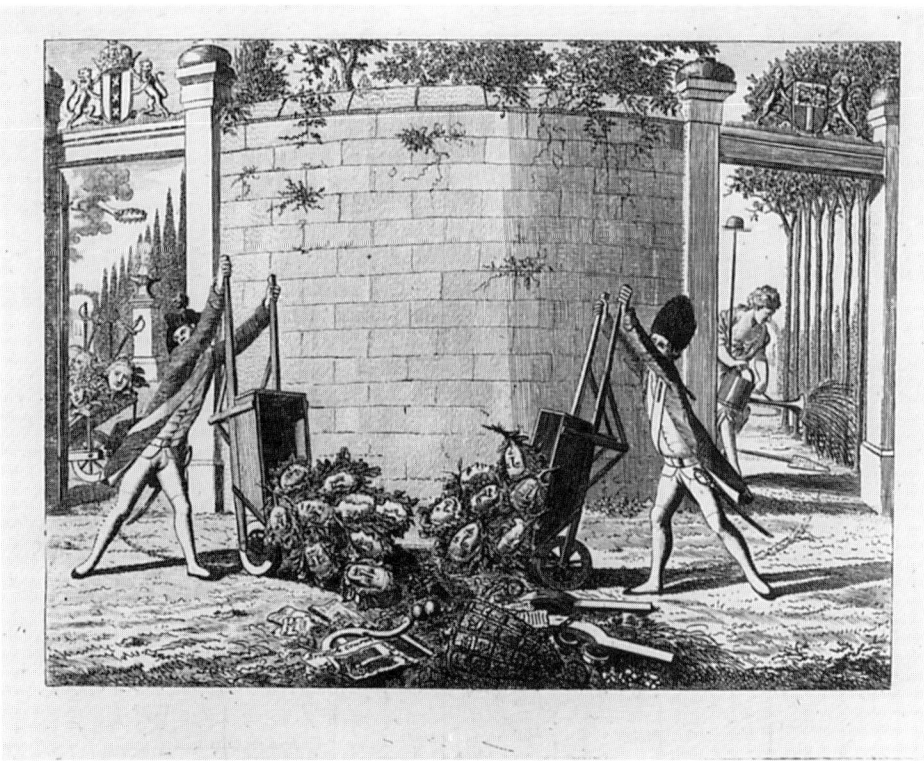

Cleaning the weeds from the garden of Holland.

CHAPTER X

Siege of the Orange bulwark of Kattenburg in Amsterdam by Patriot forces, May 1787.

In Amsterdam, windows are smashed at some Orange clubs. The Bijltjes in retaliation plunder the house of a Patriot pharmacist who lives on their island near the dockyards. The Amsterdam Freecorpsmen encircle the Bijltjes' island, bombard it and mount an attack by boats to secure the drawbridges. One of the defenders is killed.
The mob in Amsterdam takes advantage of the situation. The houses of Dedel, Beels and Rendorp are ransacked. Furniture, paintings, porcelain, everything is thrown out of the windows. Females dance around in the finery of the ladies of the house, the wine cellars are open for everyone without distinction of gender. In Paris, your head is chopped off as the ultimate measure of revolutionary punishment. In Holland, your house will be plundered and sometimes flattened to the ground.
For a Frenchman his brains, his esprit, are his most precious belongings; he carries his jewel in his head.
A Dutchman attaches the highest value to his house and his furniture.

The house of an anti-Patriot burgomaster of Amsterdam plundered by the mob, May 1787.

In May 1787 another armed confrontation between Dutchmen in uniform took place. Pieter Ondaatje did play a role therein.
Because of the split in Utrecht, there were now two bodies calling themselves the Provincial States of Utrecht; one in Amersfoort under the protection of the Stadhouder's troops and the other in the city of Utrecht under the protection of the city's 2,000 Freecorps and militia and a few thousand auxiliaries from Holland under command of the Rhine Count.
The States in Amersfoort asked the Stadhouder to order troops to encircle the city of Utrecht. The commander of the Utrecht militia, J.A. d'Averhoult, called up two companies and departed in the evening in a southerly direction with 250 men and three pieces of light artillery, each drawn by four horses, to see what is going on. Ondaatje's company was not called up.
They marched along a broad canal towards the village of Vreeswijk.

CHAPTER X

The battle of Vreeswijk between the Patriot forces of Utrecht and the army of the Prince of Orange, May 1787.

And on the dike, here at 10 in the evening, in darkness, the Utrecht forces bumped into the federal troops. Some deft reconnaissance work was done by young Utrechters, d'Averhoult showed himself a prudent and courageous commander, the cannon of Utrecht were quickly brought into position, fired, and, after some musket shots from both sides, the Stadhouder's troops turned round and ran away, leaving behind several wounded and dead. Utrecht, too, lost a couple of men.

Fresh troops arrived from Utrecht at midnight, but the battle was over. Colonel d'Averhoult dispatched Ondaatje, who had arrived with the reinforcements, to command a reconnaissance unit. Ondaatje returned with wagons full of arms and ammunition and some prisoners; he reported that the enemy had fled. He was mentioned in the dispatches which the commander sent to the Council of Utrecht.

What a pity for Pieter that he was not called up for the main force of this expedition which contributed such glory to the cause of Patriotism, the only military victory ever won in its name.

Soon he would be consoled with honorable military rank and functions. For victories in the field he would have to bide his time.

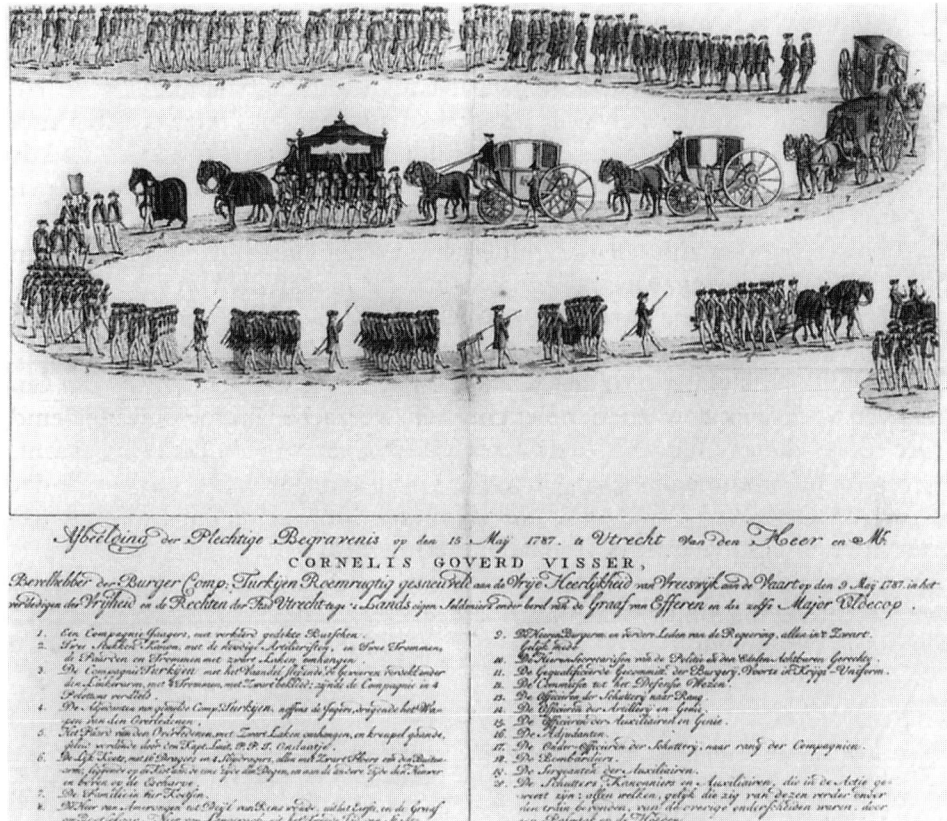

Solemn funeral of one of the heroes of Vreeswijk in Utrecht [Captain Ondaatje leads the slain hero's horse, number 5].

Utrecht acknowledged Captain Ondaatje's work for the armed forces of the city, and his leadership in the wrapping-up operations after the battle, by inviting him to play a major role in the funeral procession for one of the officers fallen at Vreeswijk. He led a horse, hobbled and covered with a black blanket to express grief for its slain master. The officer was a lieutenant-captain of an infantry company and did not ride a horse into battle. According to eye-witnesses, he had been called up from dinner and was not quite sober. He received a field-marshall's funeral and a monument.

The commander of the whole operation, J.A. d'Averhoult, who was one of the revolutionary members of the Council of Utrecht and related by marriage to the province's oldest families, had led his men superbly. He fell five years later in Paris defending the Tuilleries Palace with the Royal Swiss Guard against the mob. When the King gave orders not to resist, the mob slaughtered the Swiss. d'Averhoult preferred to shoot himself.

CHAPTER X

The French had recognised his talents and had voted him into their National Assembly, of which he had become president. No military funeral or monument for him.

Ondaatje's disappointment at having missed by a few hours the chance to become one of the heroes of Vreeswijk must have been somewhat mitigated by his appointment as Adjutant-general (general here indicates that he was an adjutant for general matters) of the united troops of Holland and Utrecht, and as Commander, Chief-Guide and Director-general of the General Secret Correspondence at the headquarters of the Rhine Count. Coordination and intelligence, Ondaatje's forte. He proudly mentioned these high-sounding functions in his autobiography, without explaining what he was actually meant to do.
Nobody knew what to do next until Prince William issued a proclamation which slammed the door firmly in the face of any moderates still inclined to take his side.
In Holland, most cities which were not Patriot-dominated were purged by "removations" of conservative councillors. No blood was shed, no property damaged.
The French called Dutch revolutions "velvet ones." Their own revolutions were made of iron and blood.
But in the Orange provinces of Zeeland and Gelderland, all gloves came off; there Patriots were actually killed and much property was destroyed.

Of the Seven Provinces, three were Patriot, two were Orange and two were split. The States General were paralyzed.
In the summer of 1787, the annual conference of Dutch Freecorps, gathered on a national level, publicly declared themselves for a new National Assembly which was to overcome provincial and local parochialism and strive for national unity. The first concerted voices announcing the new times. No more constitutional restoration.

Since the battle of Vreeswijk, troops were being concentrated: troops loyal to the Stadhouder and paid by England in Amersfoort and Zeist; troops of the States of Holland, reinforced by militia and Freecorpsmen and legionaries of the Rhine Count, in Utrecht and along the Cordon of Holland.
The decision in the now open civil war would not be brought by petitions, assemblies or removations.
The last word would be with muskets mounted with bayonets, and cannon with the motto URR.

CHAPTER XI

Tea for Mrs. Washington

In the spring of 1787 the Patriots of Holland had won the day. It seemed just a matter of time before the whole of the Dutch Republic would turn Patriot and chase the Prince of Orange over the borders.
Some people keenly felt the winds turning against them that spring. One was a young man from a family of Rotterdam Regents, called Gijsbert Karel van Hogendorp.

Gijsbert Karel van Hogendorp [1762–1834].
by J. C. FRISCH, 1780.

CHAPTER XI

The family had traditionally been adherents of the Orange faction. He had personal reasons too for feeling attached to the House of Orange.

His mother was the daughter of a Frisian nobleman, Onno Zwier van Haren, poet, grand seigneur, a Faustian figure, who ended his life convicted of incest, his castle burnt with all his books and manuscripts.

His father, councillor of Rotterdam, had squandered his money and gone to the East to remake it.

Princess Wilhelmine had helped Gijsbert Karel's mother to bring up her six children while their father was away in the Colonies. Gijsbert Karel and his elder brother had been sent to Berlin to become military cadets at the tender ages of eleven and thirteen. Gijsbert Karel was more studious than sturdy. Prince Heinrich of Prussia, bachelor-brother of Frederic the Great, made him a page at his aesthetic court where theatrical performances were staged by active dowagers and retired officers.

Gijsbert Karel returned from Prussia to serve for a while in a regiment in the Dutch Republic, but idle soldiering was not to his liking. In his free time, he studied and wrote. His mother suggested that he should take a year's leave of absence and travel to America with their kinsman, van Berckel, who had just been appointed as the first envoy of the Netherlands to the United States. Gijsbert Karel received his leave and packed a large trunk full of books on American and political subjects. To help him understand human nature, his mother had added a set of Shakespeare. Eager to study humanity and government in their state of nature, Gijsbert Karel, in June 1783, boarded "de Erfprins," the Hereditary Prince, one of the ships of the diplomatic flotilla for the New World.

He nearly ended in the other world. Storms overtook the fleet and dispersed the ships. The Erfprins lost her masts and floated around for two months, rudderless and leaking. Drinking water was reduced to one cup a day per person. Gijsbert Karel kept reading in his soaked books. It had been five months since they had set sail when a small American schooner came in sight on its way to Boston. It could only take one man on board to fetch help. Gijsbert Karel, as the only land-lubber, was sent. The schooner dropped him off at the first fishing village on Cape Anne where he mobilized help. When rescue ships reached the last known position of the Erfprins, they found only two sloops with forty men. Three hundred had gone down with the ship.

It had been Gijsbert Karel's mother who had suggested that he should travel to experience real life. He got more than she could have hoped for. He had been at life's end for months and had passed the test. He had remained calm and collected. The first night on land, walking towards Boston and traversing a pine forest he arrived on a moonlit hilltop and there his composure broke down. He was overwhelmed by a feeling of bliss, he wrote, and thanked God that he would still enjoy life.

Soon he was again enjoying his studies. He wrote frequent long letters, in French, to his mother and his father. Few eighteenth century travellers have left a more personal, incisive but also opiniated description of the American Confederation than this twenty-one year old, French-writing Dutchman. His letters and his memos merit a separate edition. Some of this material has been published without comments in the nineteenth century. More can be found in the van Hogendorp papers in the State Archives in the Hague.

As Gijsbert Karel was well connected, as he was an interesting stranger and spoke English, it was not difficult for him to meet important people, once he had bought new clothes and had tied his hair up in a tail. He did not come for sightseeing. He wanted to study the governments and the minds of the Americans. In seven months, he visited Boston, New York, Philadelphia, Baltimore and Annapolis, attended sessions of the Congress and met many of the Founding Fathers: Livingston, Trumbull, the brothers Morris, Hamilton, Jefferson, and General Washington.

The description of his meeting with Washington and his sketch of the General's character tell us more about the character of ambitious, self-conscious Gijsbert Karel. He gives us an unusual, almost self-indictive character sketch, so contradictory, but also so in line with our modern trend of great-persons-debunking, that I cannot resist the pleasure of including it here, although it will slow the pace of the main story. But as my approach to history has all along been that of strolling in an old curiosity shop, I hope the reader will continue to rummage with me.

Washington's Character.

The Americans seem to be unaware, or pretend to be uninformed, about the character of Washington. I noticed that the nearer I came to his home, the less enthusiastic people were about him. This observation failed to strike me because I was so used to regard Washington as one of the greatest men Nature ever formed.
I thought that we were still quite far away from his home when we saw in the distance a pretty house surrounded by some other smaller ones on the top of a hill which dominated the surroundings. My servant said, "I believe this is the residence of the General." We soon arrived there at full canter and a mulatto told us that in fact we were right.
I was brought to a room where Mrs. Washington and two of her friends, all dressed in middle-class fashion, were sitting together with two or three gentlemen. Upon my entering, they observed a mournful silence and looked at me with that indifferent air which had so often struck me in America. After some conversation which I kept up almost single-handedly, I heard the door behind me open and in came Washington himself.
There is so much goodness in his features that he will always dispose favorably towards himself all those who do not try to fathom the great man. But that was just what I

CHAPTER XI

wished to do and I have to confess that his expression and his first conversation did seem so plain to me that I was almost struck dumb by everything I saw.

Gijsbert Karel must at this point have given Washington the letters of introduction which he had received from Benjamin Franklin, whom he had not met, and from Thomas Jefferson, whom he had met earlier. Jefferson had written in his letter, "Mr. de Hogendorff is the best-informed man of his age I have ever seen." He would have done Gijsbert Karel more of a favor if he had written that Gijsbert Karel was interested in farming or loved fox hunting. Washington was tired of well-informed precocious visitors, and of being treated like a monument or a sphinx.

After half an hour we went to dinner. The ladies retired before the dessert. I tried to explain to the General my doubts about the proceeds of the land sale which the Congress had in mind. He understood me badly, or not at all.

Here the General probably withdrew into his shell, confronted by a young man who did not have the tact to test the waters with some small talk before plunging into the unknown deep. However, Washington did not close up completely. Gijsbert Karel continues.

He was not able to express himself concisely, elegantly or easily.

If Gijsbert Karel had been a little sensitive to the atmosphere prevailing at that time at Mount Vernon, and to the mood of the General, he would certainly have been able to elicit a more sympathetic dialogue.
Gijsbert Karel had the misfortune of visiting him just as he was still recovering from a life of eight years in the field. Only a few months before, he had returned his commission of Commander in Chief of the armed forces of the Confederation and had retired to the life of a gentleman farmer on his beloved five thousand acre plantation of Mount Vernon, overlooking the wide and tranquil Potomac. He had had no problem opening his heart to the Marquis de Lafayette whom he was expecting later that summer.
"I am not only retired from all public employments, but I am retiring within myself, and shall be able to view the solitary walk and tread the paths of private life with heartfelt satisfaction. Envious of none, I am determined to be pleased with all; and this, my dear friend being the order for my march, I will move gently down the stream of life until I sleep with my fathers." It would be another fifteen years before the General would join his forefathers, and the gentle movement down the stream of life would cover eight years as President of the United States of America.
Even the prediction that he would be "pleased with all" would prove difficult to follow. To his mother, Washington confided that Mount Vernon during the first year of his retirement there, could "be compared to a well restored tavern, as scarcely any strangers who are going from North to South or from South to

North do not spend a day or two in it." He added that he could only survive the long hours of sitting up with visitors by resorting to "the internal flame" of his own mind. He would still, as of old, rise at 4 a.m., work until 6 o'clock in his office, be in the saddle at 7 for a twenty-four miles daily tour of inspection and only sit up with his visitors at dinner and supper time. Mrs. Washington and other members of his extended family had to take care of most of the entertainment.

Lafayette had joined Washington's forces when he was only nineteen years old. When he first met Washington, he had displayed all his skills of light conversation; but he had also shown the General his real mettle by fighting rather than by questioning. He adored his General as a father. And the General who had no children himself came to consider the young French marquis as an adopted son. Lafayette called his own first-born son George Washington Lafayette and Washington consented to become his godfather. In the bloodiest days of the French revolution, this godson was smuggled out of France and given refuge at Mount Vernon. Washington was not by nature incapable of being kind to young people.

Gijsbert Karel, engrossed only in his own mood and feelings, continues.

This scene which I had hardly expected made me sink in a profound state of brooding and I went outside to pursue my thoughts. A hundred times I repeated this passage: "What a piece of work is a man! How noble in reason etc. . . . And yet, to me, what is this quintessence of dust? Man delights me not!"
In truth, I was at odds with humanity.
I passed the afternoon in the company of others. The General often withdrew to his room. He read, he dispatched letters. When he was not present, I was in good spirits. His presence upset me. All my ideas were in disarray.
Some of the gentlemen took their leave, others replaced them. I saw the General in different circumstances. Nothing of what he said or did escaped me. I observed him even when he was keeping silent.

We know that Gijsbert Karel stayed at Mount Vernon for several days, but he did not write anything about visits across the estate. Did he offer to join the General on his early morning rides? Did he try to talk about subjects which interested Washington? Or did he bore on about government revenues? Gijsbert Karel behaved like a bookworm, wrapped up in himself.

Convinced that he was not a man of genius, that he did not have great talents, abandoning the great admiration which I had for his deeds and for the qualities I had supposed he possessed, it was easier to observe him without enthusiasm and to judge him with reflection.
Until then I was so uncertain of myself that I did not dare to put anything in writing because I did only see contradictions. Now the riddle has been solved, my observations helped me to solve the problem that kept me busy. There is no more miracle, no more admiration.

CHAPTER XI

The bookworm is becoming a butterfly!

I understand everything that I have heard about Washington. Nothing in those actions which are known to people contradicts his character which is generally unknown.
I wish to retrace in a few words these actions and explain them from the point of view of his character.
Washington has delivered his country from the yoke which the most powerful country on earth threatened to impose on it, and that with inferior forces. He was constantly short of men and material. In the most critical situations, he remained unshakable. He did not take part in the party strife which rent the young Republic, the army, the Congress asunder.
He triumphed over all his rivals, over all his enemies, by his conduct alone. He has always been obeyed, respected, loved, by all parties. He has always respected civil authority, the confidence of which he enjoyed in the utmost degree. He conducted matters with great care, not confiding to any of his generals what were his innermost motives. When Arnold deserted, there were no secrets to divulge.
Easy in his manners, polite towards everyone, he seems to command the respect of those who approach him. He talks little but he does not feign taciturnity. After all his labors and glory he is going to bury himself on his estates, to enjoy in solitude and retirement a repose which has so long escaped him.
This is the true story of Washington, told after everything I have heard about him. Herein lies the source of a reputation which seems to challenge the limits of space and time. Herein lies the base of this enthusiasm for him which reigns over all minds and which makes him look like the first man of his age. Even those who deem him ambitious do not doubt his genius and join all his admirors in calling him a great man.

And Washington is an honorable man! Did Gijsbert Karel read too much Shakespeare on his rudderless ship?

Washington is tall and well shaped. He is strong. He distinguished himself in America by his manners. He is rich and his hospitality is boundless and without affectation. He has a very good heart. His slaves prove that. Their eagerness to work for him comes from respect and not from fear. He grows wheat rather than tobacco in order to have an air of ease around him and to enjoy the happiness of his people instead of the highest possible income.
His mood is even. He is not jolly, but he takes part in the pleasures of others without contributing but also without embarrassing others. He is of slow understanding and expresses himself in like manner. Changes from one subject to another seem painful to him. He does not go to the bottom of things and few subjects do interest him, hence he is not well-informed.

Thus spoke "Mr. de Hogendorff, the best informed man of his age."

Although he likes to be busy he does everything slowly. His sense of orderliness is remarkable; it is so extraordinary that that in itself would be sufficient proof that he is not a man of genius. I do not want to add that he is cold and insensible to friendship, but it is certain that I have not seen him give any proof of affection for anyone.

Gijsbert Karel was probably disappointed that Washington was not prepared, like Jefferson, to give him a proof in writing that Gijsbert Karel was the genius he thought himself to be.

He shares in that American indolence which smothers the urge to be active. He possesses so little enthusiasm and liveliness that he is embarrassed by those qualities in others. He is so little culpable of ambition that the esteem which he enjoys is a burden to him. His views are honorable, but there are those who make ill use of his name.

"Ambition should be made of sterner stuff."

This is not the character one would expect Washington to have after having studied his conduct. The virtues which he showed are firmness, generosity and patriotism.
His military talents are praised to high heaven. He is loved, respected; he has shown that he can recognize merit in others. His prudence is masterful.
The character of Washington, as I have sketched it, is responsible for that sort of firmness which is unshakable. In him it is the natural effect of the tranquility of a soul which is free of passions. His generosity, which has not the slightest taint of ostentation, is a result of that principle of good intentions which is so often smothered by passions but has been placed by Nature in all bosoms. If his generosity had been based on reason, he would have let his slaves go; but it is dominated by custom and prejudice. He shares with his fellow citizens a love for his fatherland, never blemished by ambition. That was what drove them all to revolt. Until then free from foreign taxation, they felt that submission would leave them to the mercy of their masters.
As to the military talents of the General, the stupid pride of the English generals and their ignorance contributed to his very high reputation. Besides, Washington knew the country. He was born amidst the Americans. Their character was familiar to him because he shared in it. It is well known how important the confidence of soldiers is in any military operation. The virtues of Washington were ideal to gain this confidence and, apart from that enthusiasm for the common cause, made them flock under his banners. Thereafter, the hope of reward at the end of the war kept them there. Washington had all the power he needed because nobody feared his ambition. His phlegma came him to very good staid. He never did say what needed to be said, therefore nobody could find the slightest fault with him. He could only be judged by his conduct. He treated everyone with the same politeness. The more people have reason to admire him, the more he struck them by his modesty. The less they found him susceptible to flattery, the more they praised him.
It seems that his military talents are no more than common sense, sufficient to guide him in a matter as simple as leading an army which is on the defensive amidst friends and on native fields.

CHAPTER XI

Lieutenant van Hogendorp speaks from experience.

Everything follows from the General's character as I have described it. Confidence of the soldiers, secrets well kept, order, perservance, Washington's firmness, the powers accorded to him by Congress, everything which helped to make him the instrument of the independence of his fatherland.
He is loved for the good he has done. He is respected because he has never made ill use of his influence. He has found merit because he listened to different opinions without partiality, not even to his own opinion. His judgements were based on merit. He employed those who thereby deserved his confidence.
His prudence is masterful, but it is inborn in him. In ordinary circumstances, he is apprehensive to the point of unpleasantness. In his opinions he is hesitant. He fears to be assertive in any way. I consider Washington the instrument of independence who finds his main spring in the genius of the local inhabitants, in their particular situation and in the affairs of the powers of Europe. It was the character of the General which dictated his conduct; a conduct which was not premeditated and which does not prove that he has any talents, any genius or any knowledge. He has played this great part because he happened to have been born amongst his people and not because of genius. He would not have become a great man under other circumstances or in another environment.

Gijsbert Karel had too much of an Enlightened Christian to end his character sketch, or should we by now call it a character assassination, on this note of moral relativism.

I respect him even more than before. Not because I attribute merit to him for virtues he owes to his name, but because this collection of virtues is one of the most beautiful works of the Creator, a source of happiness for mankind. This feeling of mine must be quite pure because my sensitive soul itself would not be able to love such a cold character.

Does Gijsbert Karel mean to congratulate his mother or himself?.

Washington's virtues are his simplicity, his sweetness of character, his generosity, his sangfroid. He does not have a mind embellished by knowledge, he has no vivacity, he is not ambitious, his modesty sometimes turns into embarrassment. He did not need more than an ordinary amount of common sense to conduct matters, but he did need that natural firmness and that indifference to intrigues, and to ambition which is the cause of intrigues, in order to stay on an even and sustained course of conduct. And this has been his prime merit.

As if Gijsbert Karel realizes at this point that his mother might conclude that his stay with the Americans had turned him into a Robinson Crusoe, indifferent to the rest of humanity, he changes to a totally different tune. If one was looking for a genius, there was that young officer who had come over from Europe, had stolen the hearts of the soldiers, including Washington himself, and then had conquered the English enemies on the battlefield and the American ladies on the dance floor. Everything that Gijsbert Karel had heard about him proved that he was a military genius, born to command. "Such a man must of necessity have a straight and firm character, be of a high mind and inclined to reflection, capable of expressing his feelings, and inspiring confidence and love. These qualities were possessed by the Marquis de La Fayette," whom he had sketched for his mother "from real life, that is if I have not exaggerated out of vanity, because I was told quite emphatically that people thought that I resembled him as one brother resembles the other."

After thus having assured his mother that he was still capable of generous and altruistic feelings, he concluded his description of Washington in the following way.

I never became familiar with the General, who is a cold man, fastidious, compliant, afraid to talk about his campaigns wherein he played too little of the role which is ascribed to him. He will utter his opinion, hesitantly, after you have almost forced it out of him. Or he will repeat his annoying, "Really, I don't know." He goes in and out of the room because he cannot sit still. He yawns in company or utters total banalities.

He is indifferent to the moral character and the value of those he meets unless he can use them.

And here, in the tail, we find what I believe is the reason for Gijsbert Karel's ungenerous description of Washington: unrequited admiration. Gijsbert Karel concludes for his mother.

Washington loves repose and inactivity, and in other words a life with no need to work anymore than is necessary not to fall asleep. How could you wish me to inspire any interest in a man who has no friends?

You will probably be astonished to see me sketch a portrait so different from those to which people are accustomed in Europe. But if you would know what divine Washington really achieved, if you would understand the situation in America, you would agree that my judgement does not contradict the facts which might be unknown to the vulgar people but are undeniable for the well informed.

Gijsbert Karel could produce a witness for his prosecution. He had discussed his impressions with Alexander Hamilton who had served Washington as an adjutant. He wrote that Hamilton had confirmed to him that members of Washington's family had agreed "to hide his faults and to extol his merits. His insensibility makes him impartial. The crowd admires him for his size. He chose the best officers to be his aid de camps. He appeared seldom. When during the last year of the war he did appear, and acted more himself for lack of able officers, he decreased somewhat in popularity."

Gijsbert Karel added about Colonel Hamilton, "I met no quicker wit nor opener character on my whole journey."

For his mother, he continues.

CHAPTER XI

Mrs. Washington took it amiss that I did not admire her husband. Her eyes are more perceiving than the great man's, and she has said some quite sharp things to me. That strengthens me in my opinions, because if I had been wrong she would have been less sharp. However, it is a fact that they do receive a guest very well and make him feel very much at home in their house. May I ask you, dear mother, to send something quite exquisite to Mrs. Washington, including tea of the best quality.

I did not find a letter of thanks from Mrs. Washington to Mrs. van Hogendorp. So we do not know whether it was the tea sent by Gijsbert Karel's mother, or just some other tea, which played a role in Elkanah Watson's story about his stay at Mount Vernon, less than a year later.
He was a twenty-seven year old merchant adventurer who was involved in one of Washington's favorite canal projects.
"Washington soon put me at ease, by unbending, in a free and affable conversation. The cautious reserve, which wisdom and policy dictated, whilst engaged in rearing the glorious fabric of our independence, was evidently the result of consummate prudence, and not characteristic of his nature."

Tea at Mrs Washington's with the General and George Washington Lafayette.
sketch by B. H. LATROBE, 1796.

Watson was suffering from a cold. On the first night of his visit as he was kept awake by persistent coughing, he heard the door of his bedroom opened. "On drawing my bed curtains, to my utter astonishment, I beheld Washington himself, standing at my bedside with a bowl of hot tea in his hand."

If Gijsbert Karel had been suffering from a cold instead of behaving with such apparent coldness, he might have discovered a warmer Washington.

But Gijsbert Karel was satisfied with his visit to the Washingtons. It had been an instructive experience. He had fathomed the famous General and had become quite a good judge of character. Even Mrs. Washington had been forced to agree with that. George Washington was vastly overestimated.

Thomas Jefferson, however, that was quite a different cup of tea. He had a gentle disposition. He was also vulnerable in that spring of 1784 after the recent death of his beloved wife. To judge from their correspondence, Jefferson and Gijsbert Karel struck up a warm friendship. Here was someone Gijsbert Karel could admire, because the older man treated him with interest and showed him that he was aware of Gijsbert Karel's merit. Jefferson wrote him a letter which must have been balm on Gijsbert Karel's insecure soul.

"Your thirst after knowledge, your capability to acquire it, your disposition to apply it to the good of mankind, with the ardent spirits of youth necessary to support a man against the impediments opposed to him, give your country much to hope from the continuance of your life."

Gijsbert Karel replied immediately.

"The esteem of a man of your character is a great reward of my endeavours to deserve it, but his affection makes me happy. A correspondence for the remainder of our life I did propose and do now accept eagerly. . . ."

Their correspondence continued across the Atlantic. Jefferson sent Gijsbert Karel information about government revenues. Gijsbert Karel sent Jefferson the products of his continued scribbling, including a long paper on America. How far ahead of his times Gijsbert Karel was, foreshadowing the historical and sociological insights of Tolstoi : generals do not lead but are led to victories; of Marx: man is what he eats, and of Weber: Protestants work harder and save more than other sects. This conservative Orangeman sensed the winds of change. He felt that he lived in The Age of Democratic Revolution, as Professor Palmer later would coin that period, and he knew that the Americans had started the ball rolling.

He wrote in 1784, "What is certain and undoubtable is that the example of mankind restored in all its rights is such that it strikes all nations and that its effects are profound even if they take long to become apparent. In France, I am told, the minds are in a state of agitation. The Germans suffer with impatience the yoke of a haughty nobility. In the United Provinces, power is being taken out of the hands to which it had been entrusted. An English vessel returning from the Indies and stopping over at the Comorra Islands in the Straight of Mozambique found the aboriginals in revolt against their Arab masters. And

CHAPTER XI

when they were asked for the reasons why they had taken to arms, they said, "America is free. Why wouldn't we be free too?"

Did Jefferson become tired of his over-eager student? Did the same weariness set in which Washington seemed to have felt from the first moment that he met Gijsbert Karel? Their correspondence peeters out. The last letter from Jefferson is from August 1786 when he provides his young friend with information about the finances of the American Confederation. Thereafter, "the correspondence for the remainder of our life" is dead, buried in Boyd.

By that time Gijsbert Karel had entered Leiden University and was studying law.

On his way home, Gijsbert Karel had stayed some time in London. There, too, he was instructing himself in politics and in the workings of government.

He eagerly followed the debates in Parliament. He wrote to his father that "at the view of a sincere and well-instructed young man, who by his conduct has already reconciled the various wishes of the people, he (Gijsbert Karel) was thrilled with joy at the thought that he, too, one day might be as fortunate. That would be the highest reward for his efforts."

This well instructed young man was the leader of the government, William Pitt, only three years older than Gijsbert Karel. He was a cold fish, too. But that was not apparent from the visitor's gallery at Westminster.

Back in barracks, Gijsbert Karel started to prepare himself for a career as a Dutch Regent. To become a general looked less attractive to him now.

CHAPTER XII

The Pear Drops

When Gijsbert Karel van Hogendorp came home after his travels in America, he had become sure of himself. Lafayette and William Pitt would be his examples; application and ambition his maxim.
He had lost some of his illusions, automatic recognition of his superiority and the father-figure of General Washington. He had also lost his own father. The ship, which was finally carrying van Hogendorp Sr. home with the treasures he had laid up in the East, disappeared without leaving either a man or a mouse to tell the tale of its end.
The Stadhouder gave Gijsbert Karel a private audience. He wanted to hear that the thirteen states of America were on their way to become as disunited as his own Republic. Gijsbert Karel confirmed the likelihood of such a prospect and, needless to say, backed his opinion up with a long report, far better than anything his uncle, the Dutch envoy, ever sent to the Hague in all the years that he was posted in the United States. The Stadhouder probably never read the reports of either Gijsbert Karel or his uncle, but the Prince repeated his promise that he would make Gijsbert Karel the Pensionary of Rotterdam as soon as he would be twenty-five years of age.
In the spring of 1787, half a year before this birthday, all Orangemen were removed in the Patriot purge of Rotterdam; the first of the "impediments" which as Jefferson had predicted were bound to come. Lost was Gijsbert Karel's chance to put his theories about government into practice.
The time to think, write and prepare was over. Cool judgement and cold reasoning went overboard. Gijsbert Karel learned to hate and was bent on revenge.
But he would never stop confiding his ideas to paper. The Stadhouder might well keep asking him, as his grandfather King George II had done whenever he met Edward Gibbon, "Still scribbling, Sir?"
His German schooling had left Gijsbert Karel somewhat of a German intellectual for the rest of his life. He also had a rather German adoration for Princess Wilhelmine. His self-centered memoirs for the year 1787 depict him as part of a small group which urged William V to take the lead and travel from Nijmegen, the place of his self-imposed exile, to the Hague in June 1787 to show himself to his followers and turn the tide. But the Prince by that time was afraid that he would share the fate of King Charles I of England. Van Hogendorp was disgusted when William jokingly agreed to go only if a boat would be waiting for him to take him in safety to England in case things went wrong.

CHAPTER XII

Princess Wilhelmine, wife of Stadhouder Willem V [1751–1820].
by V. GREEN, 1773.

Churchill is believed to have said of the Dutch wartime cabinet in exile in London: "The only man among them is Queen Wilhelmina." Her great great grandmother preceded her in that role some 150 years earlier.
While William finds excuses for taking the initiative and reasons for doing nothing, Wilhelmine decides to travel to the Hague to inspire the Orange party and guide it.
Prince William objects. The Princess, in front of van Hogendorp and some courtiers "with manly firmness" asks her husband: "Have you got a better plan? Say so. We have to have a plan. I am ready to follow your plan and to travel with you to make it succeed. But if you have no other plan, we should adopt mine."
The heads of the Orange party in Holland and Ambassador Harris are kept informed by Gijsbert Karel, who travels day and night between the Hague and the Stadhouder. Van Hogendorp receives a positive reaction in the Hague. He

returns to Nijmegen and finds the Princess leaving church, surrounded by people. "Yes or no?" is the only thing she asks van Hogendorp. "Unanimously yes, Madam," he replies. "Joy flashed up in her eyes."
Without any attempt to disguise their identity, the party sets off a few days later: a lady in waiting, courtiers, servants, enough to fill three coaches. Seventeen fresh horses have to be ordered for each change at the various stages. The Stadhouder's coat of arms is on the doors of the coaches. Coachmen and footmen are in their normal liveries. Princess Wilhelmine travels under the "incognito" of Princess of Prussia.

Too many people know of the secret. In the evening when the party is expected to arrive, a crowd has gathered at the Stadhouder's palace in the Hague. Everybody believes the Stadhouder will be coming with his family. Orange ribbons are hidden in coat pockets to be taken out when finally, after almost two years in exile, the beloved couple will be back in residence. The people are waiting, nobody arrives . . . except, late that evening, Gijsbert Karel and a few fellow-conspirators who inform the crowd that the Princess, wishing to join her beloved followers and on her way to the Hague, had been stopped on Holland's territory and is now waiting at Schoonhoven for permission from the States of Holland to continue her journey.
Soon everybody knows what has happened, with many conflicting details.
The Princess and her party had left Nijmegen at 5:30 in the morning, at the break of day. It was high summer, June 28. They had covered a distance of some 100 kilometers in about ten or eleven hours. The plan was to arrive in the Hague in the evening. It would be light until ten o'clock.
Just outside Schoonhoven, where the party had crossed one of Holland's large rivers by ferry, a detachment of Freecorpsmen had stopped the coaches.
We are able to follow the events of that day hour by hour from a collection of eye-witness reports and letters written by Princess Wilhelmine.
These appeared in book form some years later. Princess Wilhelmine had a copy bound in leather, stamped with a gilded and crowned W flanked by the bearers of her Prussian coat of arms, a crowned lion and a giant with a cudgel. She must often have consulted this book, the most detailed description given until this day of the adventure in which she played the leading role, one of the best known episodes of Dutch history.
The book remained in one of the Dutch Royal Palaces until 1911. I bought it at an auction years ago.
Looking over the pages and holding the beautifully bound book in my hands, I feel close to that formidable Princess, for whom I have had an admiration since I learned about the journey at school and found amongst old family papers a personal letter from Princess Wilhelmine to a Hooft, congratulating him on his marriage.
Surrounded by soldiers presenting their bayonet-mounted muskets and officers saluting with blank sabers, the party is brought to a farmhouse at a sluice on one of the canals in that watery part of Holland, the Goejanverwellesluis. There

CHAPTER XII

Princess Wilhelmine being stopped near Schoonhoven on H.R.H.'s way to the Hague, June 28, 1787.
by J. BUYS and R. VINKELES.

they are politely requested to wait. The Princess behaves with soldierly sangfroid and ignores the soldiers, who sit down without being given leave and smoke in the presence of Her Royal Highness, although they good-naturedly had offered a pipe of tobacco to the Princess and her lady-in-waiting.
Orange propaganda later tried to present Princess Wilhelmine as the victim of offensive behavior. In fact, the Princess herself told Gijsbert Karel that she could not hold a lack of manners against people who had never been taught manners.

Verblyf van HAARE KONINGLYK HOOGHIED *in Zeker boerenhuijs by de Goejan Verwellen Sluijs alwaar een Vrij- Corporist met een ontbloot Zijdgeweer de Wacht houd. Den 28. Junij 1787.*

Georg Balthasar Probst excud. A.V.

> *H.R.H. waiting in the farm and inn at the Goejanverwellesluis, together with a lady-in-waiting.*
> *The German artist has shown the members of the Freecorps in the act of committing various inexcusable breaches of protocol. Standing guard with the naked sword and smoking, drinking, and sitting cross-legged in H.R.H.'s presence without permission. The lady-in-waiting complained later that she had been escorted by a soldier with a naked sword to a place where a lady could expect not to be confronted with anything naked connected with a man.*
> by G. PROBST.

The representatives of the Defense Committee in Woerden, who arrived after a few hours at the farmhouse on the Goejanverwellesluis, make it clear that they are under instructions not to let the party continue their journey, but that the Princess is free to turn back at any time. As it is now evening, the party returns to Schoonhoven where the Princess agrees to spend the night in the local inn. From there, at 3 o'clock in the morning, she dispatches letters to the States of Holland and to the States General in which she requests permission to continue her journey and maintains that her mission is entirely peaceful. The States of Holland are not convinced of that peaceful nature and wisely delay a final answer. They do, however, approve of the conduct of the Defense Committee at Woerden.
The party wearily starts on its way back to Nijmegen.

CHAPTER XII

The farm and inn at the Goejanverwellesluis today. In the foreground Princess Wilhelmine's own copy of the book which describes the events in detail. People in the village still tell you about this turningpoint in Dutch history as if it had happened yesterday.

Prince William is beside himself with anger when he hears of the hold-up. He very bravely threatens his courtiers to march at the head of troops to rescue his Princess, but, when he calms down, writes to his children that he had always said that their mother's plan was doomed to failure and that he had been against it. Back in Nijmegen the tone of the new letter which the Princess addresses to the States becomes sharper. The States had "openly given evidence of not trusting her Royal word" – namely, that she was on a peace-mission -, and had "deliberately and forcefully obstructed her right to move about freely." She ends by insisting on "a public and satisfactory reparation for the insult suffered by her."

Van Hogendorp's private memoirs published a century later leave no doubt about the purpose of her trip. Everybody in the Orange party who knew about the secret expected her to raise the Orange flag and rally the adherents to the cause. Harris had written: "Matters must be brought to a crisis." In fact van Hogendorp had been organizing caches of arms in pro-Orange centers in Holland.

Both Prince William and the Princess write to the King of Prussia, who is led to believe that his royal sister has been forcefully detained and badly treated.
The royal brother is not a very combative person. He is musical like his uncle and ancestors. Great Frederic played the flute and composed music, the new King is an accomplished cello player and knows Haydn, Mozart and Beethoven, who all dedicated compositions to him. But after receiving the letter from his sister, he stops prescribing harmony and directs some of his troops towards the borders of the Republic.
Gijsbert Karel van Hogendorp travels to the Prussian headquarters and provides the Commander-in-chief, Ferdinand Duke of Brunswick, a nephew of the Fat Duke, with military information about access to the province of Holland.

Two months go by with correspondence to and from Berlin, deliberations of the States General and various States of the Dutch Republic. Has the Princess been insulted? Has the honor of the Prusssian King been tainted? Are the States of Holland going to apologize and punish the officers and the Defense Committee? Long-winded ruminations about that fateful day, the purpose of the journey, the possible effects, the rights or wrongs of Her Royal Highness and the authorities who stopped her, fill the elegant volume which Wilhelmine must have pondered over in later years whenever she wanted to refresh her memory. Princess Wilhelmine succeeded in convincing her brother to restore the Stadhouder by armed intervention if need be. Had she become so desperate that she saw no other way to prevent her husband from being stripped of his last powers and chased away from the Republic? Did her Hohenzollern blood in the end take precedence over her political and conciliatory side and make her fall back on her uncle's Ultima Ratio Regum, this final argument of Kings?
Only a year before, van Hardenbroek had noted that the Princess "was always in fear of intervention by a foreign power, either France or her own uncle or brother, understanding that by such a conclusion, whatever would be the outcome, the Prince would lose completely all credibility and trust!"
Until the revolutionary removations in the town of Utrecht and in the province of Holland, Princess Wilhelmine had been trying to reconcile the two parties but had confided that she feared that her husband would remain "too opiniated." She had worked hard, but in the background, often getting up in the

middle of the night to attend to her correspondence, while her husband was still up and roaming about in the Stadhouder's painting gallery. His sleeping habits were as erratic as his working schedule. He slept only a few hours at night but fell asleep at his writing desk, at dinner and sometimes even at balls.

The Orange party now relied on England for money and on Prussia for hussars; the Patriots clung to the alliance between the Republic and France. Would France be prepared to honor her obligation to defend - if necessary by arms – her ally against a foreign invasion?
The French government mounted a diplomatic campaign aimed at warning Prussia to leave the Dutch Republic alone. It disseminated reports of concentrations of French troops near the borders of the Republic, of naval preparations to assist the Sea Provinces; it detached a few French officers to the troops of the States of Holland and Utrecht.
But would France go all the way? Would France be prepared to go to war with England and Prussia over the Dutch Republic?
For more than token diplomatic support the French King needed money. France had already overspent itself by supporting the United States of America and waging war with England. It could not afford to save another Republic.
The facts of life in France started to appear through the smoke screen: a King who was rapidly losing power, an empty treasury and a new prime minister who had categorically declared to his cabinet that for adequate intervention to counter a foreign invasion of the Dutch Republic France had: pas un sou!
> We do want to fight
> and by jingo if we do
> we've got the men
> we've got the ships
> but we haven't got a sou!

For two months after Goejanverwellesluis, France continued to put up a show. The Patriots in Holland and the rest of the Republic kept up their courage while just across the eastern borders the Prussians were preparing for their invasion. A final ultimatum by the King of Prussia; then on September 13, 1787, an army of 28,000 men crossing the Rhine and entering the Dutch Republic.
The Supreme Commander, the Duke of Brunswick, was a cousin of the Prussian king and of Princess Wilhelmine. For him, Holland would be the rehearsal for an invasion planned on a much larger scale five years later: an attack on revolutionary France, stopped by the French revolutionary armies at Valmy. Goethe was an eye-witness and wrote the famous comment: "Here and now is the beginning of a new epoch in history."
Then, in 1792, Brunswick would be stopped.
His invasion of Holland still belonged to the old epoch; Brunswick could not be stopped. The Dutch pear was over-ripe and fell without much shaking.
The Prussian troops advanced on Utrecht, the first Patriot bulwark on their way to the Province of Holland. The defenders ordered the dikes to be pierced,

relying on the age-old method of inundation, but the rivers were exceptionally low that summer and the eagerly awaited flood was but a trickle. Even the Rhine Count could not make the Rhine rise.

He had finally been made the commander of the combined troops of Holland and Utrecht, although the Defense Committee omitted to confirm the appointment in writing and, worse, to inform others. Confusion and contradictory orders ensued.

The Rhine Count convinced the Committee that Utrecht was undefendable when encircled, and he was permitted to withdraw his troops to Amsterdam. In the night of September 15, the order was given to retreat. Pandemonium followed. The regular troops and the auxilliaries left for Amsterdam, the local militia and the Freecorpsmen threw away their weapons and uniforms in despair. All the trekschuiten, barges, coaches and carts were requisitioned for the general retreat.

The next morning, September 16, some advance troops from the Stadhouder's camp in Zeist cautiously approached the city gates and were welcomed with Orange flags and Orange ribbons. Otto Willem Falck went to church that Sunday thanking God for having delivered him from democracy.

Pieter Ondaatje, as adjutant of the Rhine Count and head of Intelligence, was one of the best informed persons of that hour. He believed with most of the Patriots that the French – 40,000 men – were on their way and that it was only a matter of holding out a few days until they would be on the spot.

The Patriots evacuate Utrecht in the night of September 15–16, 1787 while the Prussians are ready to occupy the town.
by G. PROBST.

CHAPTER XII

In the meantime, the Prussians advanced without much opposition, looting. They stole cash, cattle and valuables, and cut down the orchards for their campfires. Near Gouda they made away with all the newly made cheeses, tasted some and used the rest to build a dam in a ditch for an easy passage. The Orange mob plundered the houses of their Patriot compatriots.

One week after the first Prussians had entered the Republic, Prince William V returned to the Hague. The crowd was cheerful, William tearful. "There is the voice of the people," he said to one of his courtiers, when the crowd unharnessed the horses and pulled William's carriage the last part of the way.

Princess Wilhelmine reached the Stadhouder's palace in the Hague a few days later; nobody stopped her this time. On the contrary, her carriage, too, was pulled through the city by cheering followers. Van Hogendorp respectfully suggested that now might be a good time to give the citizens "some influence" in the government of their cities. "Provided it is no democracy," was Wilhelmine's answer.

It needed a second invasion seven years later to bring democracy to the Netherlands. In 1795 the French finally did arrive and made up for the delay by staying for eighteen years.

In 1787, the Dutch were in the process of establishing their own, home-grown democracy. The Stadhouder, the Prussians and the English suppressed it.

In 1787, the French might have been prepared to help the Patriots as allies and friendly neighbors if their pecuniary constraints could have been overcome. That would have needed some negotiations on behalf of a united Patriot leadership. Burgomaster Hooft and his Amsterdam banking colleagues would certainly have been capable of concluding a satisfactory arrangement to compensate France for expenses to protect the Republic against foreign invasion; but the Patriots lacked the party discipline and the national leadership necessary for such an initiative.

Now the passive nation had to pay for the Prussian invasion and for the English support, later found to be a total of 9,745,563 Dutch guilders.

Seven years later democracy came anyway in the wake of the revolutionary French armies, but now the Dutch had to pay their liberators for their democracy and the goods were not quite what they wanted.

The public purse had to be opened again. The French received 100 million guilders, a loan on favorable terms for another 100 million, and the Dutch had to pay the yearly costs of an army of 25,000 men which occupied the country. The restoration of the Stadhouder proved to be short and costly.

With the Stadhouder back in the Hague and the rest of Holland being subdued by the Prussians, all Patriots capable of fighting had concentrated in Amsterdam.

Amsterdam might still be difficult to conquer. It could be made into an island. The city was full of troops. The fleet could keep its lines open. The Prussians were only a land army. The Duke of Brunswick had his doubts. All along he had had his doubts about the justification of an armed intervention. He was an eighteenth-century gentleman, reigning in a rather enlightened fashion over his dukedom of Lunenburg, philosophically against this ham-fisted invasion of a neighboring sovereign state. He quickly found out that the Patriot gentlemen whom he met were of a higher intellectual caliber than the Orangemen, a Gijsbert Karel van Hogendorp excepted.

It so happened that in those same September days deputies of all Defense Committees, Freecorps and Patriotic societies in the whole Province of Holland were holding their annual meeting in Amsterdam. At the end of every day the minutes of the meeting would be rushed to the printer and come out the next morning, beautifully printed on large foolscap sheets. They make fascinating reading.

The Dutch mania for orderly meetings and ample discussions continued until silenced by force. Nero is making minutes while Rome burns. "Alarming tidings come in from Loenen and Nieuwersluis," two villages on the river Vecht between Amsterdam and Utrecht, valiantly defended by d'Averhoult, the hero of Vreeswijk. Burgomaster Hooft called an emergency meeting at the Town Hall. The next day von Liebeherr, who was one of the deputies to the annual meeting of Patriot forces, reported that he had been informed by Ondaatje and the Rhine Count that the French troops were actually on their way. Von Liebeherr proposed that a small committee would visit the Rhine Count and Ondaatje. This committee reported the next day that they had gone to headquarters but had not found the Rhine Count. Mr.Ondaatje, who had understood that this unexpected absence had made a strange impression, had shown the committee the copies of two letters which he had written on instructions of the Rhine Count. One letter was to Burgomaster Hooft and the other to the Defense Committee, explaining the reasons for the withdrawal from Utrecht and suggesting measures to be taken for the defense of Amsterdam. The committee reported further that "Mr. Ondaatje had repeatedly expressed himself in the strongest and most moving terms on the sincerity of the views of the honorable Rhine Count, to such extent that the committee had more than once felt strongly touched and had to declare not to have any reasons to justify to itself the doubts arisen against the Rhine Count." The committee returned, without having seen the Rhine Count, but convinced by Ondaatje that everything would be cleared up the next day.

We know from the story of Utrecht how convincing Pieter Ondaatje could be. The next day it became clear that the Rhine Count had simply disappeared without trace or, to put it in the correct military terms, had deserted.

Ondaatje had been too honest and good-hearted to believe that his friend the Rhine Count could simply have deserted his post. Rumors that he had all along been a traitor, prepared to sell out to the Orange party, were immediately resurrected. No proof, however, has been produced for such suspected treason. Twenty years later a French intelligence report on prominent persons in Holland gave the following profile of Quint Ondaatje:

CHAPTER XII

"Of Indian origin, an effervescent character, energetic, but honest and very good-natured."

Ondaatje sent a long letter to the Committee and offered himself up for detention in case he was suspected of complicity in any treacherous act, desertion or other crime. The letter contained a passionate explanation of the reasons why he had trusted the Rhine Count and a solid affirmation that he still trusted him. Perhaps the Rhine Count had left in secrecy to meet the approaching French troops to speed them up? After all, his presence in Amsterdam was not required for a short time as he had arranged the plan of defense in every detail.

The committee drily recorded that Mr. Ondaatje's letter had been duly noted. As the committee had never displayed any sign of suspicion against Mr. Ondaatje, it deemed it inappropriate and unnecessary to adopt a resolution either to detain him or to exonerate him.

Poor Pieter Ondaatje; a little less blind trust, a little more dry Dutch scepticism, would have prevented him from making a fool of himself.

The letter which Ondaatje wrote to Burgomaster Hooft had a comic follow-up. It had been dictated to Ondaatje by the Rhine Count on the day of the retreat from Utrecht. In that letter the Rhine Count explained his reasons for leaving Utrecht, referring to his orders and to the advice of the French envoy to concentrate all troops on Amsterdam and wait there for French help. Should he now enter Amsterdam with his troops or divide them over the surrounding fortified positions?

A French major was sent to Amsterdam to deliver the letter to Burgomaster Hooft in person. He arrived in the evening and left the letter at the Burgomaster's house, Hooft not being at home. The next morning the major was sent to the Committee of Defense but found nobody there. He was referred to Councillor Abbema, the man who had thrown a plate at Ondaatje's head. This time Abbema again showed little patience. He told the major that they had been wrong to have left Utrecht and that the rumor that the Prussians had entered the Republic was deprived of all foundation, in fact they were still on the other side of the Rhine border and needed more time before they could even start moving. "We do not need troops in Amsterdam, we have sufficient militia to defend ourselves," he said.

Abbema might have been good in throwing plates, but here he was wide off the mark. The Prussians had entered the Republic four days earlier and Utrecht twenty-four hours ago.

The major was sent back to the Defense Committee – that body which had omitted to publish the change of command of the troops of Holland and had given contradictory orders. The Frenchman had to wait a few hours and was told that the troops marching towards Amsterdam had to halt at Ouderkerk on the Amstel river, just south of the city. There the Rhine Count finally received some well thought-out instructions. Ondaatje was with the Rhine Count in Ouderkerk where they had planned the next moves. There was one inn eminently suitable for their stay and council of war: Paardenburg, still an inn to this very day.

Artillery pontoons in the Amstel river.

Those roads to Amsterdam which were too high to be submerged by the inundations were well guarded. In the rivers flowing to Amsterdam, pontoons were positioned with artillery.
The siege of Amsterdam started on October 1. Pieter Ondaatje soldiered on without the Rhine Count and took part in the defense. In Ouderkerk, the Prussians were actually beaten back with casualties on both sides.
In Shakespeare's time, King James I had prophesied that God would never allow Amsterdam to be destroyed because of its care for the poor. But the Prussians insisted on some clear and unmistakable signs of more wordly good behavior before countermanding the order to bombard and storm the city. Conciliatory moves were made to the Orange faction by restoring the burgomasters Dedel and Beels who had been removed in April. The chronicle states that when Burgomaster Hooft entered the Burgomasters Chamber and found himself face to face with his removed and now restored colleagues, "he seemed somewhat bashful and moved." On October 9 the Council of Amsterdam decided to capitulate.
The capitulation accepted the conditions which Princess Wilhelmine had laid down for the satisfaction which she desired and for which the Prussians had

CHAPTER XII

attacked and occupied the province of Holland. One of her conditions was the removal from all positions of government - forever – of certain persons who had displeased Her Royal Highness, seventeen in total. Plate-throwing Abbema was on Princess Wilhelmine's hit list. Henrik Hooft Danielszoon was not. But at the end of that month some Regents in Amsterdam were replaced after "cordial consultations" with William V. "Amsterdam will always remain Amsterdam and that is quite as it should be," William had confided earlier in a lucid moment to van Hardenbroek. He did not want or dare to exploit his victory. His heart was with the Regent class. A stickler for his own rights and privileges, he conceded that Amsterdam, too, had its rights and privileges and was free to elect its own government without interference. William remained against any "novelties," even if they would have been to his advantage.

William confided to the Prussian Ambassador that a balance of power between him and the Regents of Amsterdam was necessary to bridle any ambitious plans which a future Stadhouder might form to the detriment of the liberty and independence of the Republic.

Henrik Hooft Danielszoon resigned, together with his relatives Daniel Hooft Danielszoon, Jacob Hooft Gerritszoon and Daniel Hooft van Vreeland. Councillor Daniel Hooft Willemszoon was the only Hooft who was actually removed, but only because he had lost his mental capacities (had become "innocent" as they said in those days) and, therefore, incapable of determining his will, could not resign of his own free will. The fact that he could not determine his will had not been an impediment for him to remain a councillor of the city of Amsterdam for many years. Lucky the cities where members of Council are innocent.

Those who replaced them were chosen by the remaining Regents from their midst. Five Hoofts might have departed, relatives replaced them and a Corver Hooft, a nephew of Father Hooft, was thrown in to show that the Hooft name itself was not proscribed.

It was all kept within the family. The arrangements which timetabled the cooptations were slightly amended but otherwise left in place.

The party continued until January 1795, but the spirit was gone; some had been forced to leave before the dessert and against their will.

> "The Patriots in this country were little read in History, less in government: knew little of the human heart and still less of the world. They have therefore been the Dupes of Foreign Politicks, and their own undigested systems."

> John Adams to his wife Abigail, 14 March 1788.

CHAPTER XIII

Exits and Entrances

Pieter Ondaatje writes in his autobiography that after the capitulation of Amsterdam he received a hint to leave the Republic as quickly as possible. Burgomaster Dedel had prevented a full-scale occupation of the city by Prussian troops. The Duke of Brunswick was satisfied with a symbolic occupation of only one city gate. There the camping Uhlans with their fierce mustaches provided a daily spectacle for the more curious citizens of Amsterdam. No true citizen would ever forgive the person whom all felt was to blame for a foreign occupa-

Prussian Hussars encamped near one of the city gates of Amsterdam.

tion – however symbolic – of their rich and independent city: Princess Wilhelmine.

The Prussian occupation of Utrecht and Holland and the suppression of the rising influence of citizens in their own governments did not remain unnoticed on the other side of the Atlantic.
Ten years ago, the struggle for independence and for a new form of government in America had inspired the Dutch Patriots.
Now, at the Convention gathered in Philadelphia to create a national government, the old Dutch constitution was held up as an example by those Americans who wanted to preserve the independent powers of the thirteen individual states. But the outcome of the political stalemate in the Dutch Republic provided a convincing argument to others who, under the name of Federalists, wanted a strong central government. John Adams who had followed the Dutch developments on the spot for more than five years had written earlier that these "aristocratic republics" were preserved from tyranny "partly by the Stadhouder, partly by the people in mobs, but more especially by the number of independent cities and sovereignties associated together, and the great number of persons concerned in the government and composing the sovereignty, four or five thousand, and finally, by the unanimity that is required in all transactions."
In 1787, however, none of these preservatives had prevented the Stadhouder from inviting tyranny in the door.
John Adams realized that the precept "divide and remain free" was not strong enough. He came to the conclusion that the Dutch system did not have "the right mixture of monarchy, aristocracy and democracy." His friend, James Madison, writing under the pen-name "Publius," devoted one of his famous letters to the editor, later collected in *"The Federalist,"* to the Dutch United Provinces and concluded: "This unhappy people seem to be now suffering . . . from the actual invasion of foreign arms, the crisis of their destiny. All nations have their eyes fixed on the awful spectacle. The first wish prompted by humanity is that this severe trial may issue in such a revolution of their government as will establish their union."
Destruction of independence and of liberty was the result of a lack of union; this was the lesson to be learned from the latest spectacle in the Netherlands.
This time, the Dutch were giving an example to the Americans; a deterring example of what will happen if a state is not based on unifying principles.
The Philadelphia Convention, after long deliberations, proposed a federalist constitution aiming at a strong union, and it was this proposal which was finally adopted by the thirteen States of America.

Years later, Thomas Jefferson expressed his distress at the fall of the Dutch Republic, "by treachery of her Chief, from her honorable independence, to become a province of England; and so also her Stadhouder from the high position of the first citizen of a free Republic to be the servile Viceroy of a foreign Sovereign."

A year before the Prussian invasion, Jefferson had written to his young friend van Hogendorp that his preference for either of the two Dutch warring factions would depend on which one could "bring on an amelioration of the conditions of the people, an increase in the mass of happiness."

Not many Dutch considered the latest events to be an increase in the mass of their happiness; certainly not the Patriots, who had fled to Amsterdam as their last refuge. They gradually slipped away, most of them to France, the ally who had left them in the cold. Its King, His Most Christian Majesty, showed charity to the Dutch immigrants.

Big-hearted General Washington offered the "poor Patriots of Holland" welcome and freedom in America. Only two proscribed Patriots of fame took up this offer and emigrated to the United States. Most preferred to wait as close to their fatherland and as near to the sea as possible, and settled temporarily at Dunkirk, Gravelines and St. Omer.

While France established democracy under a constitution, the Dutch in exile tried to fend for themselves. The defeated Patriots had lost the illusion that a mere return to the old constitution would bring back the Golden Age. The French example seemed more attractive: demolish that entire Gothic ruin of the Dutch federation and build on its rubble a new structure designed by free and reasonable men, a new state, one and indivisible like the French prototype, with a national assembly and centralized government.

In the beginning there was one big obstacle against following the French example; France had remained a monarchy after the 14th of July, 1789. It was a monarchy with a written constitution, the first in Europe, but a monarchy. Not many Dutch Patriots were prepared to forgive William V and make him King; and William would certainly never cooperate with such a "democratic novelty."

But then choices were made easier. The King of France ran away. His coach was stopped and turned back to Versailles. Our old friend Ferdinand, Duke of Brunswick, appeared again as the man who will repair the honor of every royal person whose coach is stopped and turned back. But this time Brunswick was stopped and turned back. The French pear was not yet ripe. In fact it just started budding. A year after the attempted flight of the King, France was a republic. It would take another twenty years before France would be invaded and the House of Bourbon received its satisfaction.

CHAPTER XIII

In Utrecht, Athlone, restored as head bailiff, had the final word, at least for the time being. The case against Ondaatje was reopened; he was condemned to eternal banishment from the Province and confiscation of all his property; an empty gesture, as empty as Pieter's purse.

Ondaatje had fled to Brussels, the capital of the Austrian Netherlands. The Emperor and archreformer, Joseph II, the brother of the French Queen, had offered refuge to the Dutch Patriots.

Ondaatje lived in Brussels for three years as a private tutor.

Then he moved to Dunkirk on the coast in the most northwestern corner of France. There he published a newspaper for the Dutch emigrants and became a partner in a printing press. He also invested, thanks to French subsidies, in a fishing operation.

He now played a role in the shrimp market, too. But this one was more famine than feast.

Ondaatje was active as ever in exile. He published a set of documents on the Prussian invasion of 1787 and wrote an apology of the Rhine Count, who had emerged in Paris where no apologies could save his head, which he lost in 1794, just a day before the end of Robespierre and the Terror.

Early in 1792, France declared war on Austria. In the summer of that year, France was pronounced "en danger." From all over the country young men marched on Paris to fight for "la Patrie." The Marseillaise was heard for the first time.

The Dutch refugees wanted to form their own military unit and suggested as a name "Légion Batave." Every democrat now talked about the Batavian people after the tribe of brave Batavian Dutch in Roman times.

The most prominent soldier among them was Herman Daendels.

The Stadhouder had refused to appoint him in the place of his father in Hattum, thereby causing the removal of Orangemen in that townlet, which caused the armed occupation by the Stadhouder's troops, which had started the civil war in the Republic.

The French did not want to authorize the use of the name Légion Batave, as war with the Stadhouder, firmly allied to England and Prussia, had not yet been declared. The Dutch freedom fighters were allowed to form a "Légion Franche Etrangère," a free foreign legion.

One of the last acts of Louis XVI as constitutional King was to sign the decree forming this Duch legion. A month later he lost his liberty and his crown.

Ondaatje enlisted immediately – July 1792. His former rank of Captain was restored to him only in 1793 when the French Republic extended the war to England and the Stadhouder.

The French forces invaded the Austrian Netherlands. General Dumouriez, their commander, was the hero of the day, although politically suspect in Paris, where every hero was a threat.

Captain Ondaatje got his second chance to earn military laurels. At Vreeswijk he had come a few hours too late. He was in the first lines when the French army with its units of Dutch volunteers crossed the borders of the Republic and captured the land of Brabant and the city of Breda, an ancient seigneurial domain of the Orange-Nassau family.

In the main church, all armorial shields were torn down and the Gothic funeral tomb of Engelbert of Nassau was defaced. In front of the church, a tree of freedom was erected and spontaneous dancing by high and low was organized. Liberté, Egalité, Fraternité, ominously followed in France by the words: "ou la mort."

Onwards liberating soldiers, towards the great rivers, the frontiers of the Dutch Republic proper. The land of Brabant had not been deemed worth the honor of being a province – poor and Catholic-ridden as it was – but was only a territory administered by the States General.

Onwards to the rivers and the Republic of the Seven United Netherlands. Daendels, now very high in the French hierarchy, besieged a river fort; Captain Ondaatje led a commando raid and returned successfully.

But on the main front, General Dumouriez was thoroughly beaten by the Austrians and their Prussian allies. Knowing that in the terrible year of 1793 one single military setback meant the guillotine for the responsible officer, Dumouriez tried to rally his men to march on Paris to restore law and order there. No one wanted to follow, and he deserted to the enemy.

The French withdrew, fighting, Ondaatje with them. He ended up in Dunkirk which was besieged by the English.

In September the English were beaten back. Ondaatje took his leave from the army and moved to Calais, where he reverted to the pen. He published a local newspaper. One peaceful year for Pieter Ondaatje, while France was in the throes of the Terror.

In May he married. He was nearly thirty-six. He had been too busy since 1783. In a pamphlet from his Utrecht days, I found an amusing insinuation. Ondaatje, in one of his speeches to the Council of Utrecht, had referred to a forthcoming marriage, allegorically hinting at the cooperation between the citizens and the democratic councillors. The pamphleteer wrote that he could not understand to which marriage Ondaatje had been referring unless "this Asiatic means his own marriage to Miss van Arkel." Petronella van Arkel? The daughter of a simple Mennonite shopkeeper who was so desirable that a Regent's son married her

CHAPTER XIII

and took in his stride the social opprobrium which friends and relations heaped upon him.

Pieter Ondaatje, dashing student, warm-hearted, effervescent, swarthy, eloquent, in military uniform half of the time, should have had no difficulty in attracting the ladies. But women are not among the weaknesses held against Ondaatje by his detractors, who would certainly not have overlooked any faults if they could have found them. What we do hear, however, are references to his constant lack of money.

Strange. He came from Chetty stock, the caste of merchants and money men. He did not lack entrepreneurial courage; he was a partner in a printing house and in a commercial fishing operation and started a satyrical newspaper. But the times were not propitious for making money, unless you could get your hands in the till of arms contracts or bought confiscated property in France, speculated in paper money or went into smuggling. For such enterprises, honesty was not the best policy. And Pieter Ondaatje was an honorable man.

He married Christina Hoevenaar, the daughter of Adriaan Hoevenaar, the legal mind behind all the moves in the game of power with the Council of Utrecht. Christina had divorced Johan Christiaan Hespe, the editor of *The Political Wheelbarrowman*, thrown into jail in Amsterdam while Ondaatje was allowed to drink his tea in peace. She had been praised in the Patriot press for persistently defending her husband until he got off with a fine only. Hespe's pen was dipped in vinegar. Did she thirst for some milk of human kindness and found that in Pieter Ondaatje? He was an honorable man; after their marriage, he acknowledged a daughter born half a year earlier. Christina was twenty-seven and had three children by the Wheelbarrowman.

The Hoevenaars descended from Johan de Witt, the great statesman of the glorious years of 1650 – 1672 when the Dutch Republic had no Stadhouder and the province of Holland and the city of Amsterdam guided Dutch policy and commerce. The English had been beaten twice at sea, and Holland under Johan de Witt had organized a formidable alliance against the overbearing Louis XIV of France.

De Witt and his brother Cornelis had been murdered by the mob, incited by Orange stuivers and genever, and William III had been called up as Stadhouder. The murderers were never punished, the brothers de Witt never honored by William. Dutch liberty, for which his ancestor William the Silent had sacrificed his life and fortune, was trampled underfoot by this great grandson wherever the Regents were not strong enough to withstand him. The mob, egged on by agents of the Prince, who were rewarded by him afterwards, had torn the brothers to pieces, butchered their bodies and eaten and sold their organs.

These scenes were to haunt the Regents for more than a century and served as a constant reminder of potential mob violence. In fact, some adherents of that Prince of Orange, who became Stadhouder William IV in 1747, had in cold

The brothers Johan and Cornelis de Witt murdered by the mob in the Hague, 1672.
by S. VON SIEGEL.

blood held up the fate of the de Witt brethren to those Regents who were reluctant to elect this emergency Stadhouder.
With Johan van Oldenbarnevelt, Johan and Cornelis de Witt had become the symbols of Dutch liberty, martyrs of the thirst for power of the House of Orange. Military conquests eluded Pieter Ondaatje. At Vreeswijk, he came too late. For the liberation of the Netherlands he had been too early.
A fresh French general, Pichegru, tried again at the end of 1794. That time Ondaatje remained in Calais in the bosom of his family.

With stoicism and resilience, Henrik Hooft had faced the Orange counter-revolution. For about half a year he had been able to remain in his house on the Herengracht in Amsterdam. His old colleagues, Dedel and Beels, reinstated as burgomasters, had the decency to provide a guard in front of his house; but the old man was popular even amongst the small pockets of Orange rabble. However, a workman who had publicly shouted "Vader Hooft boven" – "long live Father Hooft" – had been condemned to stand in the pillory and to spend one year at hard labor. Demonstrations by Orangists were equally suppressed.
In the rest of the Republic, the Stadhouder's party took revenge on Patriots who had not fled.
Others, besides Ondaatje, were condemned in absentia.

CHAPTER XIII

In the spring of 1788 Hooft finally gave in to the pressing entreaties of his daughter Hester, who lived in constant fear of her father's safety. He resolved to join his compatriots in exile. He was smuggled on board of a small boat which brought him to a fishing ketch outside Amsterdam. As they approached, they found the waiting ship surrounded by fishing boats. The fishermen were known to be staunch Orangists. The skipper did not dare to take the old burgomaster with his distinctive lanky shape and unmistakable features on board in full view of these ruffians, but a heavy fog suddenly covered the scene and Father Hooft could board unseen and sail away. His admiring biographer believed that this was a heavenly fog. But Father Hooft is not yet to walk with God, like Enoch. Arrived on the coast, south of the borders, the old man started on his Odyssey. In one and a half years he visited twenty-six major cities in the Austrian Netherlands and France. "The grey wanderer was often plagued by bedbugs at night." In Paris, he witnessed the Fall of the Bastille and the beginning of the French Revolution. His old banking connections in Paris made sure that he was not plagued by bedbugs there. A much younger political colleague in Paris was the plate-throwing Abbema, running a French banking house of his own.

Hooft was received in all centers of Dutch emigration as a hero; he discreetly provided pecuniary assistance from the ample funds still at his disposal, thanks to his Paris banking connections and a wise policy of spreading his investments. The winter of 1789 and the first half of 1790 Hooft spent in Brussels, where Pieter Ondaatje had been living since the winter of 1787 with a friend from Utrecht, Jan Carel Smissaert. Smissaert was one of the few councillors who had supported the democratic movement. He had a young family and sufficient means to employ Pieter Ondaatje as private tutor for his sons. The Smissaerts came from the southern Netherlands, had settled in Utrecht in the seventeenth century and married into old nobility and Amsterdam patricians.

There were many earlier occasions when Pieter Ondaatje might have been introduced to Father Hooft. I have not found any references to personal meetings, but Father Hooft was not used to throwing dinner plates around like councillor Abbema. A meeting between Hooft and Ondaatje, if it took place, would have been too peaceful to be worth recording for posterity. Most of Father Hooft's political letters, both written and received, have disappeared, and so have Ondaatje's.

Here in Brussels they certainly did meet at Smissaert's house where Ondaatje was a member of the family and Father Hooft a regular visitor because Jan Carel Smissaert was a relative of Hooft's first wife.

Father Hooft, when still a young man of seventeen, had married a Smissaert beauty in the castle of Sandenburg near Utrecht. She had died within a year. His second wife was the only daughter of an Englishman who had started with little and left one of the largest fortunes of Amsterdam when he died at ninety-two years of age. Hooft's second wife had died before her long-living father and had left a baby girl, Hester. Hooft at thirty-two remained a widower for the rest of his life.

Hester Hooft [1748–1795].
by J. HUMBERT.

The ties between father and daughter were very close. Hester was a beauty, tender-hearted, clear-headed, with the same love of nature and gardens as her father. Their correspondence in later years is full of information about horticulture and they sent each other young plants and seeds which Hooft planted around his hovel and Hester in the gardens of her old castle of Adrichem, north of Amsterdam.
She was more than an eighteenth century lady of taste. From her father and her English grandfather, she had inherited a feel for money.
When her grandfather left his banking business to his twenty-two year old granddaughter Hester, she took over the reins herself. She was reported to have been the biggest subscriber to the first loans for the United States of America. There is a tradition in my family that Casanova fell in love with the very young Hester during his stay in Amsterdam. As he took care to wrap his story in a veil of mystery, the identity of his Hester is still a romantic enigma.

CHAPTER XIII

The choice of a husband for Hester was not based on romance. She married a Clifford, grandson of the plant collector who had employed Carl Linnaeus as head of his gardens and collections.

It was not love of plants that connected the two. Their marriage made good business sense as the Cliffords ran a similar banking house as Hester's grandfather and father – similar, but not as solid. Seven years after Hester's marriage, the Clifford bank had to stop payments and was declared bankrupt; Hester's father-in-law had retired in time and he and Hester's husband did not lose a stuiver. An uncle had also kept clear of the family's bank. He had inherited the fabulous gardens and plant collections and the priceless botanical library of his father and was that colleague of Hooft who never set a foot in the Town Hall. After eleven years of marriage and two daughters, Hester's husband died, leaving Hester to look after her father, her daughters, her business and her gardens at Adrichem.

Hester was twenty-eight and wished to remain a widow, but many men asked for her hand.

One of them was a serious seaman with direct manners and piercing blue eyes, thirteen years older than Hester and a bachelor. His proposal was made by letter – it was not the first one he made her – from a warship in the Mediterranean. His name was Jan Hendrik van Kinsbergen; he was a vice-admiral and a hero of the Battle of Doggersbank, that naval engagement in the disastrous war with England which the Dutch with some ground could claim as a victory. He had dealt with Hester's father on naval matters when Henrik Hooft was a member of the Admiralty of Amsterdam and he had met Hester before the death of her husband.

During those years, the only woman in his life had been the mother of Gijsbert Karel van Hogendorp. She had been waiting for her husband to return from the East and was worried about her young sons in the Cadet school in Berlin. When Frederick the Great had expressed the desire to meet the vice-admiral, van Kinsbergen had gone to see the boys there and had taken an interest in their education and careers. He was a strong personality, son of a soldier of German stock. A self-made man, "he had heard his first cannonball whistle by when he was nine years old," he had corresponded on naval technicalities with the English, French and Russian ministries of war and had published nautical handbooks which were translated in many languages. He had served in the Russian navy as captain, seconded by the Dutch, and had been decorated by Catherine the Great for his brave and tactical command, which led to the defeat of the Turkish fleet in the Black Sea. The Tsarina had given him a book with the dedication, "de votre amie Catherine."

He was an ardent supporter of the House of Orange and a confidant of Prince William V. A voluminous correspondence between the two is preserved. He kept his powder dry for naval advice and tried to steer clear of the growing feud between the Patriots and the Stadhouder.

Jan Hendrik van Kinsbergen [1735–1819]
by C. H. HODGES after BURKMANN.

CHAPTER XIII

When Hester Hooft accepted him, it was an ironic match: the daughter of the emblem of the Patriot movement marrying the most popular Orangist, the hero of Doggersbank and the private naval advisor of the Stadhouder.
They married in 1786. Van Kinsbergen was fifty-one, Hester thirty-eight.

That same year, civil war erupted in the Dutch Republic. Van Kinsbergen found himself between the devil and the deep blue sea, the Prince of Orange and "Father Hooft," his own father-in-law. He decided to depart on an extended trip. His wife did not like the sea. They took Hester's two girls with them and set out on a grand tour through the German states and Austria. The trip would last a full year. Everywhere they were received like royalty. Minor German Princes invited them to stay in their major palaces and gave balls and dinners in honor of the famous admiral.
The travellers followed the events in the Netherlands in the newspapers. Van Kinsbergen offered his services to William V, "In case an old sailor, who has seen a few guns being fired, can be of use, he is at Your Highness disposal." Hester worried about her father and wrote him touching letters offering to return immediately if he would need her. The Prussian invasion gave the admiral the occasion to write to the Stadhouder a letter of congratulations with "that happy event . . . which will put an end to our troubles and the miseries of the fatherland." To his father-in-law he wrote letters with observations on the best form of government, "a democracy as long as it is based on virtue, reason and patriotism." But he adds that, because of the decline of society, a regime which holds the middle between a democracy and an autocracy is best, "which I hope the Americans have founded." His letters are full of tact and filial respect.
These letters make it clear that Father Hooft's democratic ideals were not just a ploy for popularity, but convictions respected by his closest family circle as genuine.

When they heard that Father Hooft's kitchen gardens and hovel had been destroyed by the Prussian troops, they arranged for the head gardener of Adrichem castle to provide the old burgomaster with the necessary winter vegetables and greenhouse fruits.
The van Kinsbergens and the girls spent a glittering winter in Vienna. The Emperor invited them to dinner and to a masked ball for 4,000 people; more balls and dinners followed. Catherina of Russia tried to lure him back into Russian service. In order to make her offer irresistible, the Empress proposed a large pension for Mrs. van Kinsbergen and the posts of ladies-in-waiting to Her Imperial Majesty for both the Misses Clifford. The girls, twenty-one and fifteen, were much in demand. They refused many a German and Austrian princely marriage offer. Van Kinsbergen politely refused the Empress, who was not used to being refused by any man she wanted.
Hester was collecting plants and sent interesting seeds back to Adrichem.

While they were still far in Germany, Father Hooft made his escape by fishing boat in a heavenly cloud. The van Kinsbergens returned home in time to plant some of Hester's seedlings and enjoyed a peaceful summer in the Dutch Republic in the rays of the Orange sun, restored in all its brightness, while in France the first thunder of the revolution rumbled on the horizon.

That peaceful summer, a young man of twenty-six paid them repeated visits. He was not interested in van Kinsbergen's maritime pursuits nor in Hester's plants, except in one particular flower, the twenty-two year old Hesje Clifford. He had met her seven years earlier and had written to his mother, in French, "She is pretty but totally French, which displeases me." Now Hester was certainly more pretty and her French and French manners were probably less daunting to the young man who had become more wordly. He had been made Pensionary of Rotterdam, as originally promised by the Prince, a promise that was honored, although a year later than planned, thanks to Gijsbert Karel's active assistance in the Princely restoration.

Hesje's mother was not pleased with the young Pensionary's interest in her daughter. The van Hogendorps were poor, Gijsbert Karel's mother tainted by the van Haren scandal, the father lost at sea with a bad reputation, the son an ambitious Orange man.

The girl herself was not sure. After all these glittering princes, dukes and counts, why this somewhat dour, poor and self-centered young man?

Van Kinsbergen acted as the matchmaker. He had always had a soft spot for the van Hogendorps. Hester, with her innate business sense, wanted to make sure that her daughter was not wed for money. The van Hogendorps acted rather high-handedly but got their way and a dowry for the groom; and in May 1789, the young couple were married in the castle of Adrichem – Grandfather Hooft in exile in France, the van Harens cold-shouldered.

Soon after his marriage Gijsbert Karel managed to quarrel with van Kinsbergen. Before his American voyage he had written:

> Kinsbergen has extracted the secret of my heart and given me the courage not to dissimulate to myself and others any more, but to declare wholeheartedly my plan which is: to train myself under an ambassador, to study law, to acquire true merit, to penetrate all branches of government, to despise those who fail to appreciate me, to convince everyone over time of my feelings, to be useful, to be a benefactor of the common people, to abolish abuses, to thwart fools and never-do-wells, to make the good cause triumphant and in its wake to make an everlasting impression of my name on the memory of my country as long as it will exist. In one word to be in another profession what van Kinsbergen is in his.

Not a modest program for a young man of twenty in reduced circumstances. This young man, who used to refer to van Kinsbergen in his diaries as "my hero," now tells Princess Wilhelmine that he "will be careful never to have

CHAPTER XIII

Hester Clifford [1766–1826], granddaughter of Father Hooft and wife of Gijsbert Karel van Hogendorp.
by J. H. SCHEPP.

anything in common with this man." Invited by "this man," his stepfather-in-law, to be present at some naval exercises, he is jealous when he hears the Prince praising van Kinsbergen and observes that the admiral behaves "like a charlatan." Gijsbert Karel finds van Kinsbergen too ambitious!!
Hester and her husband put a brave face to the ungenerous behavior of their son-in-law. They followed the adage: "Beaucoup de cadeaux, peu de visites et surtout pas de critique!" They sent presents, visited each new child born to the couple, and behaved like magnanimous and understanding parents.

Hesje's sister married a less controversial personality, a most glittering nobleman, Jacob Unico Wilhelm, Count van Wassenaer Obdam, sole heir to the largest estate in the Republic, various castles, a town palace in the Hague and famous ancestors: a long line of admirals and a grandfather, recently discovered to be the anonymous composer of elegant baroque music, the only eighteenth century composer the Dutch produced. She had the pleasure to see her grandfather Hooft attend her wedding when she became the future Lady of Twickel with its tens of thousands of acres.

Father Hooft had finally returned to the Republic in the summer of 1790. During his exile, he had progressed from being the figurehead of the Patriots to the incarnation of the Patriotic Word. No statesman in the Netherlands has been so immortalized during his lifetime as Henrik Hooft Danielszoon, in prints, poems and in objects of daily use.

His features were depicted with a short inscription on the top of corkscrews, on drinking glasses, watches, watch-keys, snuffboxes, chinaware, and printed on silk handkerchiefs and shawls. They were even cut in wooden gingerbread forms, so that the faithful could partake of the revered Patriot father-figure in cookie shape. In the event that they just wanted to venerate his icon, porcelain manufacturers and tradesmen provided a black market with busts and mantelpiece decorations representing Henrik Hooft, with or without the temple of Liberty. Silver medals were struck in many variations with Father Hooft on one side and on the other side Joan Derk van der Capellen, that other Patriot hero or a fluffy dog – a Kees hond – the emblem of the Patriot party.

The Patriots were popularly known under the name of "Keezen" after this species of dog, the traditional watchdog of barge skippers, brave as a lion and white as Virtue.

In my family we always refer to Father Hooft as "de Kees"; an old Hooft-aunt used to keep Kees dogs all her life for that reason. I have continued in this spirit by naming our eldest son "Kees," which is short for Cornelis Pieter, linking the present generation to old burgomaster Cornelis Pieterszoon Hooft, who stood up against tyranny 400 years ago, and to Henrik Danielszoon, "de Kees" who did so 200 years later. Needless to say that my second son is called Daniel.

As a small boy I used to be intrigued by a ring with a miniature of Father Hooft's features, which could be swivelled round to display a Maiden of Liberty lifting

one finger to her lips to stop curious questions about the identity of her other side.
The wearer could show his true political hue when in trusted company but turn neutral when in doubt. Fulfilling that same wish to display or disguise, if necessary, one's Patriot sympathies were medallions covered with opaque double glass which had to be held over the flame of a candle. The heat would melt a thin layer of wax between the two layers of glass and for a moment show the face of Father Hooft until the cooling off would cover the venerable image again with a cloud of unknowing.

For some months after his return to the Republic, Father Hooft enjoyed a campaign trip through the various strongholds of Patriotism. He was recognized wherever he turned up. Sentiments were more and more openly pro-Patriot. The Orange restoration, shored up by Prussian and English troops, was unpopular. In some cities he was told to leave by the Orange-dominated town councils; in one place, armed militia actually escorted him out of town in his coach-and-four.
The next day, at an official banquet, one of the local dignitaries proposed a toast to Father Hooft and was cut short by the president who furiously exclaimed: "I do not know a Father Hooft. I only know one Father of the Fatherland and that is William I."

Hooft decided to avoid Amsterdam and settled with his sister Elisabeth, the widow of Wouter Valkenier. She was seventy-eight, four years older than her brother, and lived in a country house, Valk en Heining, on a tributary of the Vecht river near the village of Loenersloot.
Elisabeth's life maxim was: "The Lord reigns." This fitted well with Father Hooft's own religious convictions. A contemporary sketch of his life tells us that after a grave illness in later life, Hooft came to rely completely on God's guidance. "Early in the morning his valet often found him praying on his knees in front of his bed." In almost every letter to his daughter, his Christian feelings and his reliance on God's will are expressed. He certainly had had his share of personal losses and political adversities, notwithstanding the security of his money, the glory of his name and the admiration of his followers.
Every 23rd of June, his birthday, admirers came to Loenersloot to pay homage to the Father figure, or gathered at festive dinners in his honor throughout the country.
That day was an occasion for streams of new laudatory poems, sold to an eager public waiting for the Big Change.

The news from the French Republic was not encouraging. Even the fiercest democrats in the Netherlands shuddered when they read about the excesses of the Jacobins and the Terror.

EXITS AND ENTRANCES

Collection of mementos of Father Hooft, in the possession of the author and his brother. To avoid any suspicion of partiality a medal of Prince William V has been added, surrounded, however, with "Kees" dogs.

CHAPTER XIII

But after the summer of 1794 the bloodletting subsided and soon the French brothers, assisted by the Batavian refugees, were on their way again. That summer, Father Hooft was still gardening and enjoying the walks at Valk en Heining.

On August 31, 1794, he left the gardens here below for the garden of life everlasting.

Father Hooft's funeral in Vreeland in the early morning hours of September 4, 1794.

"He lives!"

The French army crosses the rivers in January, 1795.
by D. LANGENDIJK.

CHAPTER XIV

Hope and Disappointment

In 1787, the Prussians had managed to take Amsterdam because the rivers were so low that Holland could not inundate itself.
In the fall of 1794 the rivers were chock-full. The French came to a halt. Any attempt at crossing was thwarted by the Dutch and the English defending the Stadhouder's side of the river. A Siberian frost set in just before Christmas of 1794.
General Daendels, the golden boy of the Dutch soldiers in the French army, reported to headquarters that the whole country between Paris and Amsterdam was "one sheet of ice." The troops crossed the rivers over the frozen waters. Dutch resistance melted away.
The Stadhouder and his family escaped on fishing boats to England.
The French entered Amsterdam where a Batavian Revolutionary Committee welcomed them as Liberators.
Observing these arrivals and departures from his Hotel des Etats Unis in the Hague with cold detachment, was the newly arrived American resident minister. He was no stranger to the Netherlands; John Quincy Adams who fourteen years ago had witnessed his father struggling for recognition and loans for his country while he started his law studies in Leiden.

When the ice broke, a cold shower of disappointment chilled the Batavians to the bone. One hundred million guilders had to be paid to the Liberators for advice and assistance.
The former Abbé Siéyès settled the account and returned to Paris where he appeared in an evening session of the Committee of Public Safety, threw a handful of solid Dutch guilders on the table, and declared triumphantly to his colleagues, "I brought you a hundred million of these."

Another hundred million was provided as a voluntary loan at a nominal rate of interest, and 25,000 French troops had to be paid and billeted at the expense of the Dutch. But the Republic would remain independent, a sister republic of the Great Nation.
That Great Nation had in the meantime taken the Stadhouder's collection of paintings and objects of natural history, including two live elephants born in Ceylon, to Paris as "war trophies," and now benignly returned the sword of Admiral de Ruyter and the baton of Admiral Tromp as "a present by the French Nation to the Dutch People." The Dutch People were thankful to be reminded of their glorious past, and thankful to remain independent, though poorer.

Reforms were introduced, pending a new constitution. The first steps on the road to unification were made; provincial independence was definitely out of fashion.

War had always been a Union matter, so the new Military Department was not a radical break with the past. The personnel, however, was. No more courtiers of the Stadhouder. The new undersecretary was a man who had practical campaign experience, knowledge of military intelligence and the hallmark of exile: retired Captain Mr.Dr.Pieter Philip Juriaan Quint Ondaatje.

He had been late again and had missed the triumphant liberation and the dancing around the trees of liberty. He arrived three months after the French. Was he delayed because of family reasons? A daughter was born at the end of May 1795 and registered in the Hague where the Ondaatjes had taken lodgings. He started his job at the Military Department in early May.

Office hours in those days were long: from nine a.m. to three p.m. and from six p.m. to ten p.m. Accommodation was dark and cramped, stuffy in summer, smoke-filled in winter.

The difficulties facing the new Department must have made even the newest brooms lose the ability to sweep. The army had crumbled away. Most officers had been Orangists and had tendered their resignation. With a brotherly army of occupation of 25,000 Frenchmen, any reason for a Dutch army seemed gone. The navy had been decimated. Many ships had ended up in English hands. The English would look after them carefully until better days.

This English sleight of hand had been given a gloss of legitimacy by a stroke of the pen of the ex-Stadhouder.

The Prince of Orange had forfeited his due rights and privileges by abandoning his functions, and by leaving the country without the consent of his employers – the States General and the States of the various provinces. William could have had no illusions about his constitutional position under Dutch Law, which he knew better than many lawyers.

He certainly had no illusions about the fate which awaited him should he have stayed in the Republic. In the old days, he could not keep the end of Charles I of England out of his head; he now had a more recent example of the end of stubborn princes: Louis XVI of France, beheaded in 1793.

The fishing boat which William had jokingly demanded from Gijsbert Karel van Hogendorp in 1787 to take him across to England in case things went wrong had finally turned up and taken him over in those icy first days of January 1795.

Warmly welcomed by the English cabinet and King, William was persuaded to sign the most damaging letters of his whole career: the so-called letters of Kew. They contained instructions to all commanders of Dutch naval vessels and to all Governors of stations, forts and territories of the vast colonial Empire to surrender to the British King. William added the solemn assurance that everything would be returned by the British "as soon as it will have pleased God to return the fatherland to independence and to the old, established constitution."

Such an assurance was easy to give but impossible to enforce; the restitution was beyond William's power. It not only depended upon God's pleasure, but also upon the English. Besides, William must have been aware that a return to the old constitution was wishful thinking, which by now only a few in the Republic considered realistic. Even if he had remained Stadhouder he would not have been entitled to give instructions of such far-reaching consequences without previous orders from the States General and the VOC. As Stadhouder who had left his post and was now a mere private citizen, he was not entitled to give any binding instructions at all.

The English cabinet had prepared the text of the letters of Kew before William arrived. He had only to sign. But it would not have required much courage if he had been as dilatory in signing these letters as he usually was with his other correspondence. He would not have been beheaded in London for refusing to issue instructions against his mandate and the Dutch constitution. When the letters of Kew became public, accusations of high-treason were heaped on his stubborn but at least unsevered head.

Not all Dutch commanders and colonial Governors obeyed the instructions which William had issued from his English retreat.

In Ceylon, the Dutch officials had been faced with British attempts at infiltration since the days of Robert Knox. Not always had the Kings of Kandy obliged by shutting such infiltrators up in their zoo for foreigners.

In the Dutch – Kandyan war of the 1760s, the King had flirted with the British. In the Anglo – Dutch war of the early 1780s, the British had even occupied Trincomalee, one of the best natural harbors in the world. The French had dislodged them from there and had helped the Dutch to keep Ceylon. The troubled waters in 1783 had been the reason for Jacob Haafner to make his trip on foot.

Now the English tried again.

Should they suggest to the Dutch Governor of Ceylon a peaceful transfer, offering temporary safekeeping based on the letters of Kew? In that case they might be bound legally, or at least in honor, to return Ceylon once the Stadhouder would have been restored. The British East India Company decided to use force and treason.

Troops were landed on the island for surprise attacks on various coastal settlements. In the meantime secret negotiations were conducted with two Swiss brethren de Meuron, who had contracted their regiment of mercenaries to the VOC for service in Ceylon.

While the Dutch forces were fighting the English, the de Meuron regiment changed masters and now fought against the Dutch. Resistance crumbled, and in February 1796 the Dutch capitulated. The whole coast of Ceylon was taken over by the English East India Company.

CHAPTER XIV

The Dutch and the Dutch Ceylonese hoped that after a peace between France and England their position in Ceylon would be restored. The English had no such intentions and started to run things their way.

In the Netherlands the loss of almost all colonies was considered a temporary setback. When peace finally came in 1802, by the treaty of Amiens, the English kept Ceylon by way of safekeeping-charges. Soon there was war again, and the Dutch colonies were reoccupied by Britain. After the fall of Napoleon, most colonies were grudgingly given back after deduction of more safekeeping charges; the Cape of Good Hope remained English too, besides Ceylon.

The VOC, that earliest example of the successful organization of public capital and private enterprise, had been drifting into insolvency. Wars badly affected its profit and loss account and balance sheet. Soldiers on the payroll do not sell products, and forts are assets which are rather illiquid by nature.

The new regime in the Batavian Republic decided to replace the Board of the VOC, still a private limited company, by a government-appointed body to reorganize its affairs and advise on the future. A committee of twenty-eight men was appointed "for the East Indian trade and possessions."

Samuel Wiselius, one of the brightest new men of the new times, became the President. His father had been an officer in the Freecorps of Amsterdam, one

Samuel Iperuszoon Wiselius [1769–1845].

of the petitioners to whom Father Hooft had so readily lent his ear in 1787. Sam Wiselius was a witty, Voltairian spirit with political views far ahead of his time who would end his days writing dramas on Classical themes. During the next twenty years, however, he was more actor than stage writer.

Apart from some representatives of the shareholders, the rest of the Committee of twenty-eight were new men with new ideas. Some were born in the East or had colonial experience. One in particular had demonstrated his democratic zeal and paid the price for it: Pieter Philip Juriaan Ondaatje.
The Amsterdam Exchange looked down upon these political nominees with no experience in trade or administration, who thought that they could run a colonial trading operation because they were born in the East.
However, what these men lacked in commercial experience they possessed by way of political influence. President Wiselius made the Committee into an almost independent organ of the State.
A new colonial policy was being worked out by the Committee with the new National Assembly. Ondaatje had been made a member of the subcommittee of Defense and of the department which had to evaluate personnel and formulate new policies.
He was surrounded by like-thinking minds: his old brother in arms from Utrecht, von Liebeherr, and his employer from the days of his Brussels exile, former councillor of Utrecht, Jan Carel Smissaert, who had been appointed secretary to the East India Committee. Another democrat, famous in the heydays of Patriotism in Holland, joined them on the Committee, ex-Mennonite preacher and journalist, Wybo Fijnje, who had a talent for mathematics and finance.
They were all Freemasons, as were so many eighteenth century enlightened men, such as George Washington with his passion for building and land surveying for whom the cult of the Master Builder, measuring the Universe with his calipers and his all-seeing eye must have been inspiring; and Mozart who used masonic ideas in his Magic Flute. Even King Frederic the Great, that more realistic flute player, had been a Freemason.

Radical democrats, called Jacobins by their more conservative opponents, made up the majority in the East India Committee.
There might have been nearly twice as many members on the new East India Committee as there had been Lords XVII, but the amount of work was not nearly half of that of the old days.
The only territory still in Dutch hands was the island of Java and there the High Government in Batavia, nominally subservient to the board of the VOC, could afford to do as they pleased, in splendid isolation. Correspondence and messengers had to be sent by neutral - Danish and American – ships and it took at least one year to receive an answer to a letter.
Plans were drawn up for a drastic reorganization of the colonies, if and when circumstances would again permit normal communications and the exercise of

CHAPTER XIV

effective power. Reams of paper were filled to that effect, the sub-committees met at set days every week, minutes were kept, Wiselius intrigued with all the schemers and plotters at the helm of the Batavian Republic, but no amount of navigating and of steering could hide the fact that the whole ship of State, including the life-boat of the Colonies, was in tow to the ship of France, and in narrow straits at that.

The newly appointed Committee quickly adopted the way of life of the old Lords XVII. The members received a yearly salary of 4,000 guilders, more than sufficient to lead an easy life.
The dinners of the Committee became famous. In private correspondence more mention was made of the VOC's cook and wine cellar than of any other assets. Von Liebeherr ranked prominently amongst the more Lucullian members of the Committee with his nickname of Liebergott – good Lord – or Leibchen – little body. I did not find Ondaatje tarred with that brush.
But Ondaatje was an honorable man. He had a young wife, young children and old debts. And he was sent on a business trip soon after his appointment.

Some ships of the last return fleet from the East Indies had run into a port in Portugal to stay out of the hands of the English, cruising thereabouts. Ondaatje offered to go and save what could be saved. Did he not speak fluent Portuguese? He embarked in November 1796, not the ideal season for sailing, suffered shipwreck in the Gulf of Biscay, was saved by a local privateer and brought to a Spanish harbor whence he reached Lisbon overland just before Christmas. The local Dutch consul and the former VOC representative who were serving time in pleasant Lisbon did everything in their power to obstruct Ondaatje. They managed to get him expelled, but not before he had achieved the aim of his mission. At least that is the impression we get from his own brief description. He left for Madrid, where he was helped by the Dutch Ambassador Valckenaer, a prominent Patriot, reached Paris - more civilized than when he was there in the years of the Terror - and returned to Amsterdam, to his family and his friends of the East India Committee in the spring of 1797.

The Ondaatjes had moved to Amsterdam. They had rented accomodations on one of the old canals, only a short walk away from the head offices of the VOC, East India House.
While Pieter Ondaatje had been struggling towards Lisbon after being shipwrecked, Christina had given birth to twin daughters, Wilhelmina Hermina and Hermina Wilhelmina. Little Wilhelmina Hermina broke the mirror by departing to the other world in the summer after her birth.

That same summer, Ondaatje was asked to fill in for one of his colleagues on the subcommittee for internal affairs.
On the agenda was a petition submitted by one Jacob Haafner, who claimed that he had advanced the sum of 1000 Star pagodas to the commander of one

Courtyard of East India House in Amsterdam.
by H. P. SCHOUTEN, c.1790.

of the former VOC forts on the East coast of India and that he was never paid back. The claim dated from the unfortunate days of 1781 when the English were overrunning the Dutch trading posts along the coast of India.

A rather strident petitioner this Haafner.

Apparently he had been quite a successful businessman under the English in India and had left the East in 1787 with some capital. He had been travelling in France and Germany since his return to Europe and had started a family in Amsterdam. He had invested his money in French assignats and by 1796 was again as poor as when he set out.

When the "Committee for the East Indian trade and possessions" was being formed, he had applied for a position. In his application he mentioned his "perfect knowledge of the Dutch, French, English, German and Portuguese languages, bookkeeping, a reasonable style and a quick hand." However, he lacked influential friends and a democratic track record and he was passed over. If he had published his books and his views on colonialism earlier, he would have qualified on the basis of his ideas.

In the summer of 1797 he wrote again to the Committee, now demanding repayment of his 1000 Star pagodas. This demand was preceded by a cranky tirade referring to the earlier rejection of his application for a job. Once the

CHAPTER XIV

colonies would have been restored, the Committee would regret having discarded the services of such a useful and able servant. At such time, again, as in the past no doubt, "fortune hunters, adventurers, bankrupts and rakes will be sent as famished tigers amongst the unfortunate Indians." It does not seem the most appropriate introduction to a petition for the repayment of an old advance for which Haafner did not have sufficient evidence.

Nevertheless, his petition was seriously considered, a report ordered and Haafner asked to appear in person to argue his claim. Ondaatje sat in at one of the meetings. The claim was rejected, but the door left ajar; the papers were to be sent to Batavia for advice. At least half a year was required for them to reach Java, an unknown amount of time to investigate the matter and formulate the advice, and half a year for the advice to return to Amsterdam. Haafner knew very well what this meant. He reacted bitterly and threatened to appeal to the Nation in a new petition which he submitted and which was likewise rejected. The professional petitioners of ten years ago had turned into authorities and knew how to deal with petitions.

Ondaatje's and Haafner's paths had crossed. No doubt they talked to each other about Ceylon. Did Pieter Ondaatje perhaps suggest to Haafner to write about his adventures? We do not know. Spoken words have disappeared; only a few words which happen to have been written down and preserved are left to us. What other signs remain of past lives, of these creatures once made of flesh and blood? In the streets of Amsterdam and Utrecht and in the jungle of Ceylon, we had come upon their traces, "feeling sometimes with our fingers their touch upon the stones."

> "Nothing remains but the weight, the longing for the weight of a living creature."
>
> from *The King of Asine* by George Seferis.

CHAPTER XV

The Losing Horse

Not only Haafner was plagued by money worries, Ondaatje too had debts. As an honorable man, that must have bothered him. With a salary of 4000 guilders per year, he could live comfortably; but he could not quickly repay the 3000 guilders which he owed to one of his colleagues on the East India Committee, who had probably paid his debts and held a promissory note for the consolidated total.
Considering the disappearance of almost all of his correspondence, it is impossible to know the reasons for Ondaatje's precarious pecuniary position. Perhaps he just had not heeded that sound advice of Mr. Micawber:
"Annual income twenty pounds, annual expenditure nineteen six, result happiness. Annual income twenty pounds, annual expenditure twenty pounds ought and six, result misery."
Ondaatje was by all accounts generous and trusting and times were hard. As Mr. Micawber, he too must have been confident that "something would turn up." It did.

For nearly three years the Batavian Republic had been in the pangs of childbirth. The new constitution which would cast the principles of the revolution in print was very slow in coming. The democrats had been trying to introduce a constitution which would turn the Dutch Republic into a unified, centrally governed state on the model of France. They were called the Unitarists.
All the forces favoring provincial and municipal independence, under the name of Federalists, had been resisting such a constitution. They still clung to the Gothic Ruin although they admitted that it had to be modernized. Unfortunately, as so often in politics, matters had been simplified to an either-or choice. A few suggested taking a serious look at the constitution of the United States of America, now well past its seven years' itch. With its wise compromise between confederation and consolidation, it might be more appropriate to the Batavian Republic's own past than the French model, built as that was upon a long tradition of central power and abstract rationalism.
Gijsbert Karel van Hogendorp kept silent but confided his thoughts to paper. He had continued his Hamlet-like broodings about himself and everything else since his visit to General Washington. However, by this time, he had seen the light of wisdom in the American constitution of 1787 which had established such a balanced division of powers and had prevented mob-rule and guillotines.

CHAPTER XV

Another admirer of the American constitution was the Dutch Patriot Gerhard Dumbar, who did not keep quiet. He published a fine book in three volumes on American constitutions, including a translation of most of *The Federalist* papers.

During the long-winded deliberations in the new National Assembly in the Hague, one of the delegates had pointed in the direction of the American constitution as a way out of the conflict over constitutional principles. He was called Rutger Jan Schimmelpenninck. As a student, in 1784, he had written his doctoral thesis on government by the People, "De Imperio Populari," to which he had added "rite temperato," properly tempered.

Already in his student years, Schimmelpenninck had nothing of the angry young man. On the contrary, although he agreed with the democrats that the sovereign people should be given a voice, he took great care to side with those Patriots who had stressed that the People's voice should be "reasonable and respectful." When the free-thinking, and still Latin-reading public clamored for a second edition of his thesis, he made doubly sure of staying on the right side of the Patriot Regents and changed "rite" into "caute." Government by the people, cautiously tempered. Don't give the people any disrespectful ideas!

In his thesis, he quoted from the constitution of Massachusetts, John Adams' brainchild, dressed for this occasion in a Latin toga.

When Schimmelpenninck became a delegate to the National Assembly, he could himself speak as the voice of the People. When he raised his voice, properly and cautiously tempered, in praise of the American constitution of 1787, he noticed that he remained a soloist. He cautiously lowered his voice again. The great temperor knew how to keep a low profile. He had given proof of that after the Orange restoration when no one of the People had heard his voice. At that time he only spoke to and for his rich clients, whom he represented in land deals in the Mohawk valley and south of Lake Ontario, where names like Amsterdam, Rotterdam, Barneveld and Batavia still echo the patriotism of Dutch settlers who were courageous enough to put their mouth where their future was.

As things were done in the velvet way in the Netherlands, endless speeches were held and faithfully minuted; so many pipes had been emptied that a black hole could be filled with the smoke; and all the beer and punch drunk during the deliberations could easily have inundated the whole province of Holland against invading enemies.

The draft constitution had become thicker and thicker. People called it "the Thick Book." As so many times before, matters were in a stalemate. But the Dutch had been shown by their French brethren how stalemates should be resolved in a manly, less velvety way. Recent French history teemed with coups all named after the month in which they had taken place, now renamed with classical sounding names to distinguish this modern era of mankind: Thermidor, the end of Robespierre; Vendemiaire, a right-wing uprising put down by a young artillery officer called Napoleon Bonaparte; and Fructidor, the coup in which the army had strengthened the hand of the corrupt Directoire in Paris.

French troops were at hand in Holland and willing to give a hand to the few decisive Unitarists who were resolved to push a Unitarist Constitution through in a manly way.

Their bandleader, by now well versed in musical and theatrical surprises, was Pieter Vreede.

Ondaatje's colleague on the board of the East India Committee, Wybo Fijnje, the Mennonite minister turned journalist turned Lord XVII, was prepared to forget his Mennonite principles of not bearing arms as long as someone else would brandish the sword for him.

The small group plotting a coup needed two things: French soldiers and Dutch guilders.

French soldiers they had. The French Ambassador was backing them. The French Commander in Holland had instructions to be helpful.

Dutch guilders they had not. But their radical friends on the East India Committee came in handy. Thanks to some clever manoeuvering, Wiselius had been able to build up a considerable cash balance unknown to the shareholders.

Some palm greasing in France was felt to be necessary. Wiselius was asked whether he was prepared to send Ondaatje, since "a well-oiled tongue is required in Paris." Why not send von Liebeherr with him? Wiselius seems to have replied that they had better not send his "Indians" to France.

Not all of the correspondence between the coup-leaders is preserved, but it is clear that by January 1798 Pieter Ondaatje had been fully informed about the plans. Wiselius, too, was drawn in. His letters mention soldiers who will be arriving. The coup-leaders wrote to Wiselius about 1000 m. from the B. (1000 mille – 1 million – from the bank?). One of the Directors in Paris had demanded one million for his help.

Some days before 22 January 1798, Wiselius, von Liebeherr, Fijnje and Ondaatje have all travelled to the Hague and are staying at the former headquarters of the VOC, which had recently been turned into an inn in the drive for cost-cutting.

Here, in the "Council of India," these East India men meet the conspirators and General Daendels, Commander of the Dutch Forces. Wiselius has left us a report – perhaps apology is a better word – in which he writes that he declared himself firmly against an armed intervention.

There were reasons to expect that a Unitarist breakthrough was about to take place in a purely political way. What would become of Batavian independence if the army would be used in internal political controversies? It would soon be the ultimate arbiter of Dutch affairs. He states that he was not alone in his refusal to back a coup, but neither from Wiselius' report nor from the papers of other eye-witnesses can one conclude whether Pieter Ondaatje declared himself for or against a coup. Did Ondaatje manage to sit on the fence for some time?

CHAPTER XV

Pieter Vreede [1750–1837].

Wiselius pleads for mitigation of certain measures proposed by the coup-leaders against their adversaries, such as confiscation of property. He writes that he visited the French Ambassador to convince him that harsh punishment for political opponents was unwise and un-Dutch. Then he returns to Amsterdam. With his report, a passport is preserved. Apparently the liberty which the French had brought did not include free travel. In the days of the Patriots, Princess Wilhelmine might have been stopped, but nobody asked her for her passport. Wiselius' passport for his return to Amsterdam mentions amongst his fellow-travellers P.P.J. Quint Ondaatje, but Ondaatje did not return with Wiselius.
He had made up his mind. While Wiselius was pleading with the French Ambassador, Ondaatje had gone to fetch their fellow Freemason, Pieter Vreede, who was ill in his home town in the South. Vreede had been chosen by the conspirators to be their leader. Ondaatje returned with Vreede, who was suffering from a headcold. Informed about the coup, he did not get cold feet. That night, the eve of the coup, he wrote to his wife: "Adieu, aristocrats, until tomorrow."
General Daendels had never suffered from cold feet in all his life, rather from a hot head. He had offered to assist with some of his men. The French Ambassador was only too happy that Dutch soldiers were volunteering to do the dirty work.

In the night of January 21–22, 1798, the National Assembly is purged. A number of members accused of aristocratic and federalist tendencies are arrested in their homes; other members arriving for a morning meeting of the Assembly are debarred and only a rump is admitted to the meeting. This rump now declares itself a constituent body which will not disperse until a true constitution will have been established. They swear an oath of hatred against "A Stadhouder, aristocracy, federalism and anarchy."
They declare the deputies who have been severed from the rump as having forfeited their seats; they annull all provincial sovereignties and set up an interim Executive Directory of five, in imitation of the French Directoire.
Since 1795, the Republic had had no true executive body. The provinces had still run finance, justice and police, as of old, and war and foreign affairs had been conducted by committees from the National Assembly. Vreede became the First Director, Fijnje joined the team. The French Ambassador arrived at the end of the purged session to bestow embraces and bring the congratulations of the Great Nation. Wiselius had just in time escaped complicity.

For Pieter Ondaatje, the temptation to play an active role in this exciting drama had been too great. He could not resist the thrill of being in the middle of a revolution again; nightly meetings where strategy was discussed and plans of action. He had been asked to go with one of the conspirators, van Langen, to fetch the new Leader. He went.
What did they discuss on their way back in the coach to the Hague? A fact is that, shortly after the coup, Ondaatje is offered the post of secretary of the "Agent of Home Police and Internal Correspondence."

The new regime had created a number of "Agencies," precursors of the later ministries. For the first time in the Dutch Republic, there would be a central administration of Justice, Finance, National Education, Economics and Internal Affairs, then called "Home Police." That Agency included internal security and the supervision of roads, waterways and dikes, the ultimate form of internal security, for with leaking dikes large parts of the Netherlands would disappear under water.
Wiselius had been asked to become the Agent for the Marine but had refused. Other Agents had to be more or less coerced to accept.
One of these was Isaac Jan Alexander Gogel. He belonged to the radical Unitarists and edited a newspaper called *De Democraten*. He was born in Amsterdam to German parents; active and successful in the world of small brokers in stocks and bonds and insurance policies, one of the first Dutch statesmen with practical ideas of social engineering; slightly obsessed by inequality, "great fortunes are a blight on society;" inspired by a wish to contribute to the creation of wealth and an equitable division of the burden of taxation.
Seven years younger than Pieter Ondaatje, he had only come into his own after 1787, the year of the Orange-restoration. He had secretly prepared the demo-

cratic revolution which all Dutch knew would be coming in the wake of the French revolution and had belonged with Samuel Wiselius to the same crypto-democratic societies in Amsterdam.

Gogel had been the only Dutchman of intellectual substance to have recommended the introduction of a Revolutionary Tribunal – complete with the guillotine – to set the liberation of the Netherlands on the right footing. Once that liberation had taken place, however, he had used his razor-sharp mind to write for his bloody-minded newspaper.

Now, as Agent of Finance, he would be given the chance to put the knife into the financial muddle inherited from the old regime and perform some financial and fiscal cutting and pruning.

He had already worked out a general plan of taxation.

Gogel and Ondaatje had become acquainted during the last two years and belonged to the same democratic and Freemason circles in Amsterdam.

Van Langen had proposed someone for the post of Agent of Home Police, one Abraham Jacques LaPierre, "who had been devoted to our principles." LaPierre came from the same cloth manufacturing circles as Vreede and van Langen and had been superficially involved in some minor revolutionary sinecures. An anonymous French report on leading Dutch personalities, some ten years later, the same which had characterised Ondaatje as "effervescent, energetic, but honest and the most good-hearted person in the world; has talents and an Oriental vivaciousness," writes about LaPierre: "A chameleon. Little talents, much pliability, eager for money." Gogel later wrote that LaPierre belonged to "those toadies and careerists who are prepared to lick the devil's ass to get what they want."

No wonder that van Langen observed that Ondaatje was not satisfied with being offered the job of secretary to such an ass licker and chameleon with little talents.

But Pieter Ondaatje accepted. His position as member of the East India Committee was kept open for him.

Wiselius, for his part, might have kept an arm's length distance from the new Directors; he could not prevent them from getting their hands in the till of the VOC.

We know from later revelations that the Directors drew bills of exchange on the secret balances of the East India Committee for various payments which they wanted to hide from public scrutiny.

Most of it was used for bribes.

Under the heading "miscellaneous" figured a subsidy for the French theater in Amsterdam and 3000 guilders for P. Quint Ondaatje, six days after he had been appointed secretary to the Agent of Home Police.

Did Ondaatje get carried away by his "effervescent character" and "Oriental vivaciousness" when he accepted a rather inferior position under an inferior character?

Or did 3000 guilders make Pieter Ondaatje bet on the wrong horse? For a wrong horse it was, this new regime of Directors. It lasted only five months.
In those five months the Vreede government managed to alienate almost everyone, the French in the first place, the conservatives, the radicals, Wiselius, even their own Agent Gogel and, last but not least, General Daendels.

Herman Willem Daendels [1762–1818]
by C. JOSI.

At a dinner in June 1798, in the French Embassy in the Hague, Daendels fished out of his pocket the latest issue of a broadsheet called *The Constitutional Fly*, the successor to *The Political Wheelbarrowman*, equally published by J.C. Hespe, Mrs. Ondaatje's first husband. He had changed from a carrier of venom into a gadfly. His sting carried more poison than ever.
Daendels, full of good French wine, erupted in a furious accusation of the Vreede government, pointing at Hespe's Fly and praising its contents. The Ambassador immediately reported Daendels' words to the government. The next day Daendels was summoned for a private dressing-down, but he had already departed post-haste to Paris where the foreign minister, Talleyrand, had

CHAPTER XV

been prepared by Wiselius and von Liebeherr with solid Dutch guilders (from the VOC) to order the French in the Batavian Republic to assist matters to take their course.

Daendels returned having secured French complicity in Paris.
In the Hague, a dinner for 160 guests is arranged in Daendel's honor. The French commander attends. No table decorations, no odes by Vreede, but toasts galore against the Vreede government.
The next day the Directors summon the Agent for Home Police to report on the dinner. LaPierre asks to be excused because of illness. His second in command appears instead, Mr. P.P.J. Quint Ondaatje, who must have felt even more embarrassed than in the days of the vanishing Rhine Count. This general – Daendels – had not only vanished but, worse, turned up again.
The government decides to take harsh measures. The French supreme commander will be dismissed, the sponsors of the Daendels' dinner arrested, tried by special tribunal and executed on the spot if found guilty.
Before noon, rumors fly in the Hague that a guillotine is being erected in front of the Assembly on the same spot where Johan van Oldenbarnevelt was beheaded 180 years ago.
The French commander goes to see Vreede, Fijnje and van Langen, and gives them the impression that he will keep things quiet if the Directory refrains from hasty action.
The three Directors sit down to lunch in one of the rooms of the stately building which, until four years before, had housed the representatives of the City of Amsterdam to the States General. The directors have the French Ambassador as a guest.
The French commander alerts Daendels who immediately marches to Amsterdam House with some of his soldiers. The lunch is roughly interrupted. Vreede and Fijnje jump out of the window and flee through the gardens and out of Dutch history. Van Langen is arrested.
Daendels reads a warrant signed by Gogel and some other Agents, ministers who are toppling their own government. The French Ambassador is roughed up; Daendels knows he is going to be withdrawn by Paris anyhow. Daendels then proceeds across the road to het Binnenhof, the cluster of buildings housing the government and the National Assembly. The most notorious radical members of the National Assembly are arrested and the meeting is dissolved. The chairman is pushed to the ground and his velvet sash, the sign of his dignity, is removed by force. A coup, and not a velvet one this time.
Not that armed coups were unknown in the history of the Dutch Republic. The Princes of Orange, Maurits and William III had intervened by arms, in Amsterdam in 1618, and in Utrecht in 1674. No arms had been needed to install William IV. He had been thrust upon the reluctant Regents by the mere threat of mob violence, by the reminder of the fate of the de Witt brothers.

Arrest of citizen S.J. van Langen, one of the Executive Directors, June 12, 1798.

In the eighteenth century, the first armed coup had been masterminded by Pieter Ondaatje in Utrecht in 1786, although the iron fist had been hidden in a velvet glove.
The first coup of 1798 had been staged by Ondaatje's friends; he had been one of the main conspirators.
The second coup of that year, the coup of Daendels, went ahead without Ondaatje; he was not even one of the rebels but a civil servant in Home Police responsible for law and order.

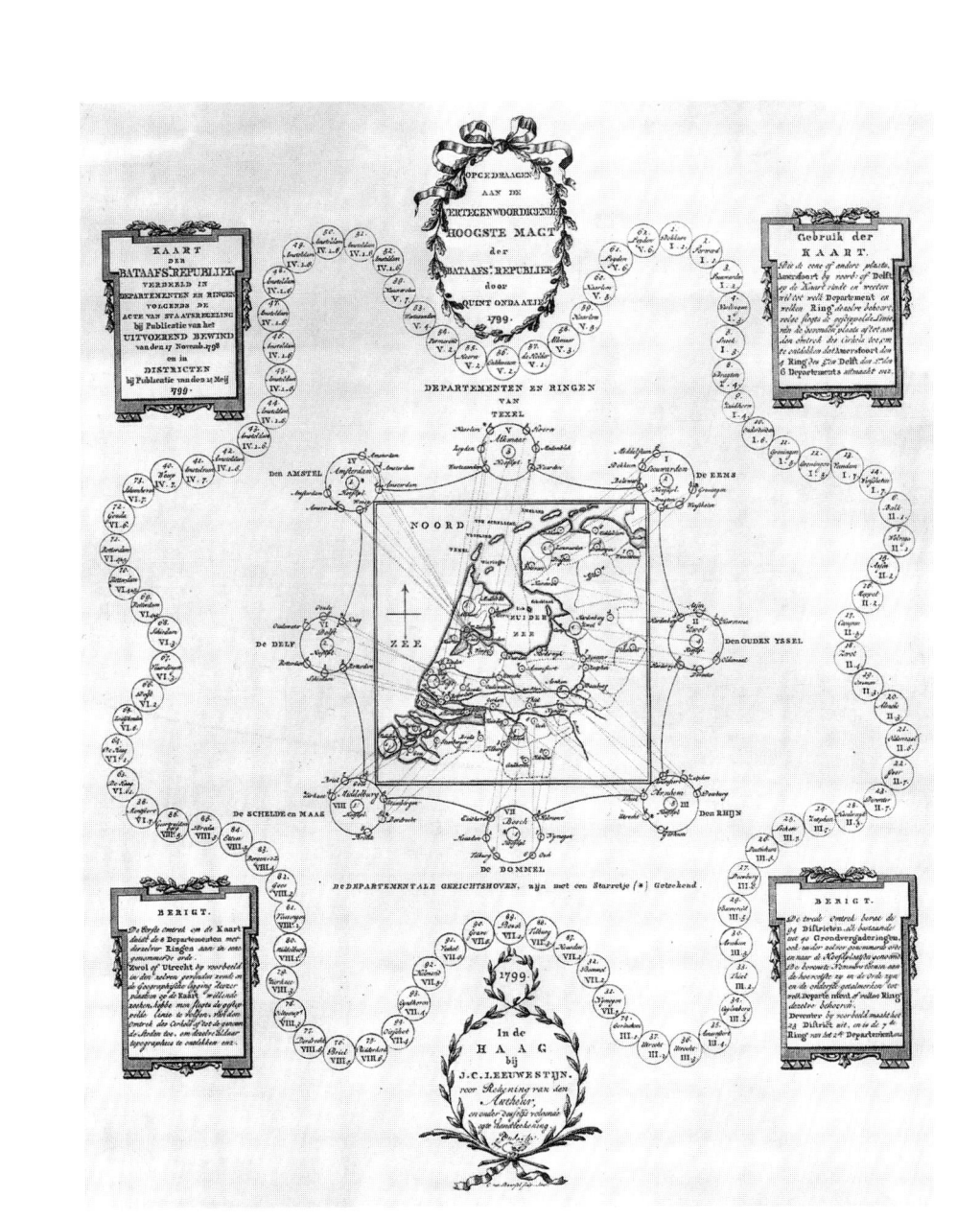

CHAPTER XVI

Shadows And Clearance

The new regime which took the reins of power after the coup of Daendels immediately called a general election. A new Executive Directory was formed: the Agents who had backed the coup stayed on, amongst them Gogel and LaPierre.
Between the summer of 1798 and early 1800, the Netherlands came close to representative democracy and saw the beginning of centralised government. The state of public finances and the international situation, however, severely limited any growth along those lines.
In France, Napoleon Bonaparte had become the effective leader of the nation. All countries allied with France were expected to contribute to the French war effort. The national debt of the Batavian Republic kept rising and the State's creditworthiness diminishing.
Gogel could scoop and scoop into coffers and pockets; the results were drops in a sea of swelling public deficit and debt.

In winter, disastrous floods swept over the lowland estuaries of Holland and Zeeland. Besides internal security, Ondaatje was also responsible for waterways and dikes. Municipal archives in the Netherlands still contain letters written by him in his own hand with detailed instructions about dike repairs.

In an effort to break the old parochial habits of provincial sovereignty, the provinces of the Republic were regrouped, a needlessly grieving exercise, undone two years later. Pieter Ondaatje, between police work and dike repairs, found time to draw a topographical map of the new departments.
With the dedication of this map to the National Assembly by way of a parting gift, Ondaatje resigned in December 1799 from the Agency of Home Police and Internal Correspondence. He left the Hague and moved back to Amsterdam where he resumed his position on the East India Committee.
Why did he resign?
Could he no longer bring himself to serve under the self-serving opportunist LaPierre?
The main reason why he wanted to leave the Hague and look for a change of air might be found with his family.
Six children had by now been born to him and Christina, of which one, a twin girl, had died soon after birth. The other twin girl died on November 8, 1799, in the Hague. Four days later a little girl followed, not yet one and a half years

CHAPTER XVI

old, and in another four days his second daughter, born in May 1795, was dead.

In eight days, the Ondaatjes had lost three children; only two of the six were left.

The move to Amsterdam did not bring Pieter Ondaatje more luck.

In May 1800, the East India Committee was dissolved. After 197 years in business, the old VOC was liquidated and the State took over its assets and liabilities.

A new body of nine members was formed to run what was left of the colonial affairs of the Dutch Empire. Wiselius was reappointed as chairman. Ondaatje and von Liebeherr were passed over.

Ondaatje did not remain long in Amsterdam.

On July 4, 1800, an advertisement appeared in a newspaper announcing that Mr.P.P.J. Quint Ondaatje would open a practice in the Hague for drafting and submitting petitions. He informed the public that he would charge a fixed fee not exceeding a modest, reasonable and appropriate compensation. He must have lived so modestly in the Hague that even his address there is no longer traceable.

While we lose track of Ondaatje scribbling humble petitions for clients in the Hague, we pick up the track of Gijsbert Karel van Hogendorp who had been scribbling far from humble schemes and ideas since he lost his job as Pensionary of Rotterdam in 1795.

At Father Hooft's funeral in September 1794, in the last days of the Orange restoration, Gijsbert Karel, as Orangeman and Pensionary of his city, had not been present.

Father Hooft had been buried in the small church of Vreeland, a seigniorial domain of the Hoofts. Because of his popularity, the authorities in Amsterdam were afraid of anti-Orange disturbances if he would be buried in the family vault in the Nieuwe Kerk next to the Town Hall on the Dam Square. Admiral van Kinsbergen had a funeral monument designed for his father-in-law in Vreeland, but before it could be executed, the French Liberation took place and the old admiral had to worry about being executed himself as one of the leaders of the now proscribed Orange party. The new regime put van Kinsbergen behind bars, a cause of grave worries for Hester Hooft.

Van Kinsbergen was soon released and joined his wife. On his advice, she decided to make her son-in-law Gijsbert Karel van Hogendorp a partner in her banking house.

In the spring of 1795 Hester died, which inspired her son-in-law to write later, "I became a rich man from being poor."

He behaved ungenerously towards the old admiral in a dispute over Hester's will and ended up with the castle of Adrichem, some houses in Amsterdam, the banking business and, after the death of his wife's sister, Margot van Wassenaer, Father Hooft's house on the Herengracht in Amsterdam as well.

During the next ten years or so Gijsbert Karel lived in Amsterdam, and at Adrichem in the summer.

In the house on the Herengracht where Father Hooft, John Adams and Joan Derk van der Capellen tot den Pol had discussed plans for a republic based on democracy, Gijsbert Karel van Hogendorp sat brooding on plans for a restoration of the House of Orange. While in the early years of the new century – in the shadow of France – "aristocrats" and Orangemen were compromising with their honor and conscience and sliding back into positions of power under the new regime, Gijsbert Karel issued an uncompromising proclamation, stirring up his countrymen to recall the Prince of Orange as the only safeguard of the true interests of the people.

No one was stirred.

Prince William himself was more interested in the negotiations which had started for a compensation for his lost rights and privileges than in a return to the Netherlands as a shield for the people.

Gijsbert Karel had to wait twelve years before he could issue another proclamation which that time did stir up general enthusiasm.

In those years he led the life of "a small businessman and a big rentier."

The only time he tried to become a big businessman he ended up with a smaller capital. He invested a large amount of his wife's money in a land development scheme in the Cape Colony of South Africa, which had been restored to the Dutch in 1802 but was lost again to England in 1806.

Practice differed from ideas on paper and dealt a blow to all Gijsbert Karel's good hopes.

Far more hopeless was the situation for Pieter Ondaatje at the end of 1802. A political broadsheet of that time mentioned that Ondaatje – and some others – had been abandoned by the government and "do not know what to do to earn a crust of bread."

In fact, Ondaatje would take whatever crust of bread came his way.

He went into journalism again and contributed to some political satirical journals: Hespe's *Gadfly* and *The Political Thunderbolt.*

In 1803, all of these political gadflies, thunderbolts and wheelbarrowmen were silenced on orders from France.

When the short-lived peace of 1802 was announced, Ondaatje applied to be sent to the East in a military capacity. He wrote in his autobiography that he had been promised the rank of colonel to which he was entitled, but which he never received "because they had dragged him into politics."

"Dragged?" By what means? Ondaatje here is less than honest with himself. "Because his palm had been greased with 3,000 guilders" is closer to the truth.

The peace did not last. The East retreated behind the horizon, political satires were forbidden, Ondaatje sank back into the clerical activities of a petty lawyer.

CHAPTER XVI

He had by now moved back to Utrecht, abandoned by the heirs of the regime which Ondaatje and his fellow democrats had helped to establish in that city. He was not in exile abroad where, after all, there had been hope that the French Brethren would go to make the Netherlands safe for democracy, but abandoned in misery, in Utrecht of all places, the town where Ondaatje had enjoyed his greatest hours.
Those French Brethren had turned out to be tyrants, far worse than the Prince-appointed Regents of the Town Hall. The Batavian Republic now lived in the shadow of a self-appointed Emperor.
Gogel, too, had been left to his own devices, his general taxation plan abandoned; Wiselius removed from East Indian affairs; von Liebeherr returned to the East.

Did Pieter Ondaatje, the son of a Reformed Minister, in the midst of his misery, in the trough of despondency, call out to his God? Not the Deist God of Liberty of 1785, nor the Master Builder of the rationalist Freemasons, but the God of the Psalmist who expects a broken spirit, a broken and contrite heart?
Did he feel that whatever valley of shadows he might be crossing he could with David hope to hide beneath the shadows of God's wings until this storm would pass?

The whole country passed through a valley of shadows.
The clergymen might well compare it to the Israelites travelling through the Sea of Reeds. The Dutch people were travelling along the bottom of the sea with walls of water on either side: the National Debt, sky high, tottering over, ready to submerge the nation. French Tyranny, like Pharaoh, followed close behind, threatening to lead the unwilling ally into captivity. Where was the Moses to bring them safely to the other side and with his rod keep the walls of debt from tumbling down?
As a prophet of old, Gogel was called back from the wilderness. He was the only one who could stave off impending national bankruptcy.
As for the pursuing Egyptians, only God could help. He would, in His time.
Gogel was not keen to come to the rescue of a regime which had eliminated all democratic people from government. He knew his medicine would be bitter and that he would not be able, as Moses, to change the taste to sweetness.
He returned as Secretary of State for Finance after his conditions had been accepted: unification of finances and taxation, to be administered by a central department and no reduction of interest payments on the national debt.
Napoleon had tried to convince the Batavian government that the easiest way out of the annual deficit would be a reduction to one-half or one-third of the interest paid on the national debt.
Total revenue was by now taken up entirely by payments of interest, leaving nothing for the other expenses of the central government and the war effort.
Gogel, who had started life as a stock broker and not as a professional soldier, realized that arbitrary reduction of interest payments would destroy the bor-

rowing capacity of the State for many years to come and would hit those holders of debt who had been patriotic enough to invest in Dutch paper, while leaving scott-free those who held foreign debt.

As a further condition for being prepared to show that he did not carry the nickname "the bulldog of the Treasury" in vain, Gogel had stipulated a free hand in staffing his new Department of Finance. Gogel knew what had to be done. He also knew who could help him to do it. He surrounded himself with clever and decisive collaborators.

A decree of 29 November 1805 appointed Ondaatje as advising Council of Finance and as member and permanent Secretary of "the Council of Adjucation of the Means at Sea and on Land" – a Council of War Bounty – at an annual salary of 3,500 guilders.

The Council of War Bounty had to declare on the legality of war prizes and to apportion those made.

The Council of Finance was Gogel's rod.

The emperor's shadow lay over everything. It assumed a human form, the weight of a living creature, albeit a light-weight and very much a puppet: the great temperor, Rutger Jan Schimmelpenninck. He now carried a high profile and the venerable republican name of "Grand Pensionary." The word "pensionary" reminded people of the weight given to the Dutch Republic by Johan de Witt under that title. After only one year, Napoleon pensioned off the Grand Pensionary and moved his own brother, Louis Napoleon, on the stage with an even higher title, King of Holland, definitely un-Dutch and un-republican.

Under these two shadow reigns, Gogel was given free rein to run his Ministry.

He liked to call his team at Finance "children of the Minister." Not shadows, but children.

As a child of the Minister, Pieter Ondaatje spent four years in hard and productive work. Gogel established the base of modern Dutch taxation. This legacy is a monument to him more difficult to destroy than anything in bronze or stone.

The seat of government was transferred from the Hague to Amsterdam. The Ondaatjes moved thither in 1808.

King Louis, who became popular because of his dedication to become a Dutchman and his attempts to distance himself from his Imperial brother, admired the honest and blunt Gogel. Frictions, however, developed. Gogel had difficulty compromising, he lacked the adaptability of the chameleon. He resigned in 1809, but all of "his children" were retained at their post.

In 1810, Napoleon annexed the Netherlands to France. The Egyptians had finally overtaken the small sea-treading nation. Gogel's rod could no longer protect them. The walls of debt came falling down. Interest payments on the national debt were reduced by two-thirds. The former Republic of the Seven

CHAPTER XVI

*Napoleon visits Amsterdam, October 1811.
Gogel is indicated by a small arrow.*
by M. I. VAN BREE.

United Netherlands was geographically disunited into several French Departments.
Gogel was asked by Napoleon to resume office as Intendant General de Finance. He accepted in order to save the flotsam and jetsam after the cataclysm.
The Emperor came to inspect his new Departments in 1811.
There Gogel stands, old for his years, unfit from spending all his waking hours behind his desk, surrounded by French worthies and deferential Dutchmen, collaborators of Imperial France, all in the same white breeches pulled up high and exposing the merest hint of obesity. Even the Emperor could not hide his paunch when not on his high horse.
The painting could be called "The Triumph of Collaboration."
No Hoofts.
No Gijsbert Karel van Hogendorp, although even Gijsbert Karel had had his weak moments and had made it known at the heydays of Napoleon's success that he was willing.
And Daendels? He had continued to serve the French and been sent by King Louis to Java, the only part of the East Indies left to the newly-baked Kingdom of Holland, whence he had soon been removed by the English.

No van Kinsbergen. He had excused himself, being unwell and seventy-six years old. King Louis had honored him by making him Count of Doggersbank. Napoleon had overtrumped that by creating him a Comte de l'Empire and a French Senator.

Not many could resist the blandishments of titles, offices and money offered by the firm of Bonaparte Bros. Samuel Wiselius was one of the few who never wanted to have anything to do with them.

Who is the oriental looking person behind Gogel? One of his children? Ondaatje perhaps?

If so, he was included in absentia. The painter anyhow must have composed the painting in his studio. Napoleon would not sit still for one minute; Gogel would be too busy to pose beside a horse.

By the time the Emperor visited Amsterdam, Ondaatje and his family had moved to France. He had accepted an offer to become member of the Conseil des Prises in Paris, the supreme court in matters of war bounty.

To the former Prosecutor-General van Maanen, now President of the Imperial Court of Justice in the Hague, Ondaatje wrote when being offered this post: "Times are really too hard to decline such an offer. Lucky is he – and particularly a father of a numerous family – who can praise himself to have the generous attention of a sensitive friend of mankind who is prepared to support him, especially in times as we are now experiencing, wherever and however it may be. . . ."

This was quite a different tone from the one in which Ondaatje used to address the authorities twenty years before, or even seven or eight years earlier, when he contributed to satirical periodicals.

Still, apart from undisguised gratitude, natural to his good-hearted character, a slight tongue-in-cheekness can be detected in the tone of the letter as if he wants to tease van Maanen by reminding him that both had learned how to trim their sails to the wind.

Van Maanen was the biggest chameleon of all the Dutch statesmen of those times. He had studied with Sam Wiselius in Leiden and had believed in the same Patriot ideals.

As Prosecutor-General, he had served every regime from the French Liberation to King Louis Bonaparte. In that capacity he had been after the journalist Pieter Ondaatje in 1795 and around 1802. He had prosecuted Vreede, van Langen and Fijnje and unearthed the financial scandals of their short reign, including the pay-off of Ondaatje's debts. He had investigated Gijsbert Karel van Hogendorp when his Orange proclamation became public.

Under King Louis of Holland, van Maanen served as Minister of Justice. After Napoleon had annexed the Netherlands, he made van Maanen President of the Imperial Court of Justice in the Hague.

Ondaatje was not ashamed to confess that he, too, a democratic republican by origin as van Maanen had been, would accept a well-paid job even from an autocratic Emperor.

CHAPTER XVI

It meant moving to Paris.
There, in the capital of half of Europe, Ondaatje, his wife and their children witnessed the decline and fall of the Emperor and the Great Nation.

In the Netherlands, that decline was greeted with a swelling chorus of "Oranje Boven" – "Orange forever" – the traditional cry when the people wanted a change.
But which Orange?
William V was dead. His eldest son, now going by the name of William VI, had had his spells of chameleon-like behavior. He had sat admiringly at the feet of First Consul Bonaparte. He had negotiated with Emperor Napoleon about compensation for the losses of the House of Orange in the Netherlands.
He had quarrelled with the English government, fought under the Prussians, and made up with England again.

The swelling chorus of "Oranje Boven" was soon accompanied by some dramatic action.
While Prussian, Russian and Austrian troops were approaching from the East, in Amsterdam the mob – in true Dutch fashion – went on a rampage and sacked the houses of the hated French. In one night, the city was cleared of all French custom posts and police offices. Illuminated by the fireworks of the blazing symbols of French oppression, the French authorities fled the city. The citizens' militia – organized under the French as the Garde Nationale – removed the French eagle from their uniforms, donned Orange bows and kept the mob under control. The mob has a tendency to overdo things.
But the mob is useful when it comes to the take-over of power. In the name of the people, the militia officers installed some trusted and respected citizens as the new Provisional City Council.
Like cautious merchants, this Provisional Council steered a middle course: the mob was kept in hand, no rebellious steps were taken, for the French were close by in Utrecht and might return at any moment.

In the Hague, the French had withdrawn without fireworks.
Gijsbert Karel van Hogendorp who had been living there for some years took heart. The plans for a restoration had been lying ready in his drawer. A proclamation drawn up by Gijsbert Karel was handed round and posted on public buildings. It started and ended with "Oranje Boven."
It announced that "the Government" proclaimed the Prince of Orange "High Authority" and postulated: "The old times are coming back." Gijsbert Karel had been planning all his life how he could bring back the old times.
He invited as many old-timers to his home as he could reach, all of them with impeccable Orange credentials.
These "legitimate" authorities were to call back the Prince of Orange and appoint him as a new Stadhouder. They were also to appoint Gijsbert Karel as

the new Pensionary with full executive powers. Sovereignty would revert to the old provinces.

Only twenty old gentlemen turned up. They were afraid of the French and wanted to wait. A second meeting was convened, this time with an equal number of Orange and Patriot former Regents. This meeting . . . appointed a commission to study van Hogendorp's proposals. The old times had come back indeed. But Gijsbert Karel in his earlier days had shown that he could act when others dithered. Then he was twenty-four, now fifty-one, old for his days, plagued by gout – a typical Regent's affliction – which made him immobile just at the time when everything around him was moving.

As a young man, he had prepared the way for Princess Wilhelmine, and she had taken the lead. Now he took the lead to prepare the way for her son. When he was twenty years old, he had nearly gone down with his ship, the Erfprins, the Hereditary Prince. Now he would raise the hereditary prince who was laying low.

The General Administration assumed by the Triumvirate in the name of the Prince of Orange, November 21, 1813, at the home of Gijsbert Karel van Hogendorp.
by J. W. PIENEMAN.

Van Hogendorp and two retired officers from old aristocratic families, near neighbors in the Hague, declared themselves the General Administration. They knew they would be shot if the French would ever lay hands on them.

This General Administration sent emissaries to all major towns of Holland to unite the hesitant magistrates to the power in the Hague. For about ten days in that November month of 1813, Gijsbert Karel van Hogendorp was the undisputed rallying force of the self-liberation of the Dutch, confined to his chair by gout.

Gijsbert Karel knew very well that without the support of Amsterdam his plans would come to nought. His link with the big city was a thirty-five year old man, captain in the Amsterdam town militia, recently appointed secretary of the triumvirate in the Hague: Anton Reinhard Falck.

Anton Reinhard Falck [1777–1843]
by P. DAGOBERT after BANGNIET.

Another Falck? Yes, the nephew of Otto Willem Falck of Utrecht whose face Ondaatje had saved when Otto Falck had tried to escape disguised as a groom. Anton Reinhard had been a young boy when this uncle and his own father were coping with the troubles of Council in Utrecht. He remembered a visit by Ondaatje and von Liebeherr, "excited young men" to his parents' house. They had first politely inquired if Mr. Falck Sr. could see them at home. The aim of their visit was to press old Falck into becoming a patron of the Freecorps. Falck declined and they told him in his own house that they would henceforth consider him as an enemy of the Freecorps.
The Falcks had moved to Amsterdam after the Prussian invasion. Anton Reinhard's father had been appointed to a special committee of the VOC. After all, he knew Indian matters from experience and had married – on his return journey – the daughter of the Governor of the Colony of the Cape of Good Hope.
Anton Reinhard had a quick mind, a great interest in the Classics and a sense of humor. In 1795 and 1796, his father had sent him on a tour through France. After studying law at Leiden University, he became a barrister in Amsterdam, refusing to serve the Emperor, except as captain of the militia of Amsterdam.

There, the mob was fiercely pro-Orange, the Provisional City Council guardedly. "Our Fatherland can be restored by Orange, not for Orange alone. The citizens of Amsterdam will sacrifice everything for the liberation of their Fatherland, much for the House of Orange, but will not support a revolution exclusively aimed at an Orange-Restoration."
This was the dignified message given to the emissaries of the triumvirs from the Hague. The patrician families from Amsterdam had not forgotten the counter revolution of 1787. They had not forgotten the unwholesome effects experienced each time a Prince of Orange had been called back by the mob.
But some people had learned some lessons in those nineteen years in which more had changed than in two centuries and were prepared to draw a veil over the past.
One of them was Samuel Iperuszoon Wiselius, the witty, Voltairian democrat. Another was Daniel Hooft Danielszoon, one of the three Daniel Hoofts removed from the Council of Amsterdam in 1787 after the restoration of the House of Orange.
He was by now a sixty-year-old gentleman of refined literary taste and vast cultural knowledge.
Daniel Hooft and Wiselius were both members of the Patriot Club "Doctrina et Amicitia."
As a member of Doctrina, I have myself tasted something of proudly independent Amsterdam with its mixture of businesslike solidity and liberal political views which has continued to inspire the Club from its early days in the 1780s.

Once more Wiselius acted behind the scenes. He even appeared in the limelight for a brief moment together with Daniel Hooft when they visited the Provisional

Council of Amsterdam. Hooft had been appointed to that body by the militia. Together they urged the cautious and hesitant members to accept the turn of the tide and take the initiative before the mob or the Hague would force their hand.

While Provisional Council deliberated, a handful of horsemen appeared at one of the city gates. Falck led them into the city. Provisional Council realized to its relief that they were not the returning French. Their mustachios were fiercely un-French and their language Russian. They were a band of Cossacks, an advance guard of the approaching Allies.

The old flag of the United Provinces – with an Orange banner – was hoisted above the cupola of the Town Hall. The bells played the tune of Wilhelmus of Nassau, which would become the Dutch national anthem.

The triumvirate had proclaimed the Prince of Orange "High Authority," but where was that High Authority?

It shows how little the Prince of Orange had himself worked for his own restoration that, when the moment came – and it had been coming for nearly a year – his followers did not even know where to find him and had to send emissaries both to London and to Berlin to look for him.

Departure of Prince William V from the beach at Scheveningen, January 18, 1795.

Arrival of Prince William VI on the beach at Scheveningen, November 30, 1813.

On the famous painting of the Proclamation of Independence, we see the triumvirs and many now forgotten dignitaries, and even some Misses van Hogendorp, but not the Prince of Orange himself, the object of the proclamation.
It shows how original and excentric van Hogendorp's initiative was.
The Prince of Orange was totally unaware of van Hogendorp's actions.
He was eventually found in London, returned on an English ship, and delivered by fishing boat to the beach at Scheveningen, almost at the same spot where he had left with his father and been seen off by Admiral van Kinsbergen nearly nineteen years ago.
The fishermen at Scheveningen who had carried the small and podgy William V on board now hauled in the tall and trim figure of William VI.

Van Hogendorp had reserved the title of Sovereign Prince or Grand Duke of Holland for him. The Netherlands were too small for a King and, besides, Napoleon's brother had made that title odious to the Dutch people.

Furthermore, van Hogendorp had romantic reactionary ideas about the position and powers of this restored Super-Stadhouder which were not shared by many and certainly not by the Prince of Orange.

Van Hogendorp could not move because of the gout. The Prince on his way to the Hague could hardly move because of the crowd. His first visit was to one of the other triumvirs. Only late that evening did he finally go and see the man to whom he owed so much. Van Hogendorp described the moment: "I told him that now all my wishes had been fulfilled and offered my hand in expectation of his hand. That hand came, but not spontaneously, and that was the only time." The only time that the Prince of Orange went out of his way for Gijsbert Karel van Hogendorp.
The emissaries of the triumvirate in Amsterdam showed that they had a better understanding of what the times required than van Hogendorp. When the Prince arrived in Amsterdam the day after his visit to van Hogendorp, they had already issued a proclamation concocted with Wiselius, Daniel Hooft and their Doctrina colleagues: "It is not a William VI which the Dutch people have asked to come back. . . . It is William I, who as Sovereign Prince according to the wishes of the Dutch, appears amongst the people."
The Amsterdam patrician families did not like that tone at all. Amidst general rejoicing, the grand houses on the Herengracht kept the curtains closed.

William realized that he had no choice but to accept sovereignty from the hands of "the people" – whatever the English might say about such a dangerous precedent – and, after some back-room negotiations, he appeared in the windows of the Town Hall on the Dam square, now called the Palace since King Louis had taken up residence there:
"Dutchmen, you have expressed your will. Your trust, your love puts the sovereignty in my hands. It must be so. I will sacrifice my hesitations and follow your wishes. I accept what the Netherlands is offering me, but I only accept it under the guarantee of a free constitution."
It sounds rather stilted and not very spontaneous, but the democrats of Doctrina could be satisfied.

The democratic Patriots of 1785 would have been satisfied too. Had not Ondaatje and von Lieberherr travelled to the Hague and shown themselves at the military parades of William V in the hope of forming an alliance between the people and the House of Orange?
But would Father Hooft have been satisfied? Would Cornelis Pieterszoon Hooft, that burgomaster at the start of the Golden Age with his system of aristocratic republicanism?

Aristocrats and patricians were given a symbolic final voice. A few months later the Prince of Orange was "inaugurated" as Sovereign Prince, not crowned, by

a meeting of notables in the Nieuwe Kerk in Amsterdam, adjacent to the Palace-Town Hall. Beneath him lay unmoved the remains of the Regent dynasties who had been the rivals of his House for over 200 years.
Only after Napoleon's second coming and defeat did he finally become King of the Netherlands.

One advantage of the new situation was that the Prince of Orange as Sovereign could reward his followers in a way which did not cost the Treasury a stuiver and which was even more appreciated than pensions or positions: he could enoble whomever he wanted.
Gijsbert Karel van Hogendorp was made a hereditary Count. That cost less than a handshake.
Everyone who had played even a minor role in the Restoration was enobled. Falck was made a Jonkheer, van Kinsbergen too, although he had already been made Count of Doggersbank by King Louis and Comte de l'Empire by Napoleon. Wiselius was considered too radical to receive a title; but, as he was known to be good in working behind the scenes, he was made Head of Police in Amsterdam. Converted poachers make the best gamekeepers. He was probably the only Head of Police who wrote with success for the theater.
The King, who was reserved and closed-up by nature, had not forgotten the closed curtains on the Herengracht.
Most of the Patriot Regent families of Amsterdam were left in the cold while the warm shower of titles was pouring down on smal-town dignitaries, minor military men, sycophants and heroes of the day. Even notorious collaborators of the French were honored with titles provided they had turned coat in time. A rare example of a man who had held high office in Batavian and French times and did not turn his coat was Isaac Jan Alexander Gogel. His friend van Maanen had turned like a weathervane and had immediately been appointed Minister of Justice.
Gogel had left with the French. He could not accept a return of the House of Orange, for him the symbol of feudalism and iniquity. He remained in France until the Emperor released him from his oath of loyalty. Upon his return to the Netherlands, he was offered the Ministry of Finance where one of his "children," Elias Canneman, had been standing in for him. Gogel refused, bought a small starch and blue works and, stiff as a rod, ended his days mourning the betrayal of all hopes for liberty, equality and fraternity in this new age of domesticity, inequality and selfishness.

And Pieter Ondaatje? He was late again.
In 1795, he had not been on the spot when the era of liberty for the Netherlands was ushered in by the French. In 1813, he was still ruling on the legality of French war bounty. But bounty was now made at the expense of France.
He was in Paris when the Allies entered that city. He adressed a petition to the new Dutch Sovereign. Formulating petitions for others had been his main

CHAPTER XVI

business in his earlier dark years, now he himself is the humble petitioner. He asked to be considered for the post of Dutch Consul in Paris, but the Ministry of Foreign Affairs rejected his offer. Politically unacceptable. The future must have looked uncommonly dark for him in the spring of 1814.

A ray of light and grace unexpectedly brightened Ondaatje's darkest moment.

William I came to Paris for the peace conference with the Allies. Anton Reinhard Falck accompanied him as Secretary of State, the highest position under the new Dutch Sovereign. He heard about Ondaatje, renewed the acquaintance with the "excited" student of his youth and arranged an audience with the Monarch for Ondaatje. William I – unlike the Bourbons who were returning to Paris at the same time – had learned from the past and was prepared to forget. Ondaatje offered his services. They were accepted. He returned with his family to the Netherlands.

Two letters from Pieter Ondaatje are preserved in Falck's papers. Without those letters we would only know the barest of outlines of the end of the story of the demagogue for democracy, Pieter Quint Ondaatje.

The first letter to Falck was written from Middelburg, the capital of the province of Zeeland, and dated 10th March 1816:

Highest esteemed Benefactor!

For all I have enjoyed since my return from Paris I have surely to thank the best of Monarchs, our fatherly Sovereign. This goes without saying. But, Patron sans pareil, what would have become of me and my nearest without you? What extraordinary luck [I cannot call it coincidence] has made you take us under your high protection? Has this not come only from you yourself? Our acquaintance – I dare not call it friendship – was not that close that it could give any cause whatsoever to those special and touching favors which I have received from you.

No, really. If I reflect on everything again, no tie on earth connected me to your magnanimous heart, but, I repeat it again with thankfulness, what would have become of us without you?

I ascribe everything to my favorable genius which has influenced you by way of speaking in my favor at the most appropriate time of my life. No, not at all! I owe everything to the good, favorable and liberal thoughts which you have entertained for me and my family.

Accept, dear Patron, our most heartfelt gratitude! Keep us in your permanent high protection. On the other side of the broad seas, and in the country of my birth, you will live unceasingly in our thankful hearts. Everywhere I will bless your memory and will make it blessed.

God be with you. Farewell,
 your most grateful Ondaatje.

This is quite a different tone again from the letter of thanks to van Maanen. The "force des choses," as that ice cold professional revolutionary St. Just in

Paris had called the real world, after Rousseau, had finally overtaken the excited young student, the idealistic revolutionary, the witty pamphleteer, the soldier ready to sacrifice his life for liberty and equality, the colonial reformer, the child of the reformer of the Ministry of Finance.

To serve an Emperor who was, after all, himself a child of the revolution which Ondaatje had considered as the liberation of mankind, was one thing.

To praise and thank the son of the Pernicious Hand, to accept the favors of that son, invested with more absolute powers than the Stadhouder ever had, was another thing.

In the Netherlands, the revolution had not eaten its children. But its children, if they wanted to eat, had to eat many of their words.

However Ondaatje is an honorable man. The thankfulness expressed in this letter to Falck sounds genuine.

He throws himself into the future. What future for a man of fifty-eight?

Back to the East. Not exactly to "the country of my birth," but back to another tropical island, another jewel in that necklace of emeralds to which the Dutch East Indies have been compared, the island of Java.

Ceylon was lost to the Dutch. His father and mother had died there, both still in Dutch times. His cousins and nephews were now serving the English, they were becoming pillars of the Anglican Church and forgetting their Dutch and Portuguese.

King William had appointed Ondaatje to the civil service, of the first class, in the Dutch East Indies.

Troops were levied, trained and on the point of being sent to the East when they had to be marched southwards instead to beat Napoleon at Waterloo.

Their training center was in Harderwijk, where I was garrisoned myself 150 years later in the same barracks, which had hardly been modernized in all those years. In freezing winter days, through snow and ice, we had to cross the parade grounds on the way from our unheated quarters to the washrooms to shave, wash and brush our teeth with freezing water. We were not going to fight under the tropical sun; we were learning Russian, hence this training for the Siberian cold.

The Ondaatjes who had been waiting for a whole year to be transferred to Java had been living on half-pay, graciously accorded by the King: a down payment of 700 guilders and 100 guilders a month. This was about half of what Ondaatje had received in his days at the East India Committee, without perks and perquisites.

The dispatch of troops and civil personnel was delayed by the desperate state of the Dutch navy and merchant marine.

An old French warship had been requisitioned and renamed "the Nassau." The ship was not in good shape and the ship chandlers had delivered foodstuff of inferior quality.

CHAPTER XVI

Finally, all Ondaatjes – Pieter spoke of ten persons – packed up and proceeded to Vlissingen, a naval center in Zeeland, where the Nassau was lying in the roads. Further delays in supplying the ship and accommodating it for passengers; delays because of bad weather, March squalls.
Pieter Ondaatje wrote another letter to Falck. All his money was spent while they had been waiting for the ship to sail. He included a letter for the King and begged Falck to deliver it – personally if at all possible – with a word of recommendation. "We need instant, quick and ample assistance."
At the end of March 1816, the Nassau finally set sail.

What a difference with that voyage forty-three years ago from Ceylon to the Republic of the Seven United Netherlands.
Now Pieter is departing from the Kingdom of the Netherlands, Ceylon no longer Dutch, to the island of Java.
Then he was going westward, with the rising prospect of a Dutch education and a high position upon return. Now he is sailing eastward into the sun setting over his fifty-eight years.

The next letter gives an account to his Patron Falck of the vicissitudes of the voyage.
It is a cheerful letter, one would say, the report of an "excited" young student. Falck was sure to appreciate such cheerfulness. Falck, who once said that they had made the revolution in Amsterdam "with a laugh."
Within twenty-four hours after their departure, the "Nassau" ran aground on a sandbank and had to be rescued by English vessels. Did the irony escape Ondaatje? The English had just rescued the entire ship of the Dutch State and put a new captain on board.
Because of the doubtful condition of the ship itself it put in at Rio de Janeiro. From here, Ondaatje sent a letter ending with: "Do not forget that I am attached to you and your interests until death! P. Ondaatje."

On the 19th of October 1816, the Nassau arrived at Batavia, after six months at sea.
"Some families have had to suffer somewhat longer" between their arrival and the commencement of their jobs.
"Among them can surely be counted the family of Ondaatje. Old Mister Ondaatje had suffered a stroke already in the roads and appeared to be slightly confused upon arrival in Batavia. He had to survive with his family on half-pay and would have starved without the help of generous people."
This is the last sign of life we have of Pieter Ondaatje, now "old Mister Ondaatje," taken from a report by a high colonial official.

Ondaatje had been made a member of the Supreme Court of Justice in Batavia. He obtained some months' leave to restore his health, but no Falck, not even a King, could help him anymore.
On April 30, 1818 – one and a half years after he had arrived in the East – he died, fifty-nine years old.

The God of Liberty had finally lifted him out of all shadows into everlasting light.

The "Kees" dog at Valk en Heining confides Patriot secrets to the author.

CHAPTER XVII

Missing Links

We drive along the river Vecht in thick fog.
The parks and mansions, admired incognito by Czar Peter the Great of Russia and King Frederic the Great of Prussia, emerge one by one from the grey mist and fade away, mere silhouettes.
Modern changes are obscured, only eighteenth century contours stand out and the timeless shapes of bare old trees.
In Vreeland, we cross over to the river Angstel near the medieval castle of Loenersloot; clammy walls rising from a swampy moat crowned by a crow-haunted tower. On the other side of the river which is no wider than a moat and almost level with the road, lies Valk en Heining.
Even in the gloomy, inward-looking winter afternoon the house seems to radiate color and warmth. Ochre walls and a gilded sundial against the facade, subdued and toned down, but just strong enough to bring to mind the music of Scarlatti and Vivaldi.
Have we fallen under the spell of the genius loci?
In fact, Scarlatti and Vivaldi are often played in the conservatory, built as a wing to the house. The chatelaine is an accomplished flutist and gives concerts where once tender plants used to wait for balmier days.

Before we actually hear music, we are welcomed at the gate by a friendly dog, to our delight a Keeshond. Is it the incarnation of Patriotism greeting us on our pilgrimage to Father Hooft's last earthly dwelling place?
We take our time to pay homage to the incarnation who wags his tail and most of his fluffy body and treats us to his version of a flute sonata of Scarlatti.

When I discovered a bundle with private correspondence of Father Hooft in the State Archives amongst the van Hogendorp papers, I noticed an annotation on its covers in Gijsbert Karel's own hand: "Found by me in the library at Valk en Heining."
How clearly did I see before me the grandson-in-law, arriving in haste at Valk en Heining upon the news that Burgomaster Hooft was dead, offering to help the octogenarian sister to sort out her brother's belongings.
Father Hooft's son-in-law, Admiral van Kinsbergen, was away on duty. He was commanding the fleet in Zeeland against the approaching French. At Father Hooft's burial in Vreeland only Count van Wassenaer followed the bier. Did

CHAPTER XVII

Gijsbert Karel fear to be seen with the symbol of Patriotism? Even at the burial of that symbol?

But he did go to Valk en Heining according to his own written statement, found letters in the library, and took them with him. Did he come to look through Father Hooft's papers to make sure that anything which had to do with Patriot politics, anything anti-Orange, anything which might possibly compromise him, the husband of the granddaughter of the dead Burgomaster, would disappear? How can we otherwise explain the total lack of anything political in the Hooft papers preserved by Gijsbert Karel.

Father Hooft did not act as if he had anything to hide. He had stayed in Amsterdam for half a year after the restoration and had only left because of the repeated entreaties of his daughter. He remained defiantly the head of the Patriot movement even in exile and after his return to the Republic.

His role and position were known to everyone. His house had been protected by the restored pro-Orange faction in Amsterdam. There was no reason for him to destroy any papers. During the whole time he was in self-imposed exile, his house in Amsterdam had been left untouched.

He "bent down for no one except for the Almighty."

When Hooft was a young man, Prince William's father on a visit to Amsterdam had asked Hooft to come and discuss some matters. At that time, he had kept Hooft waiting. Hooft had sent a courtier with the message: "In another ten minutes Hooft will be gone to the Exchange." For an Amsterdam Regent, the Almighty came first, Amsterdam second, the Exchange third and only thereafter other things, including the Stadhouder.

For more than two centuries the Regent dynasties of Amsterdam had considered themselves above the opinion of the Princes of Orange, certainly above public opinion.

I find it unlikely that Father Hooft, a convinced democrat but very much an Amsterdam Regent by birth and profession, would have stooped to lock himself up in his cabinet to burn some of his papers. It is more likely that van Hogendorp, who during the French period had constantly been hiding his own papers, ready to burn them at the first sign of danger, burnt all Patriot material found in the library at Valk en Heining and only kept some personal letters for his wife as a souvenir of her grandfather.

Lost are the letters from John Adams and Joan Derk van der Capellen.

A fire is burning in the eighteenth century fireplace in the library of Valk en Heining. The Keeshond has posted himself in front of the fire. No Patriot papers will be burnt while he is on guard!

Through the large windows on one side the elms on the edge of road and river are visible in the last blanketed light of day. The windows on the other side overlook the garden behind the house, gravel walks, clipped hedges and scrolled box-edged flower beds, now empty, all fading into the darkening greyness.

We have tea in the dining room, unchanged since the time when the old brother and sister Hooft were having their meals there together. We walk over the boards

A log fire is burning in the eighteenth century fireplace at Valk en Heining. The "Kees" dog has posted himself in front of the fire. As long as he is on guard no Patriot papers will be burned.

of the music conservatory, recently cut from some of the elms in the park, over 250 years old. Father Hooft had walked in their pristine shade.

In the teahouse on the river, designed by Daniel Marot, the architect of King-Stadhouder William III, the lady of Valk en Heining lights candles. There is no electric light and darkness now has covered the mansions on the river.

We both had Swedish mothers and learned the song of Santa Lucia when we were children. The Saint who brings light to Swedish homes on December 13, represented by the mistress of the house, bearing a tray with coffee or mulled wine and carrying a crown with candles on her head. We both had been "star children" for our mothers on Santa Lucia and were suddenly reminded of our childhood in Holland when the Germans had cut off electricity at the end of the war and let the country sink into darkness every night.

At that time, the light-bringing Saint became the symbol of hope for our parents' friends, who came to our homes at Santa Lucia's feast. To Christopher's and Eliane's amazement, we sang Santa Lucia together while lighting the candles in the teahouse of Valk en Heining.

The Keeshond took it all in his stride and did not utter a sound. But when we took our leave, he gave us as a parting gift, again his version of a flute sonata of Scarlatti.

Bright sunshine spoils the subtle shades of history.

As we are retracing our steps until we meet those of our ancestors of two hundred years ago, we are glad that we are treading amongst dampened contours; it deepens our vision.

On their retreat from Utrecht to Amsterdam in September 1787, Ondaatje and the Rhine Count had halted in Ouderkerk on the Amstel, where they waited for further orders from the city. There they had completed the plan of defense. Where better could Christopher and I plan our next moves than in the old inn of "Paardenburg" in Ouderkerk on the Amstel.

In the morning we had walked along the canals of Amsterdam and visited the places where Pieter Ondaatje had lived and worked. East India House is well-preserved, now used by the University; trade exchanged for learning.

Where Father Hooft's triumphal coach-ride began, in front of the Town Hall on the Dam Square, now the Royal Palace, a taxi-stand reminded us of our modern age.

We continued walking, past the Shrimp Doelen, now part of the University Library, to Father Hooft's house on the Herengracht. In the first decades of our century the owner had gathered between its walls the largest private collection of items concerning the House of Orange; 1842 objects were listed in the catalogue of its auction.

When we drove to Ouderkerk for lunch in "Paardenburg," Christopher and I talked about the descendants of Pieter Ondaatje and Christina Hoevenaar. Christopher knew that they had not returned to Ceylon.

I had come across a recent genealogical study which indicated that the four surviving children had married in the Dutch East Indies.

One son had become a professional soldier, an officer in the Engineering Corps, mentioned honorably in dispatches during some military operations. He was made a knight of the highest order for valor and received a statue somewhere on Java.

The soldier Ondaatje was honored by a statue, but the democrat is still waiting for one.

This soldier had a son who was a professional soldier, too; he died young without children.

The other son of Pieter Quint Ondaatje followed a career in the colonial administration and ended as Governor of a part of the wild island of Borneo. He retired to the Netherlands and died in the Hague. He must have been bitten by the Haafner bug as he got into trouble with his superiors for defending the local people against what he saw as injustices by the government.

This Ondaatje junior, a chip of the old block, had a son who also worked in the colonial service but did not attain the same heights as his father. He married twice, both times Christian Chinese women. His second wife had gone through life under the name of Lie Kwie Moy until she was baptised and had her name changed to Theodora Quint.

She gave the grandson of Pieter Quint Ondaatje three sons, but none of them was named Quint Ondaatje although their mother's name change would have seemed to lead to that.

These sons were born a hundred or more years ago. The genealogical study did not list their children, only mentioned that one of the sons had died in the Netherlands in 1969 and that the two others had chosen Indonesian nationality in 1951.

While I was still explaining the family tree of the Dutch Ondaatjes to the Ceylonese Ondaatje, we had arrived in Ouderkerk on the Amstel.

Before we entered Paardenburg, I casually mentioned that I had invited some guests for luncheon, a gentleman and two young ladies. I was greatly amused when Christopher, shaking hands and saying "Christopher Ondaatje," heard the gentleman reply "Eduard Ondaatje." After more than two hundred years, a Dutch Ondaatje and an Ondaatje of the Ceylonese branch shook hands.

As could be expected, the main course of the lunch consisted of shrimps. Our only table decoration was a bouquet of Dutch tulips.

No fog came to our assistance when we went to Ceylon to look for the old Ondaatjes there.

The wood of family trees which we entered in our search recalled Haafner's forests of Ceylon. Darkness in the shadows of leaves and branches, intertwined with creepers; out of reach, a hint of some exotic flower or fruit. A flash of birds, most often hidden in the shades, the toned-down twittering of their voices, like Homer's ghosts of human beings gone.

CHAPTER XVII

A family reunion. After more than two hundred years the Ceylonese and the Dutch branch of the Ondaatjes are meeting.

I had hoped that we could start our genealogical foot tour through the island of Ceylon in Jaffna, like Jacob Haafner. But the Tamil Tigers do not encourage historical expeditions. In fact, the Dutch Reformed Church in Jaffna, where the father of Governor Iman Falck lies buried and where Pieter Ondaatje's father preached, had been obliterated by fighting just before our visit to Sri Lanka. One should not look for old graves where there are too many fresh ones.
Wolvendaal Church in Colombo has been left in peace. The seething life of the East pulsates in the Pettah district around the church; inside nothing moves. The caretaker quickly changes from sarong into dark trousers and with a big smile on his dark face greets me and says that he is "de koster," the sexton.
I am in a Dutch eighteenth century church. Whitewashed walls, high windows filtering the light to cooler hues, the benches and pulpit of dark wood, the gentry's bench like a private theater box with elegant drawing room chairs. A hardstone floor with tombstones larger than the remains they cover, each one with the coat of arms of the deceased in low relief and with names, dates and Scripture texts in every style and form.

>   *Under this slab in a*
>   *coffin*
>   *lies the dead corpse and*
>   *sleeps*
>   *of. . . .*

The Wolvendaal Church in Colombo with Governor Falck's hatchment on the wall.

CHAPTER XVII

The koster plays some psalms on the organ, music still sung in Holland, composed in Calvin's Geneva in the sixteenth century, garbled by the koster into Sinhalese – Portuguese dancing rhythms.

Armorial shields hang on the walls: for the wife of van Angelbeeck, the last Dutch Governor who had to capitulate to the English in 1796, and for his daughter; and a large pyramidical composition crowned with the falcon of Iman Willem Falck, who was nicknamed "the Black Crow," and was considered the best Governor of Dutch Ceylon.

I find his tombstone, next to the one of the wife and only grandson of Joan Gideon Loten, the naturalist Governor and brother of the Utrecht Burgomaster of Pieter Ondaatje's time.

They were all reburied here, slabs and all, with English colonial pomp and military ceremony in the early 1800's, when the old church in the fort of Colombo was demolished.

The eighteenth century church registers are all kept, crisscross, in a cupboard with glass doors in the sacristy. They smell strongly of camphor.

I am interested in the seventeenth century when Dr. Ondaatje went to the fount of the old church and became a Christian. Those registers are kept elsewhere says the sexton.

I come closer to the Ondaatjes in the cool reading room of the National Archives of Colombo. The director, Dr. Garvin Wimalaratne, is a magician who seems to be keeping at least three balls in the air at the same time. While we talk to him in English about Ondaatjes and eighteenth century topography and I throw Dutch expressions around with him, he manages to handle several phone calls and other visitors or petitioners in Sinhala without giving any one of us the idea that he is busy. He knows Dutch and has worked in the State Archives in the Hague. He is a worthy successor to a line of distinguished archivists of Ceylon, who studied, translated and used the 7,000 odd volumes of material which the Dutch left after their 150 years on the island.

There I am leafing through volumes with mysterious sounding names, "Colombo Four Gravets School Thomboes." Pages and pages covered with clear eighteenth century Dutch handwriting giving precise information about landed property in each district under Dutch rule.

There they are, all the Ondaatjes of Ceylon. For a brief moment each one materializes before my eyes in a name written in sloping flourishes two and a half centuries ago, rarely noticed since then, died and forgotten for more than 200 years. A name and some dates under the heading:

"Chettys, inside"

MAGDALENA JURIE ONDAATJE	BAPT. 31 OCT. 1723
FRANCISCO TAMBIUNNA	MARRIED 26 NOV. 1729
CHILDREN SABINA	BAPT. 24 FEB. 1732
FRANCISCA	20 JULY 1738
JOAN ONDAATJE	10 AUG. 1729
SABINA PAULA	MARRIED 7 SEPT. 1732
	27 APRIL 1726, DIED 1790
MANUEL	20 JUNE 1738
THOME JURRIA ONDATIE	MARRIED 28 FEB. 1746
JOELIANNA FRANCISCA	
ANDERA JURY ONDATIE	9 MARCH 1722
ANNA ROEDERIGA	MARRIED 17 MAY 1733
MICHIEL JURI ONDATIE	OPPERM
ADRIANA PERERA	
ANDONE	BAPT. 1772
AGIDA	1777
FRANCISCO ONDATIE	BORN 1744
SABINA PIERIS	
MATEO	BAPT. 1747
MARIA	1750
PAULO ONDATIE	1721 OBIT 1780
LOLIANNA PIERIS	
PHILIP JOERIE ONDAATJE	
FRANCINA PIRIS	25 June 1797

I realized that I was lost and stuck, as Haafner had been in front of his deep ravine full of impenetrable brushwood. Here my travel companion did not offer to creep through so that we could link up a rope bridge.
That was unnecessary, we had already found the treasure. It lay scattered about in Thomboes and church registers. We only had to link the jewels together into "a necklace of emeralds." We needed a jeweller. Who else should this be but Dr. Wimalaratne.

Christopher asked him if he could provide the missing links; the link between Christopher and the founder of the family, the seventeenth century ancestor who came from Tanjore to cure the Dutch Governor's wife, and the link between

CHAPTER XVII

Pieter Quint Ondaatje and Christopher's direct forefathers. Dr. Wimalaratne was prepared to add another ball to the many he had in the air already.
That gave me time to go and look for Dutch Colombo.
Immediately I lost track again.
I wanted to have a photograph taken of Christopher in front of the portrait of Governor Falck. After the picture taken of Christopher looking disparagingly at the Stadhouder's chair in Utrecht, I wanted to balance the scales by having Christopher immortalized looking gratefully at Iman Falck. Iman Falck had been the benefactor of young Pieter Ondaatje, and his nephew Anton Reinhard Falck of old Pieter Ondaatje.
I had read that the Presidential Palace in Colombo housed a series of portraits of Dutch governors of Ceylon.
In the early 1900's, a Dutch diplomat visited the English Governor in Colombo and discovered that amongst the collection of portraits of former Governors at Government Lodge there was not a single Dutch one. Holland offered to present the missing links and after much searching in private collections and illustrated books, pictures of eight Dutch Governors were identified. The State Academy of Arts in Amsterdam selected a team of contemporary Dutch artists to paint eight portraits of similar format, each in the style of the period of the subject. In this way, a portrait of Falck was painted. The artist had to use the one original picture of Falck, in profile only. It is a watercolour done by Reimer,

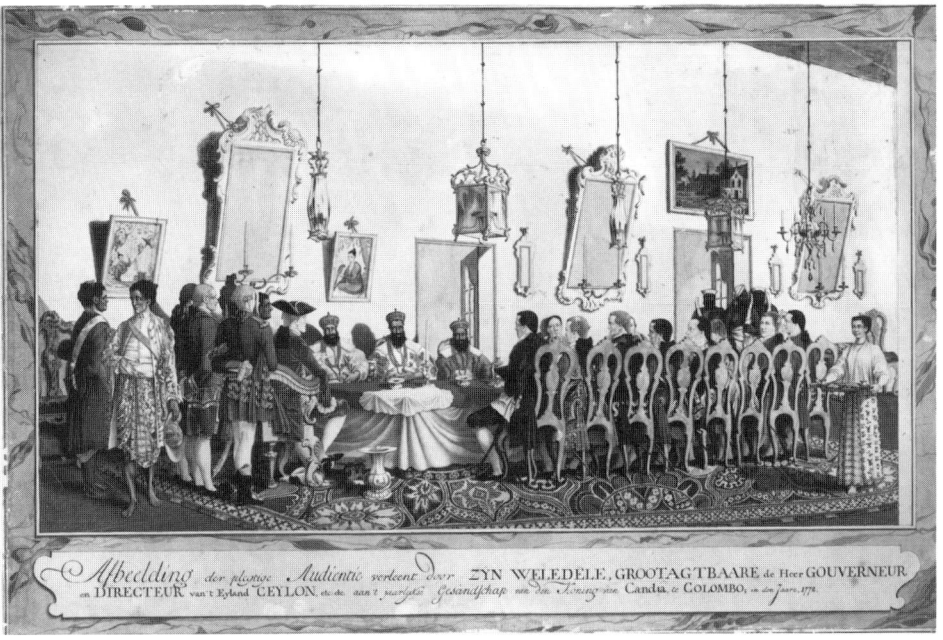

Envoys of the King of Kandy received by Governor Falck in Colombo, 1772.
by C. F. REIMER.

The lost portrait of Governor Falck, photographed by Nihal Fernando.

a German soldier of fortune who had a natural talent not only for painting but also for surgery. He became an under-surgeon in Colombo in Falck's days and thereafter a land-surveyor and ended his days in Batavia as a Lieutenant-Colonel and Director of Fortifications. A man of many parts.

On this watercolor, Falck is seen to receive Ambassadors from the King of Kandy in the reception hall of Government House. The Ambassadors look rather like Russian Orthodox prelates.

President's House in Colombo was occupied by the wife of President Premadasa. Because of the security situation, a special appointment long in advance

CHAPTER XVII

had to be made. While still in Canada, I had set it all up. When we arrived in Colombo, I reconfirmed the appointed day. We were given to understand that we did not need to be so specific. For about three weeks the session for a photograph in front of the portrait of Falck was kept pending. Then a few days before our departure, an official called me to say that the portrait was not in President's House. Mrs. Premadasa, already some time ago, had ordered the portraits to be removed to the National Archives.

I set out for the National Archives again, but nobody there had ever received the portraits of the Dutch Governors. I got deeper and deeper enmeshed in the impenetrable shrubbery. High officials who "knew Mrs. Premadasa well" offered to locate the portraits but either got enmeshed too, or were wiser and avoided the brushwood.

I was still involved in correspondence about the portrait when President Premadasa was assassinated by a fiery device supposedly planted by the Tamil Tigers. The missing Falck would not have been the only unsolved mystery which he took with him into the grave.

Two friends from our trip to Yala Wildpark knew about the portrait. Nihal Fernando, Sri Lanka's best known photographer, had taken pictures of the portraits some years ago, and Ismeth Raheem had written about them.

We continued to track the old Ondaatjes of Ceylon not on paper, not on canvas, but on stone.

One afternoon Christopher took me to St. Thomas', "their" church. It is indeed. The Ondaatje name outnumbers all other ones on the floor slabs and on the tablets on the walls. The wizzened little man, dark face, white Anglican robes, who sits in front of the simple barnlike edifice fills out with joy and pride when he recognizes the benefactor and his sister, who are doing him the honor of a visit.

The church was built in early English times on the spot of an earlier Catholic church in a former residential suburb called Mutwal, now a part of the overcrowded and ugly harbor section. The open yard and the old trees around St. Thomas' Church barely withstand the pressure of a whole village of shanty homes built right against the precinct walls. Garbage lies around in large piles, complete with mangy dogs; crows feed off the refuse and a stench of decay spoils the view over the harbor. The churchyard is green and overgrown. Loose gravestones have been arranged along a border of roses.

One stone is entirely covered with Tamil script.

In early English times, the church was sometimes called the Malabar Protestant Church, referring to the congregation and its old ties with South India, then called the Malabar coast.

The church inside is pleasantly cool. Some schoolchildren are doing homework on the benches. One wall tablet bears a dedication by Christopher, his brother Michael and their two sisters to the memory of their parents. Another tablet expresses the gratitude of the parish to Christopher for his liberal gifts to the church.

Gillian and I crawl over the floor and try to decipher the texts on the tombstones.

Profane feet wear out the names and dates of mortals, even the most sacred texts, on tombstones. The feet themselves leave no impression. Only Saints sometimes leave us a lasting imprint of their feet; Saint Stephen's in the snow, radiating heat "though the frost was cruel," and Lord Buddha's footprint on Adam's Peak. We do not hear about Christ's footprints. He wrote with His finger in the dust and gave His message in words which do not wear out: "Whoever is without sins, let him throw the first stone."

>REVd. MAs. J. ONDAATJE Mar.Por.
>   preacher died 15th April 1791 aged 33
>   and his wife
>CHRISTINA FERNANDO
>   died 2 Sep 1811 aged 45
>   DONA MARIA CONSTE
>   widow of
>MICHL J. ONDAATJE Doct of TOW
>   died 21 Aug 1827 aged 98

Doctor of town Michael Juriaan Ondaatje lived to an old age. Born under the Dutch, he saw the British take over when he was in his sixties and cured them of spleen and drink for many more years. He had the same names as the first and famous Doctor Ondaatje a hundred years before him.

This Doctor of town has survived in folk memory on Sri Lanka. When Christopher and I visited former President J.R. Jayawardene who with his eighty-seven years is emulating the Doctor in longevity, he told us a story about him. The Doctor had been asked to go to Kandy to cure Queen Muttu Kanamma Devi or was it Queen Venkadayammal, her sister? Both were beautiful South Indian Princesses married to King Sri Wikrama Rajasinghe.
The British had not yet invaded the interior.
Guided and guarded by the King's soldiers, the Doctor made the journey through the mountains, which for most Europeans who had dared to undertake it unescorted, had become a voyage of no return. In Kandy, he was received at an audience in the throne room where he was asked to kneel down in front of a curtain surrounded by prostrate nobles. The curtain was withdrawn to reveal another curtain through which a veiled shape became visible. That curtain too was drawn aside, and, after several more, each one more transparent than the preceding one, the Queen was revealed in her full splendor and beauty, seated on a throne.
She graciously welcomed Doctor Ondaatje in Tamil, who still kneeling at a distance replied in the same language and in the formulas prescribed by Court etiquette.

CHAPTER XVII

Dutch envoys received by the King of Kandy.
by JAN BRANDES, 1785.

Over the next days, the Doctor was regaled with further audiences and royal apparitions, during which the purpose of the Doctor's visit was gradually broached. Finally, Doctor Ondaatje was given an indication that the Queen's medical complaint lay in Her Majesty's legs. By now the old Doctor's own legs were bothering him. He had been on his knees for a long time and had not come closer to the royal legs.
He respectfully suggested that he could not get to the bottom of things unless the Queen would deign to submit the royal legs to a medical examination.
Doctor Ondaatje was immediately sent back to Colombo.
The consultation, however, not having had any beneficial effect on the Queen, Doctor Ondaatje was eventually invited back and was given the opportunity to inspect the Queen's legs and cure Her Majesty completely .
Was this long-lived doctor the grandfather of the Reverend Johan Jurgen Ondaatje, who became the first colonial chaplain of St. Thomas Church in 1825 and who was the great great grandfather of Christopher?

Christopher takes me to a large graveyard in one of the spacious, English colonial suburbs of Colombo where his direct ancestors are buried.
His great grandfather was Philip de Melho Jurgen Ondaatje (1831–1887), Crown Counsel of one of the districts of the island and married to Frances Sophia Morgan (1839–1920). The Morgans were pure British and had settled in Ceylon early in the nineteenth century.

Their son, Philip Francis Ondaatje, was Christopher's grandfather. Both Michael and Christopher have written about this grandfather and his estate in Kegalle, where Christopher took me for a visit. This grandfather married a Jonklaas; his son, Mervyn, a Gratiaen, all considered "Burghers."

Burgher, now spelled burger in modern Dutch, means citizen. In nineteenth century Ceylon, the word Burgher was used to describe those inhabitants who descended from European families who had settled on the island in the Dutch days and had continued to live more or less in a European way.

The descendants of the Portuguese were not called Burghers but Tupaz and were rather looked down upon as they had abandoned their Western ways.

A Portuguese name alone does not indicate that the bearer descends from a Portuguese ancestor. Most Sinhalese and Tamil who went over to Christianity in great numbers in Portuguese times would choose a Portuguese family name. Hence the hundreds of de Silvas, de Suzas, Fernandos and Pierisses in the telephone book of Colombo today.

In British times, the highest level of local society after the British themselves consisted of the "Burgher" families.

Mounting nationalism in the 50's and 60's, in which everything Sinhalese was revered and all immigrants from outside despised (although the Sinhalese had also come from abroad), made many "Burghers" emigrate to Australia and Canada. When we visited the island, this extreme nationalism had spent its force; but the effects are irreversible.

By strict definition, the Ondaatjes would not be considered "Burghers," as the founder of the family was not a European.

In the eighteenth century, the Ondaatjes had been classified as Chetties. Chetty was a Tamil synonym of the name of the third caste, that of the vaisya or traders, merchants and farmers; the first caste consisted of the priests, the second of the warriors.

The Sinhalese, although Buddhists, had preserved that same caste system.

Birds of one feather flock together, and it was therefore no wonder that when the biggest traders of that age, the Dutch, had gained a foothold on Ceylon, the trading Chetties came over in droves from Southern India to set up shop in Colombo.

Once the Chetties had established roots, they would want a physician who understood their needs and traditional ways of medicine. Such a physician would not necessarily be a Chetty or Vaisya himself. Among the Ondaatjes on Ceylon, and, as we found also among the Dutch Ondaatjes, the family tradition claims that the first Ondaatje who came to Ceylon as a doctor was of the Brahmin – or priestly – caste.

A court physician, such as Doctor Ondaatje in Tanjore, could hardly have belonged to the merchant caste but would in all likelihood have been a professional fulltime doctor with a profound knowledge acquired by study and practice of herbal medicine, astrology and spells and charms, and those doctors came from the Brahmin caste.

CHAPTER XVII

His descendants, who had become Christians and had therefore given up their distinctive Brahmin way of life, would be living in the Christian Chetty community of traders in Colombo and would over time have been classified as Chetties. They could not have been ranked as Brahmins anymore, as that would have implied that they had remained Hindus.
Later, in English times, the Ondaatjes were prominent in typical Burgher occupations such as the civil service and the law; Sri Lanka to this day follows Roman Dutch Law. They also married into English and Burgher families. Quite quickly they became absorbed into the Burghers of Ceylon.
Already in 1817 Ondaatjes appeared on petitions submitted to the authorities by the Burgher community.

Tamil, Sinhalese, Burghers,
Patriots, Orangemen, French,
Hoofts, Pesters, van Hogendorps,
Ondaatjes, Falcks, Haafner.
As Christopher and I were tracking our families of two hundred years ago in Amsterdam, Utrecht and on Ceylon, we came across the footprints of all of these and many more who had joined the track. Living creatures rose out of these prints; we were walking with Princes of Orange, Kings of Ceylon, burgomasters, citizens and burghers.

Some of the walkers had joined hands and supported each other on their way. The fathers of Governor Iman Falck and of Pieter Ondaatje, as young men, had sailed to the Dutch Republic in each other's company. Anton Reinhard Falck reached out his hand to Pieter Ondaatje when he was losing his way.
More often, those whose paths had crossed fell out with each other. Burgomasters opposed Princes, the Ceylonese resisted the Dutch, Patriots clashed with Orangemen, citizens crossed their councillors, the Prussians, in agreement with England, invaded Holland to suppress freedom, the French to restore it; the English fought the Americans, took Ceylon from the Dutch, and brought them a King instead.

As we kept following the footsteps, we found the wanderers fall in line.
The daughter of Henrik Danielszoon Hooft, the symbol of Patriotism, married the hero of the Orange party, Admiral van Kinsbergen;
Father Hooft's granddaughter became the wife of the restorer of the House of Orange, Gijsbert Karel van Hogendorp.
Hooft's nephew's great great grandson, my own grandfather, married the great granddaughter of the nephew of Lieutenant-Stadhouder Pesters and my own godchild, a daughter of my first cousin Hooft, married the last male member of the de Pesters family.
Daniel Hooft Danielszoon, removed from government by Stadhouder William, helped to restore William's son as King William.

Samuel Wiselius, who had supported revolutionary governments for nineteen years, ended his days as Head of Police of the legitimate government.
Pieter Ondaatje, demagogue for democracy, died as Chief Judge of a colonial High Court of Justice.

Less than two centuries later the English, hand in hand with the Americans and Canadians, liberated Holland and lost Ceylon; the Dutch brought portraits of Dutch Governors to the Ceylonese, which they lost.

The footprints which we followed most closely were those of Henrik Danielszoon Hooft and Pieter Ondaatje, the aged burgomaster of mighty Amsterdam and the young university student from the colonies.
These two were far apart in age and background, as far as Ceylon is from Holland.
Their tracks ran parallel during political upheavals and civil war in the Netherlands; they continued to run together in the dust of exile.
Their road led to the future, to democracy. Their traces left a lasting impression.

Regrets Only

In this book I have tried to introduce Dutch history with the help of some table decorations embellishing a banquet held in Amsterdam in 1783. For those readers who like to get their facts straight, I have to confess that although John Adams, as envoy of the United States of America had been invited to this dinner as one of the guests of honor, he had had to apologize. The negotiations for a peace treaty between his country and England required his presence in Paris. I have omitted to mention the other guest of honor because he does not play a role in my story. He was the pensionary of Amsterdam, van Berckel, whose brother had just been appointed first envoy of the Dutch Republic to the United States and would be sailing out later that year together with his young nephew Gijsbert Karel van Hogendorp who does play a part in this book, and a very important part at that.

In describing this dinner which stood so clearly in the sign of Liberty, I have allowed myself some further poetic licence. I used as an illustration a print which was published a few years later at the occasion of a very similar dinner, at the same location, with Father Hooft in the chair again.

BIBLIOGRAPHY

Adolus de Opmerker, *Staatkundige bijdragen* (Utrecht, 1784).
Angevent, W. J., *Het gevecht bij Vreeswijk 9 mei 1787* (Jaarboek Oud-Utrecht, 1987).
Anthonisz, R.G., *Governor Falck's audience to the Kandyan ambassadors in 1772* (Journal of the Dutch Burgher Union of Ceylon, (JDBUC), 2, Colombo, 1909).
Anthonisz, R.G., *The Dutch occupation of Kandy in 1765* (JDBUC, 21, Colombo 1932).
Arasaratnam, S., *Dutch power in Ceylon, 1658–1687* (Amsterdam, 1958).
Arends, H., *Beknopt verhaal van de zevenjaarige troublen in de Vereenigde Nederlanden, voornaamlijk te Amsterdam van 1780 tot 1787, onder de Stadhouderlijke Regeering van Prins Willem de Vijfde* (Amsterdam, 1789).
Authentique Bijlagen tot de Gebeurtenissen van den 12 Juny 1798 (Amsterdam, 1799).
Authentique Bijlagen tot de Geschiedenis der Omwenteling van 22 January 1798 en van het Arrest en Ontslag van 28 leden der Nationale Vergadering (Amsterdam, 1799).
Balbian Verster, J.F.L., *Burgemeesters van Amsterdam in de zeventiende- en achttiende eeuw* (Zutphen, 1932).
Baldaeus, Philippus, *Naauwkeurige Beschryvinge van Malabar en Choromandel . . . en het machtige Eyland Ceylon . . .* (Amsterdam, 1672).
Beaufort, Henriette L.T. de, *Gijsbert Karel van Hogendorp, Grondlegger van het Koninkrijk* (Rotterdam, 1948).
Beaufort, W.H. de, *Brieven van en aan Joan Derk van der Capellen tot de Poll* (2 delen, Utrecht, 1879–93).
Bellamy, Jacobus, *Gezangen* (Amsterdam, 1785)
Bellamy, Jacobus, *Gezangen mijner jeugd en naagelaaten gedichten* (Haarlem, 1790).
Blok, P.J. en Molhuysen, P.C., *Nieuw Nederlandsch Biografisch Woordenboek* (10 delen, Leiden, 1911–37).
Boeles, W.B.S., *De Patriot J.H. Swildens* (Leeuwarden, 1884).
Boels, Henk, *Binnenlandse Zaken. Ontstaan en ontwikkeling van een departement in de Bataafse tijd, 1795–1806* ('s-Gravenhage, 1993).
Boer, M.G. de (red), *Het Dagboek van Jacob Bicker Raye, 1732–1772* (Amsterdam, z.j.).
Bosch, Bernardus, *Gedichten, dl 3* (Leiden, 1803).
Bossard, Mr J.C. en Spier, Jo, *Aan d'Amstel en het IJ. 100 jaar bouwen en brouwen* (Uit de geschiedenis van de Amstelbrouwerij 1870–1970, Amsterdam z.j.).
Bouwens, R.L., *Aan Zijne Committenten* (Amsterdam, 1797).
Boxer, C.R., *The Dutch seaborne empire 1600–1800* (London, 1965 / Harmondsworth, 1973).
Boyd, J.P., ed,. *The papers of Thomas Jefferson* (Princeton, N.J., 1950)
Breen, Dr Joh. C., *Napoleon in Amsterdam* (Jaarboek Amstelodamum, 1931).
Brohier, R.L., *De Wolvendaalsche kerk* (Colombo, 1957 rev. ed.)
Brohier, R.L., *Land, maps and surveys* (2 vols., Colombo, 1950–51).
Brohier, R.L., *'Adams Berg'* (JDBUC, Colombo, 1930).
Brugmans, H., *Opkomst en bloei van Amsterdam* (Amsterdam, 1944).
Bruin, Dr R.E. de, *Burgers op het kussen* (Zutphen, 1986).

Bruin, Renger de, *Revolutie in Utrecht* (Utrecht, 1987).
Bruin, R.E. de, *De tweede ronde* (Jaarboek Oud-Utrecht, 1987).
Burg, Mr Dr V.A.M. van der, *Zeist en het geslacht de Pesters* (Van de Poll-Stichting, Zeist, 1981).
Burmannus, Johannes, *Thesaurus Zeylanicus* (Amsterdam, 1737).
Butterfield, L.H. et al., eds., *The Diary and Autobiography of John Adams* (4 vols., Cambridge, Mass., 1961).
Byvanck, W.G.C., *Bataafsch Verleden, 'Dorus Droefheid'* (Zutphen, 1917).
Campen, Mr J.W.C. van, *De Stadskelder (Jaarboek Oud-Utrecht, 1930)*
Capellen, Joan Derk van der, *De wekker van de Nederlandse Natie* (Zwolle, 1984).
Capellen tot den Pol, Joan Derk Baron van der, *Aan het volk van Nederland. Het Democratisch Manifest* (1781), (Uitgegeven door W.F. Wertheim en A.H. Wertheim-Gyse Weenink, Amsterdam, 1966).
Carlyle, Thomas, *History of Friedrich II of Prussia called Frederick the Great* (Leipzig, 1858–1865).
Casie Chitty, Simon, *The Tamil Plutarch* (Jaffna, 1859).
Catt, Heinrich de, *Tagebuch* (R. Kosser in Publicationen aus den K. Preuzischen Staatsarchiven, Berlin, 1884).
Chevalier, J.W., *Vader Hooft in Groningen* (Groningsche Volksalmanak van 1879).
Christiaans, P.A., *Ondaatje* (De Indische Navorscher, jrg 2, 1989 nr. 4).
Cobban, A., *Ambassadors and Secret Agents. The diplomacy of the First Earl of Malmesbury at the Hague* (London, 1954).
Colenbrander, H.T., *Aanteekeningen betreffende de vergadering van Vaderlandsche Regenten te Amsterdam 1783-87* (Bijdragen en Mededelingen van het Historisch Genootschap (B.M.H.G.), deel 20, Amsterdam, 1899).
Colenbrander, H.T., *Brieven van G.K. van Hogendorp 1788–93* (B.M.H.G. 31, 1910).
Colenbrander, H.T., *De Bataafsche Republiek* (Amsterdam, 1908).
Colenbrander, H.T., *De patriottentijd, hoofdzakelijk naar buitenlandsche bescheiden* ('s-Gravenhage, 1897–1899).
Davies, Mrs C.M., *Memorials and Times of Pieter Philip Juriaan Quint Ondaatje* (Utrecht, 1870).
Democraten, de, (3 delen, Amsterdam, 1796–1798).
Dichterswoningen te Utrecht door C. L. v.d. G. (maandblad Oud-Utrecht 1947).
Dirks, J., *De Uitgewekenen uit Nederland naar Frankrijk 1787–1795* (Amsterdam, 1868).
Dudok van Heel, Dr A.C., *De familie van Pieter Cornelisz Hooft* (Jaarboek Centraal Bureau voor Genealogie, 1981).
Dumbar, Gerhard, *De oude en nieuwe Constitutie der Vereenigde Staten van Amerika, uit de beste schriften in haare Gronden ontvouwd* (3 delen, Amsterdam 1793–1796).
Dunning, Albert, *Count Unico Wilhelm van Wassenaer (1692-1766), A master unmasked or the Pergolesi-Ricciotti puzzle solved* (Buren, 1980)
Echte Bescheiden omtrent het waar gebeurde bij de aanhouding van mevrouw de prinses van Oranje-Nassau in het jaar 1787 (Amsterdam, 1787).
Eeghen, Dr I.H. van, *Dertig jaar archiefonderzoek Casanova - Symons - Hooft* (Jaarboek Amstelodamum, 1978).
Eeghen, Dr I.H. van, *Inventarissen van de familie-archieven Heshuysen, Hooft, Hooft van Woudenberg* ('s-Gravenhage, 1960).
Eenige aantekeningen wegens het gebeurde in Utrecht in 1786 en 1787 (In Kroniek van het Historisch Genootschap, Utrecht 1870 en 1871).
Elias, J., *De vroedschap van Amsterdam 1578–1795* (2 delen, Haarlem, 1903-5).

Eyk, P. van der, *Nieuwe Nederlandsche Jaarboeken, of vervolg der Merkwaardigste Geschiedenissen die voorgevallen zijn in de Vereenigde Provinciën, de Generaliteits-landen en de volkplantingen van den Staat* (Amsterdam / Leiden, z.j.).

Falck, A.R., *Gedenkschriften* (Uitgegeven door H.T. Colenbrander, Rijks Geschiedkundige Publicatiën, kleine serie 13, 's-Gravenhage, 1913).

Ferguson, D., *Joan Gideon Loten, the naturalist governor of Ceylon (1752–1757) and the Ceylonese artist De Bevere* (Journal of the Royal Asiatic Society, Ceylon Branch, (IRASCB), 19:58, 1907–1908).

Freeman, D. S. *George Washington, A biography* (New York).

Fruin, Robert, *De tijd van de Witt en Willem III* (2 delen, 's-Gravenhage, 1929).

Fruin, Robert, *Geschiedenis der Staatsinstellingen in Nederland tot den val der Republiek* (Uitgegeven door Dr H.T. Colenbrander, 2de bijgewerkte druk 1922, ingeleid door Prof. Dr. I. Schöffer, 's-Gravenhage, 1980).

Gaastra, Femme S., *De geschiedenis van de VOC* (Zutphen, 1991).

Gabriels, A.J.C.M., *De heren als dienaren en de dienaar als heer. Het stadhouderlijk stelsel in de tweede helft van de achttiende eeuw* ('s-Gravenhage, 1990).

Gedenkstukken der algemeene geschiedenis van Nederland van 1789 to 1840 (Uitgegeven door H.T. Colenbrander, 10 delen in 21 banden, 's-Gravenhage, 1905–1922).

Geijl, Dr P., *Oranje en Stuart* (Utrecht, 1939).

Geijl, Dr P., *De Bataafsche Revolutie*, and *Patriotten en N.S.B.ers* (In: Studies en Strijdschriften, Groningen, 1958).

Geijl, Dr P., *De patriottenbeweging 1780–1787* (Amsterdam, 1947).

Geijl, Dr P., *De Witten-oorlog. Een pennestrijd in 1757* (Amsterdam, 1953).

Geijl, Dr P., *Kernproblemen van onze geschiedenis* (Utrecht, 1937).

Geijl, Dr P., *Revolutiedagen in Amsterdam, Prins Willem IV en de Doelistenbeweging* ('s-Gravenhage, 1936).

Gelder, Dr H.A.E. van, *De levensbeschouwing van Cornelis Pieterszoon Hooft, burgemeester van Amsterdam 1547–1626* (Amsterdam, 1918, heruitgave Utrecht, 1982).

Goonetileke, H.A.I., *A bibliography of Ceylon. A systematic guide to the literature on the land, people, history and culture published in western languages from the 16th century to the present day*, (3 vols., and suppl., Bibliotheca Asiatica: 5,14 Zug 1970, 1976).

Goor, J. van, *De VOC op Ceylon* (In: Het machtige Eyland Ceylon en de VOC, 's-Gravenhage, 1988).

Goor, J. van, *Jan Kompenie as schoolmaster. Dutch education in Ceylon 1690–1795* (Groningen, 1978).

Graaff, H.J. van de, *Brieven van en aan H.J. van de Graaff 1816–1826.* (Uitgegeven door P.H. Kemp, Batavia 1901, 1902).

Grijzenhout, F., *Feesten voor het Vaderland* (Zwolle, 1989).

Groen van Prinsterer, G., *Handboek der Geschiedenis van het Vaderland* (Amsterdam, 1895).

Grondwettige Herstelling van Nederlands Staatswezen (2 delen, Amsterdam, 1784–6).

Haafner, J., *De werken van* (Bezorgd door J.A. de Moor en P.G.E.I.J. van der Velde, Zutphen, 1992–1997).

Haafner, J., *Lotgevallen en vroege zeereizen* (Amsterdam, 1820).

Haafner, J., *Reis te voet door het eiland Ceylon* (Amsterdam, 1810).

Haafner, J., *Reize in eenen palanquin; of lotgevallen en merkwaardige aanteekeningen op een reize langs de kusten van Orixa en Choromandel* (2 delen, Amsterdam, 1808).

Haasse, Hella S., *Schaduwbeeld of het geheim van Appeltern* (Amsterdam, 1989).

Hardenbroek, G.J. van, *Gedenkschriften* (Uitgegeven door F.J.L Krämer en A.J. van der Meulen, Dl. I–VI, Werken Historisch Genootschap, 3de serie 14, 17, 24, 36, 39, 40, Amsterdam, 1901–1918).

Hartog, J., *De Patriotten en Oranje van 1747–1787* (Amsterdam, 1882).
Hedendaagsche Historie of tegenwoordige Staat van alle volken, delen XXI en XXII, *tegenwoordige Staat van Utrecht* (Amsterdam, 1758 en 1772).
Heniger, J., *Hendrik Adriaan van Reede tot Drakenstein (1636–1691) and Hortus malabaricus. A contribution to the history of Dutch colonial history* (Rotterdam / Boston, 1986).
Historical Journael van tghene ghepasseert is vanweghen drie schepen ghevaren uyt Zeelandt naer d'Oost-Indien, onder 't beleyt van Joris van Spilbergen. Anno 1601 tot in 't Eylant Ceylon (Delft, 1605).
Hocks, Else, *Paus Adriaan VI* (Amsterdam, z.j.).
Hoek, D., *Casanova in Holland* (Zaltbommel, 1977).
Hogendorp, G.K. van, *Brieven en Gedenkschriften* (4 dclcn, 's-Gravenhage, 1866–1887).
Hooft, Cornelis Pietersz, *Memoriën en Adviezen* (Uitgegeven door Dr H.A.E. van Gelder, Utrecht, 1871, deel I; Utrecht, 1925, deel II).
Hooft, Pieter Cornelisz, *Nederlandsche Historien* (Amsterdam en Leiden, 4e druk, 1703).
Horst, D. van der, *Van Republiek tot Koninkrijk. De vormende jaren van Anton Reinhard Falck, 1777–1813* (Amsterdam, 1985).
Hulzen, A. van, *Utrecht in de patriottentijd* (Zaltbommel, 1966).
Jets Zaakelijks voor Utrechts burgers; of het Adieu van de Pesteriaansche lijftrauwanten. (anoniem pamflet, 1783)
Israel, J. T., *Dutch primacy in world trade, 1585–1740* (Oxford, 1989).
Jong, M. de, *Joan Derk van der Capellen, Staatkundig levensbeeld uit de wordingstijd van de moderne demokratie in Nederland* (1922).
Jorissen, Th., *Anton Reinhard Falck, Herinneringsrede* (Amsterdam, 1877).
Jorissen, Th., *De overgave van Amsterdam in Januari 1795* (Amsterdam, 1884).
Jorissen, Th., *De patriotten te Amsterdam in 1794* (Amsterdam, 1875).
Kluit, M.E., *Cornelis Felix van Maanen tot het herstel der onafhankelijkheid* (Groningen, 1953).
Kluit, W.P. Sautijn, *De Duinkerksche Historische Courant* (Bijdragen voor Vaderlandsche Geschiedenis en Oudheidkunde (B.V.G.O.), 3e reeks, 4, 1888).
Kluit, W.P. Sautijn, *De Politieke Kruyer* (B.V.G.O.). 3e reeks, 1, 1882).
Kluit, W.P. Sautijn, *Janus; de Politieke Blixem; en beider gevolg* (Ned. Spectator 347, 1867).
Knox, Robert, *An historical relation of the island Ceylon* (London, 1681).
Knox, Robert, *An historical relation of the island of Ceylon* (Second edition together with his autobiography, edited by J.J.P. Paulusz, 2 vols, Sri Lanka, 1989).
Knuttel, W.P.C., *Catalogus van de pamfletten-verzameling, berustende in de Koninklijke Bibliotheek* (9 delen, 's-Gravenhage, 1889–1920; herdruk Utrecht 1978).
Kok, Jac. en Fokke, J., *Geschiedenissen der Vereenigde Nederlanden voor de vaderlandsche Jeugd* (25 delen, Amsterdam, 1793–1795).
Koolemans Beijnen (red.), *Historisch gedenkboek der herstelling van Neêrlandsch onafhankelijkheid in 1813* (4 delen, Haarlem, 1912–1914).
Kroes-Ligtenberg, Chr., *Dr. Wybo Fijnje (1750–1809). Belevenissen van een journalist in de Patriottentijd* (Assen, 1957).
Leeb, I. Leonard, *The Ideological Origins of the Batavian Revolution. History and Politics in the Dutch Republic 1747–1800* (The Hague, 1973).
Lennep, Mr J. van, *Feestrede ter viering van het vijfenzeventig jarig bestaan des genootschaps Doctrina et Amicitia te Amsterdam* (Amsterdam, 1864).
Limburg Brouwer, P. van, *Het leven van Mr Samuel Iperuszoon Wiselius* (Groningen, 1846).

Ludovici, Leopold, *Lapidarium Zeylanicum of Ceylon* (Colombo, 1877).
Luzac, E., *Hollands Rijkdom . . . behelzende den oorsprong van den Koophandel, en van de Magt van dezen Staat . . .* (4 delen, Leiden, 1780–3).
Malone, Dumas, *Jefferson & The Ordeal of Liberty* (New York, NY., 1969).
Marel, van der, *De afstamming van Paus Adriaan VI* (Maandblad Oud-Utrecht 1927).
Motley, J.L., *The Rise of the Dutch Republic* (London, 1903).
Motley, J.L., *The United Netherlands* (London, 1904).
Mout, Dr M.E.H.N., *Plakkaat van Verlatinghe 1581* ('s-Gravenhage, 1979).
Muller, F., *De Nederlandsche geschiedenis in platen: beredeneerde beschrijving van Nederlandsche historieplaten, zinneprenten en historische kaarten* (4 delen, Amsterdam, 1863–1882; herdruk Utrecht, 1970).
Naber, Joh. W.A., *Prinses Wilhelmina* (Amsterdam, 1908).
Naber, J.W.A. (red.), *Correspondentie der Stadhouderlijke familie 1770–1820* (6 delen, 's-Gravenhage, 1931–1936).
Nauwkeurig Historisch Verhaal van de verrichtingen der Pruisische Troupen voor Amsterdam (Amsterdam, 1788).
Nijland, J.A., *Leven en werken van Jacobus Bellamy 1756–1786* (2 delen, Leiden, 1917).
Nypels, G., *Hoe Nederland Ceylon verloor* (1908).
Omstandig en Echt Relaas van het geen, zoo bij 't aanhouden van Haare Koninglyke Hoogheid Mevrouw de Princesse van Oranje en Nassau, op deszelfs Reis aan de Vlist tussen Schoonhoven en Haastrecht, als by deszelfs Arrivement aan de Goejanverwelle-Sluis, en verblyf aldaar is voorgevallen, op Donderdag den 28 Juny (Amsterdam, 1787).
Ondaatje, Christopher, *The man-eater of Punanai* (Toronto, 1992).
Ondaatje, Mathew, *Peter Ondaatje of Ceylon* (In: The Leisure Hour, Colombo 1867, reprinted in the Ceylon antiquary IX part 1, Colombo, 1924).
Ondaatje, Michael, *Running in the family* (Toronto, 1982).
Ondaatje, Mr P.Ph. Juriaan Quint, *Bijdragen tot de geschiedenis der omwenteling in 1787* (2 delen, Duinkerken, 1791–1792).
Ondaatje, M.P.J., *A tabular list of original works and translations published by the late Dutch government of Ceylon at their printing press at Colombo* (JRASCB, 1865).
Palmer, R.R., *Much in Little: The Dutch Revolution of 1795* (In Journal of Modern History, XXVI, 1954).
Palmer, R.R., *The Age of Democratic Revolution. A political history of Europe and America, 1760–1800* (2 vols. Princeton 1966/67).
Pater, Dr J.C.H. de, *De familie Falck in de patriottentijd* (Amsterdam, 1943).
Paulus, P., *Het Nut der Stadhouderlijke Regering* (Alkmaar, 1772–3).
Paulus, P., *Verklaring der Unie van Utrecht* (4 delen, Utrecht, 1775–7).
Peyster, Henri de (ed.), *Journal de G.K. van Hogendorp pendant les troubles de 1787* (B.M.H.G. XXVII).
Pfau, Theodorus Philippus, *Geschiedenis van den Veldtogt der Pruissen in Holland, in MDCCLXXXVII* (Amsterdam, 1792).
Pijman, G.J., *Bijdragen tot de voornaamste gebeurtenissen, voorgevallen in de Republiek der vereenigde Nederlanden* (Utrecht, 1826).
Politieke Blixem, de (Leiden, 1797–1798).
Politieke Kruyer, de (10 delen, Amsterdam, 1782–1787).
Portengen, Dr Alberta J., *De begrafenis van Vader Hooft te Vreeland* (Jaarboekje Nifterlake, 1918).
Post van den Neder-Rhyn, de (11 delen, Utrecht, 1781–1787).
Potjewijd, K., *Onderzoek naar de betekenis en oorsprong van de positie van Jan Pesters en Willem Nicolaas Pesters in Utrecht in de achttiende eeuw* (Ongepubliceerde doctoraalscriptie, z.j.).

Prud'homme van Reine, Dr R.B., *Jan Hendrik van Kinsbergen 1735–1819* (Amsterdam, 1990).
Raat, A.J.P., *Enige voorwerpen uit de nalatenschap van Joan Gideon Loten (1710–1789)*, (Tijdschrift voor de Geschiedenis der geneeskunde, natuurwetenschappen, wiskunde en techniek, 2, 1979).
Raat, A.J.P., *Joan Gideon Loten (1710–1789) en zijn collectie van platen en dieren uit Ceylon* (In: Het machtige Eyland Ceylon en de VOC, 's-Gravenhage, 1988).
Raven-Hart, R., *The Dutch wars with Kandy, 1764–66* (Colombo, 1964).
Raven-Hart, R. (transl. and ed.), *Germans in Dutch Ceylon. Von der Behr (1668), Herport (1669), Schweitzer (1682) and Fryke (1692)*, (Colombo, 1953).
Raven-Hart, R. (transl. and ed.), *Heydt's Ceylon, being the relevant sections of the 'Allerneuester geographische- und topographischer Schauplatz von Afrika und Ost-Indien', Wilhemsdorf 1744* (Colombo, 1952).
Reimers, E. (ed.), *Memoir of Joan Gideon Loten 1752–1757* (Selections from the Dutch Records of the Ceylon Government no. 4, Colombo, 1935).
Reimers, E. (ed.), *The Dutch Parish Registers (School tombo's) of Ceylon* (Colombo, 1950).
Reinders, Henk, *De Pesters en de Niënhof* (van de Poll-Stichting, Zeist, 1987).
Rijn, G. van, en Ommeren, C. van, *Atlas van Stolk. Katalogus der Historie-, Spot- en Zinneprenten betrekkelijk de geschiedenis van Nederland* (10 delen, Amsterdam, 1895–1933).
Rogge, C., *Geschiedenis der Staatsregeling voor het Bataafsche Volk* (Amsterdam, 1799).
Rogge, C., *Tafereel van de Geschiedenis der Jongste Omwenteling* (Amsterdam, 1796).
Romein, Jan & Annie, *Erflaters van onze beschaving* (4 dln, Amsterdam, 1938–1940).
Sas, N.C.F. van, *Politiek als leerproces: het patriottisme in Utrecht 1783–1787* (Jaarboek Oud-Utrecht, 1987).
Schama, S., *Patriots and Liberators. Revolution in the Netherlands, 1780–1813* (New York, 1977).
Schimmelpenninck, Rutger Jan, *De Imperio Populari, caute temperato* (1784).
Schulte Nordholt, J.W., *Gijsbert van Hogendorp in America, 1783–1784*, Acta Historiae Neerlandicae, X (1978).
Schulte Nordholt, J.W., *Voorbeeld in de verte. De invloed van de Amerikaanse revolutie in Nederland* (Baarn, 1979). Translated by H.H. Rowen, *The Dutch Republic and American Independence* (London, 1982).
Schutte, G.J., *De Nederlandsche Patriotten en de Koloniën* (Groningen, 1974).
Schutte, G.J., *Willem IV en Willem V* (In C.A. Tamse, red., Nassau en Oranje in de Nederlandse geschiedenis, Alphen a/d Rijn, 1979).
Sillem, J.A., *De Politieke en Staathuishoudkundige Werkzaamheid van I.J.A. Gogel* (Amsterdam, 1864).
Silva, R.K. de, en Beumer, W.G.M., *Illustrations and views of Dutch Ceylon 1602–1796* (London / Leiden, 1988).
Someren, J.F. van, *Bibliotheek der Rijksuniversiteit te Utrecht. Pamfletten etc.* (Utrecht, 1915).
Thorbecke, J.R., *Historische Schetsen* ('s-Gravenhage, 1872).
Vaderlandsche Chocolaad (Amsterdam, 1796).
Veeger, L., *Het verlies van Ceylon aan de Engelsen* (In: Het machtig Eyland Ceylon en de VOC, 's-Gravenhage, 1988).
Veer, Paul van 't, *Daendels, Maarschalk van Holland* (Zeist, 1963).
Vijlbrief, I., *Van anti-aristocratie tot democratie. Een bijdrage tot de politieke en sociale geschiedenis der stad Utrecht* (Amsterdam, 1950).
Voltaire, *Précis du Siècle de Louis XV* (Maastricht, 1781).

Vreede, G.W., *Bijdragen tot de geschiedenis der omwenteling van 1795–1798* (Amsterdam, 1847–1851).
Vreede, G.W., *Friederike Sophie Wilhelmine, gemalin van den Stadhouder Willem V en Laurens Pieter van de Spiegel, Raadpensionaris eerst van Zeeland, daarna van Holland* (Utrecht, 1868).
Vreede, G.W., *Geschiedenis der diplomatie van de Bataafsche Republiek* (Utrecht, 1863).
Vreede, G.W., *Mr Laurens Pieter van de Spiegel en zijne tijdgenooten* (Middelburg, 1874–1877).
Vreede, P., *Mijn Levensloop* (Hilversum, 1994)
Vries, Joh. de, *De economische achteruitgang der Republiek in de achttiende eeuw* (diss. G.U. Amsterdam, 1959).
Wagenaar, C.W., *9 mei 1787: een merkwaardige datum uit den Utrechtschen Patriottentijd* (Utrechtsch Jaarboekje, 1905).
Wagenaar, J, *Vaderlandsche Historie, vervattende de geschiedenissen der Vereenigde Nederlanden.* (Door J. Munniks). Amst. 1781–1787. 17 dln.
Wagenaar, J, *Vaderlandsche Historie. Ten onmiddelijke vervolge van Wagenaar's Vaderlandsche historie.* (Door P. Loosjes). Amst., 1788–1789. 3 dln.
Wagenaar, J, *Vaderlandsche historie vervattende de geschiedenissen der Vereenigde Nederlanden, zints den aanvang der Noord-Americaansche onlusten. Ten vervolge van Wagenaar's Vaderlandsche historie.* Amst., 1786–1811. 48 dln.
Washington, George *The Papers of George Washington,* Confederation Series, ed. W.W. Abbott (Charlottesville and London).
Wedgwood, C.V., *William the Silent* (London, 1944).
Wieder, F.C. et al (red.), *De reis van Joris van Spilbergen naar Ceylon, Atjeh en Bantam 1601–1604* (Werken van de Linschoten-Vereeniging, nr. 38, 's-Gravenhage, 1933).
Wijk, F.W. van, *De Republiek en Amerika 1776 en 1782* (Leiden, 1921).
Wijnen, H.A. van, *Vorst Willem, het is alles Uw schuld* (Amsterdam, 1987).
Winter, Jhr Dr P.J. van, *Het aandeel van den Amsterdamschen handel aan den opbouw van het Amerikaansche Gemeenebest* (Werken Ned. Econ. Hist. Archief 7, 9, 's-Gravenhage, 1927, 1933).
Winter, P.J. van, *American Finance and Dutch investments* (Arno, New York).
Wit, Dr C.H.E. de, *De Nederlandse revolutie van de achttiende eeuw 1780–1787* (Oirsbeek, 1974).
Wit, Dr C.H.E. de, *De strijd tussen aristocratie en democratie in Nederland 1780–1848* (Heerlen, 1965).
Wit, Dr C.H.E. de, *Het ontstaan van het moderne Nederland 1780–1848 en zijn geschiedschrijving* (Oirsbeek, 1978).
Witte van Citters, Jhr J. de, *Contracten van Correspondentie en Andere Bijdragen* ('s-Gravenhage, 1873).
Zappey, W.M., *De economische en politieke werkzaamheden van Johannes Goldberg* (diss. G.U. Amsterdam, Alphen a/d Rijn, 1967).

PROVENANCE OF THE ILLUSTRATIONS

Rijksmuseum-Stichting, p. 25; 38; 49; 83; 108; 153; 169; 173; 182; 186; 189; 194; 197; 199; 209; 212; 213; 230; 234
The Natural History Museum, London, p. 109
Archiv fur Kunst und Geschichte, Berlin, p. 120
Overijssels-Museum, Zwolle, p. 36
Amsterdams Historisch Museum, p. 129; 206
Stichting Iconografisch Bureau, Den Haag, p. 41; 137; 171; 176; 210
Universiteitsbibliotheek, Leiden, p. 10; 13; 123
Stichting Atlas van Stolk, Rotterdam, p. 46; 59; 131
Topografisch-Historische Atlas of the municipal archives, Utrecht, p. 18; 56; 111; 112; 114; 135
Historisch-topografische Atlas, Gemeentelijke archiefdienst, Amsterdam, p. 60; 132; 133; 161; 163
Gemeentearchief, Amsterdam, p. 121
Algemeen Rijksarchief, Den Haag, p. 200
Koninklijke Verzamelingen Den Haag, with gracious permission of H. R. H. Princess Juliana of the Netherlands, p. 20
Koninklijk Instituut voor Taal, Land- en Volkenkunde, Leiden, p. 15
Jonkheer P. C. Hooft, Den Haag, p. 177
Christopher Ondaatje, London, 96; 98
H. T. J. T. Modderman, Monaco, p. 220; 223; 226
The author, p. 9; 24; 27; 30; 32; 53; 64; 72; 75; 86; 89; 92; 97; 99; 103; 127; 128; 130; 134; 150; 154; 157; 179; 180; 238
Private collection, through the Mount Vernon Ladies' Association, Mount Vernon, Virginia, p. 146

The portrait of Pieter Quint Ondaatje on p. 18 is a "physionotrace" drawn by Fouquet and engraved by Chrétien, Cour St. Honoré à Paris, and is here rendered in reverse.
The illustration on p. 46 is after a drawing by Anthony Ziesenis, dated 1783 and engraved by his son Reinier Ziesenis in 1796.

INDEX OF PERSONAL NAMES

Abbema, Balthasar Elias 117, 124, 160, 162, 170
Adams, Abigail 162
Adams, John 6, 7, 38, 39, 43, 47, 52, 114, 116, 162, 164, 192, 222, 239
Adams, John Quincey 48, 183
Adolus the Observer 54, 81
Angelbeeck, governor van 228
Anna 88, 90, 105
Antrim, Baron of 76
Arkel, Petronella van 167
Aristotle 116
Arlandes, Marquis d' 54
Athlone, Count of 76, 77, 166
Averhoult, J. A. d' 133–136, 159

Beethoven 155
Beels, Marten Adriaan 124, 125, 129, 131, 132, 161, 169
Bellamy, Jacobus 53, 58, 59, 73, 74, 79
Berckel, P. van 138
Berckel, pensionary van 239
Berger, Cypriaan 110
Bevere, Pieter de 107, 108
Bicker, family 51
Bicker, J. B. 124
Bourbon, House of 165, 216
Brunswick Lunenburg, Ferdinand, Duke of, 156, 158, 159, 163, 165
Brunswick, Louis Ernest, Duke of 40

Calkoen, Abraham 125, 129
Calkoen, Eliane 125, 224
Canneman, Elias 215
Capellen tot den Pol, Joan Derk van der 26, 36, 37, 45, 47–52, 53, 58, 59, 62, 63, 71, 81, 115, 125, 177, 203, 222
Casanova 171
Catherine the Great 172
Charles I, King of England 149, 184
Charles V, Emperor 29, 33
Christian, Danish King 26
Churchill 42, 150
Clifford, George, 172
Clifford, Hesje 175, 176
Clifford, Margot 176, 202
Clifford, Pieter 125, 172
Conste, Dona Maria 233
Cornwallis 49
Crusoe, Robinson 144
Cruz, Manuel de 94, 95, 96, 102

d'Edel, Adriaan Floriszoon, pope Hadrian VI 124
Daendels, Herman 166, 183, 193, 194, 196–199, 201, 206
Dam, beadle van 76
Darwin, Charles 96
David 204
Davies, Mrs. C. M. 6
Dedel, family 124

INDEX OF PERSONAL NAMES

Dedel, Willem Gerrit Salomonszoon   124, 125, 128, 129, 131, 132, 161, 163, 169
Dumouriez, General   167

Enoch   170

Falck, Anton Reinhard   210–212, 216–220, 232, 236
Falck, Iman Willem   94, 117, 226, 227, 228, 230, 232, 236
Falck, Mr. Isaac   111
Falck, Otto Willem   84, 85, 94, 111, 117, 118, 157, 211
Fernando, Christina   233
Fernando, Nihal   232
Fijnje, Wybo   187, 193, 195, 189, 207
Franklin, Benjamin   140
Frederic II, King of Prussia named the Great   41, 63, 87, 90, 119–122, 138, 172, 187, 221
Frederic William II, King of Pussia   120, 155, 156
Frederik Hendrik, Prince of Orange   31

George II, King of England   40, 42, 149
George III, King of England   42, 43
Gibbon, Edward   149
Goethe   17, 156
Gogel, I. J. A.   195–198, 201, 204–206, 215
Graeff, family de   51
Gratiaen, family   12, 235

Haafner (Haffner), Jacob   87, 106, 185, 188–191, 225, 226, 229, 236
Hamilton, Alexander   145

Hardenbroek, Gijsbert Jan van   41, 42, 43, 45, 46, 52, 63, 76, 77, 79, 116, 117, 125, 155, 162
Hardy, Thomas   99
Haren, van, family   138, 175
Harris, Sir James   119, 120, 123, 150, 155
Hasselaer, family   51
Haydn   155
Heinrich, Prince of Prussia   138
Hespe, Mr. Johan Christiaan   58, 77, 124, 168, 203
Hoevenaar, Adrianus   58, 69, 71, 77, 80, 168
Hoevenaar, Christina   58, 77, 168, 188, 197, 224
Hogendorp, Gijsbert Karel van   137–152, 155, 158, 159, 172, 175, 176, 191, 202, 203, 206–210, 213–215, 221, 222, 236, 239
Hogendorp-van Haren, Mrs. van   138–146, 172, 175
Hohenzollern   155
Homer   225
Hooft, family   26, 51, 124, 162, 206, 236
Hooft, Cornelis Pieter (Kees)   177
Hooft, Cornelis Pieterszoon   26, 27, 33, 34, 35, 37, 52, 177, 214
Hooft, Daniel   177
Hooft, Daniel Danielszoon   162, 211, 212, 214, 236
Hooft, Daniel Willemszoon   162
Hooft, Daniel, Vrijheer van Vreeland   162
Hooft, Elisabeth   178
Hooft, Gerrit Corver   162
Hooft, Hester   170–176, 202
Hooft, Henrik Danielszoon   6, 7, 24, 26, 37, 45, 47–53, 81, 89, 115, 124–131, 158–162, 169–181, 187, 202, 203, 214, 221, 222, 224, 235, 237
Hooft, Jacob Gerritszoon   162

INDEX OF PERSONAL NAMES

Hooft, Pieter Corneliszoon 27, 31, 32, 124, 125
Hooft, Willem Janszoon 26
Huydecoper, family 51, 124

James I, King of England 161
Jayawardene, J. R. 233
Jefferson, Thomas 2, 43, 114, 139, 140, 143, 147, 148, 149, 165
Jonklaas, family 12, 235
Joseph II, Emperor 166, 174

Kataragama 95
Kinsbergen, Jan Hendrik van 172–176, 202, 207, 213, 215, 221, 236
Knox, Robert 100, 101, 105, 185

Lafayette, George Washington 141, 146
Lafayette, Marquis de 140, 145, 149
La Pierre, Abraham 196, 198, 201
Langen, van 195, 196, 198, 199, 207
Lie Kwie Moy 225
Liebeherr, Boguslav Friederich von 58, 69, 78, 80, 112, 159, 187, 188, 193, 197, 202, 204, 211, 214
Linnaeus, Karl 125, 172
Livingston, William 50, 139
Locke, John 66
Louis XIV, the Sun King 21, 39, 168
Louis XVI, King of France, 119, 165, 166, 184
Loten, Arnout 57, 82, 83, 86, 107, 109, 228
Loten, Joan Gideon 107–109, 228
Louis Napoleon, King of Holland 205–208, 214

Maanen, C. F. van 207, 208, 215, 216, 218
Madison, James 164
Marie-Antoinette, Queen of France 119
Marot, Daniël 224
Marx, K. 80, 147
Maurits, Prince of Orange 31, 33, 34, 36, 39, 40, 46, 49, 198
Melho, de, family 12
Melho, Philippus de 12, 90
Melho, Simon de 9
Meuron, de 185
Micawber, Mr 191
Montesquieu 116
Morgan, Frances Sophia 234
Morris, brothers 139
Mozart, W. A. 71, 87, 155, 187
Moses 204
Muttu Kanamma, Queen 233

Napoleon Bonaparte 186, 193, 201, 204–208, 217
Nassau, Engelbert of 167
Nassau, Counts of 30
Nero 159
Nijs, Adriaan de 58, 80

Oldenbarnevelt, Johan van 45–47, 169, 198
Ondaatje, family 6, 7, 12, 225, 226, 228, 229, 232, 233–236
Ondaatje, Christopher 6, 7, 9, 11, 12, 16, 73, 74, 76, 77, 89, 95, 99, 100, 101, 104, 105, 109, 110, 224, 225, 226, 229, 230, 232–236
Ondaatje, Rev. Willem Juriaan 12, 90, 94, 226
Ondaatje, Eduard 225
Ondaatje, Gillian 11, 233
Ondaatje, Hermina Wilhelmina and Wilhelmina Hermina 188

INDEX OF PERSONAL NAMES

Ondaatje, Rev. Johan Jurgen 234
Ondaatje, Rev. Mas. J. 233
Ondaatje, Mervyn 235
Ondaatje, Michael 232, 235
Ondaatje, Doctor Michael Jurian 53, 233, 229
Ondaatje, Michael. J. 233
Ondaatje, P. P. J. (Quint) 6, 7, 9, 10, 11, 12, 16, 17, 18, 19, 23, 33, 37, 53, 54, 58–85, 87, 89, 90, 94, 108, 109, 112, 116, 117, 118, 126, 133–136, 157, 159–161, 163–170, 184, 187, 188, 190, 208, 211, 214–219, 224, 230, 236, 237
Ondaatje, Philip de Melho Jurgen 237
Ondaatje, Philip Francis 235
Ondaatjes listed on p. 229 not in this index.
Oranje, House of and Princes of 33, 34, 37, 40, 41, 42, 49, 74, 138, 167, 171, 208, 211, 215, 236

Paine, Thomas 43
Palmer, R. R. 147
Pesters, family (de) 55–57, 236
Pesters, Jan, Heer van Cattenbroek 55, 56, 57
Pesters, Willem Nicolaas (Klaas) (ex-colonel) 55, 56, 57, 71, 75, 79, 82, 117, 236
Peter, Czar 121, 221
Philip II, King of Spain 29, 31, 33
Pichegru, General 169
Pitt, William the Younger 42, 43, 148, 149
Pitt, William the Elder 42, 43
Premadasa, Mrs. 231, 323
Premadasa, President 232

Quint, Pieter 19
Quint, Theodora 225

Raheem, Ismeth 95, 96, 100, 104, 105, 232
Raja Sinha II, Emperor 15, 16, 105
Reael, family 125
Reede, F. C. R. van, Milord, Athlone 76, 77, 166
Reimer, C. F. 230, 231
Rembrandt 57
Rendorp 124, 132
Renswoude, Hendrik van 73, 76
Reynolds, Sir Joshua 107
Richard II, King of England 42
Rhine Count, the; Prince Frederic III of Salm-Kyrburg 122, 123, 126, 133, 136, 157–161, 166, 198, 224
Robespierre 164, 192
Rousseau, Jean Jacques 65, 66, 217
Rozier, Pilatre de 54
Ruyter, Michiel Adriaanszoon de 47, 183

Saint-Simon 52
Salm-Kyrburg, Prince Frederic III of, See Rhine Count
Santa Lucia 224
Scarlatti 223, 226
Schimmelpenninck, R. J. 192, 205
Schubert 104
Seferis, George 190
Shakespeare, William 35, 106, 138, 142, 161
Siéyès, Abbé 183
Sichterman, Mr Jonathan 67–71, 77, 78
Silva, Rev. Petrus de 10
Smetana 104
Smissaert, Jan Carel 170, 187
Spilbergen, Joris van 13, 14
Sri Wikrama Raja Sinha, King 233
St. Just 216
Stephen, Saint 233

INDEX OF PERSONAL NAMES

Stuart, Anne, Princess 39
Stuart, Mary, Princess 39

Talleyrand 195
Tirion, Isaac 100, 101
Tolstoi 147
Tromp, Maarten Harpertszoon 47, 183
Trumbull, Jonathan 50, 139

Undati, Undatee 79

Valckenaer, J. 188
Valkenier, Wouter 178
Venkadayammal, Queen 236
Vérac, Marquis de 241
Vimala Dharma Suriya, Emperor 13, 14, 15
Vivaldi 223
Vondel, Joost van den 125
Vreede, Pieter 37, 45, 123, 193–198, 207

Washington, George 38, 39, 48, 51, 122, 139–149, 165, 187, 191
Washington, Mrs. 137, 139–147
Wassenaer Obdam, Jacob Unico Wilhelm, Count of 176, 221
Waterhouse, Benjamin 23
Watson, Elkanah 146, 147
Weber 147
Weert, Sebald de 12, 14, 15

Wilhelmina, Queen of the Netherlands 150
Wilhelmine, Princess of Prussia 41, 120, 122, 138, 149–155, 158, 161, 162, 164, 175, 194, 209
William, Count of Nassau, Prince of Orange, 'the Silent' 30–35, 39, 45, 46, 168
William III, Stadhouder, Prince of Orange 34, 39, 40, 41, 46, 54, 55, 76, 168, 198, 224
William IV, Stadhouder, Prince of Orange 34, 39, 40, 41, 42, 54, 168, 198, 222
William V, Stadhouder, Prince of Orange 34, 39, 40–43, 51, 53, 58, 60, 61, 63, 64, 69, 74, 76, 80, 81, 119, 123, 129, 136, 137, 149, 150, 154, 155, 158, 162, 163, 172, 174, 184, 185, 203, 208, 212, 213, 217, 220, 236
William VI, Prince of Orange, later King William I 59, 208, 209, 212–219, 236
Wimalaratne, Dr. Garvin 228, 229
Wiselius, Samuel Iperuszoon 186–188, 193–198, 202, 204, 207, 208, 211, 215, 236
Witt, Cornelis de 168, 169, 198
Witt, Johan de 168, 169, 198

Yvoy, Paul d' 59, 71

Zeelandus 54